The Open University

D1146870

A207 FROM ENLIGHTENMENT
TO ROMANTICISM, c.1780–1830

Unit 1
Course Introduction: Enlightenment and the Forces of Change

Block 1
Death of the Old Regime?

This publication forms part of an Open University course A207 *From Enlightenment to Romanticism, c.1780–1830*. Details of this and other Open University courses can be obtained from the Course Information and Advice Centre, PO Box 724, The Open University, Milton Keynes MK7 6ZS, United Kingdom: tel. +44 (0)1908 653231, e-mail general-enquiries@open.ac.uk

Alternatively, you may visit the Open University website at http://www.open.ac.uk where you can learn more about the wide range of courses and packs offered at all levels by The Open University.

To purchase a selection of Open University course materials visit the webshop at www.ouw.co.uk, or contact Open University Worldwide, Michael Young Building, Walton Hall, Milton Keynes MK7 6AA, United Kingdom for a brochure. tel. +44 (0)1908 858785; fax +44 (0)1908 858787; e-mail ouwenq@open.ac.uk

The Open University
Walton Hall, Milton Keynes
MK7 6AA

First published 2004. Reprinted 2005

Edited, designed and typeset by The Open University.

Printed and bound in Malta by Gutenberg Press.

ISBN 0 7492 8595 8

1.4

Mixed Sources
Product group from well-managed forests, and other controlled sources
www.fsc.org Cert no. TT-CoC-002424
© 1996 Forest Stewardship Council

FSC

The paper used for this book is FSC-certified and totally chlorine-free. FSC (the Forest Stewardship Council) is an international network to promote responsible management of the world's forests.

Contents

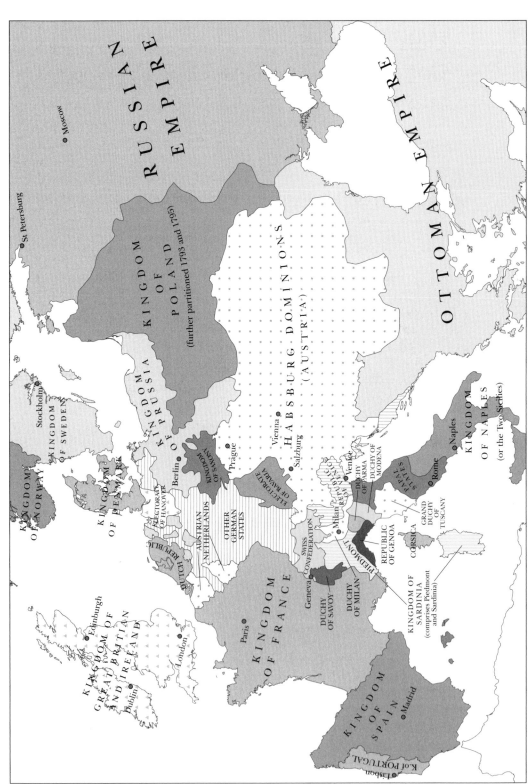

Europe in 1789.

Unit 1
Course Introduction: Enlightenment and the forces of change

Prepared for the course team by Linda Walsh and Antony Lentin

Contents

Study components

Weeks of study	Supplementary material	Audio-visual	Anthologies and set books
1	AV Notes	Video 1	–

Objectives

By the end of your work on this unit you should:

- have gained a basic understanding of the cultural climate that existed as the historical period we shall be studying began;
- understand the main characteristics of the Enlightenment;
- be aware of some of the cultural shifts and trends leading from Enlightenment to Romanticism.

1   Introduction

> What a change there was between 1785 and 1824! There has probably never been such an abrupt revolution in habits, ideas and beliefs in the two thousand years since we have known the history of the world.
>
> (**Stendhal**, *Racine and Shakespeare*, 1825; 1962 edn, p.144)

In this course you will be studying, through a variety of texts, a period of 50 years or so during which European culture underwent one of the most profound and far-reaching changes in its history. This occurred against a background of political and social turmoil and transformation equally unprecedented, marked by revolution, war and the beginnings of industrialization. The period saw the interface of two fundamental cultural movements on which you will be focusing: Enlightenment and Romanticism. The transition from the first to the second has been described as 'the greatest single shift in the consciousness of the West that has occurred' (Berlin, 1999, p.1), one that 'cracked the backbone of European thought' (Isaiah Berlin, quoted in Furst, 1979, p.27), and it continues to impact on our ways of thinking in the twenty-first century.

In order to help you get to grips with the nature and scale of the cultural changes that took place, we intend in this first unit to offer a 'map' of the conceptual territory, the intellectual and cultural climate you'll be exploring. We shall give most attention here to the Enlightenment, since it forms the fundamental background to the following units of Block 1 and to the course in general. As we proceed in this Course Introduction, we shall point forward to some of the key texts of the course, but we shall continue to concentrate largely on the Enlightenment, drawing your attention to the major figures and works characteristic of this movement. We shall ask you to watch parts of the introductory video (*Aspects of Enlightenment*), in which some important aspects of the Enlightenment are discussed further, and to attempt the corresponding exercises set in the Audio-Visual Notes. We shall also outline briefly some of the main changes that began from about 1780, principally with regard to the shift towards Romanticism. The characteristics of Romanticism, and the ways in which they relate to your course texts, will be discussed in greater detail in the relevant units and in the Course Conclusion.

As you work through this unit please bear in mind the learning objectives specified above. At this stage of the course you are asked simply (1) to gain a basic understanding of the cultural climate that existed as the historical period we shall be studying began; (2) to grasp the main characteristics of the Enlightenment; and (3) to be aware of some of the cultural developments leading from Enlightenment to Romanticism. You will encounter in this unit a great deal of supporting detail that you will *not* be expected to memorize. As you progress through the course, you may wish to reread some or all of the unit, and may then be in a better position to absorb some of its detail, or to relate its main points to the texts you encounter in later units. When you reach the end of the course, you may find it helpful to revisit Unit 1 in order to establish a firm framework for your revision of the texts and the themes that bind them together.

In order to help you to work smoothly through the unit, we have highlighted in bold the summary points that we expect you to absorb in this first week of study. We have also highlighted in bold at their first mention the names of the institutions, historical phenomena and authors of texts that feature prominently in the course. Note that in subsequent units we have used bold type to indicate terms that can be found in the glossary at the end of the block.

2   The Enlightenment and its mission

'The Enlightenment' is used to refer:

1   to a chronological period (roughly, the middle and late decades of the eighteenth century between around 1740 and 1780), often also called 'The Age of Reason'; and

2   to the unprecedented focus on a particular set of values, attitudes and beliefs shared by prominent writers, artists and thinkers of that period.

There were changes of emphasis depending on date: it is common to distinguish, for example, between early and late Enlightenment attitudes, while the half-century beginning around 1680 is often thought of as the pre-Enlightenment. There were also different 'varieties' of Enlightenment depending on national, social and political contexts. The sweep of the Enlightenment was enormous: from Lisbon to Saint Petersburg and from Edinburgh to Naples. Enlightenment culture spread from one nation to another, defining a pan-European consciousness of tremendous force. Each nation added its own dimension. In France, for example, there was a much greater sense of opposition to the (Catholic) Church than in England, where the religious establishment was perceived to be far less oppressive. It is agreed that the Enlightenment was at the height of its influence in the 1760s and early 1770s. Of its most representative figures in France, Voltaire died in 1778 and Diderot in 1784 (see Figures 1.1 and 1.2). There is also a consensus that certain key attitudes characterize what we may describe as an Enlightenment outlook.

The Enlightenment consisted, in essence, of the belief that the expansion of knowledge, the application of reason, and dedication to scientific method would result in the greater progress and happiness of humankind. The Enlightenment outlook was buoyant, reformist and humanitarian. The archetypal Enlightenment thinker was confident that

Figure 1.1 Jean-Antoine Houdon, Voltaire, 1778, bronze, 45 x 20.8 x 21.2 cm, Louvre, Paris. Photo: Getty Images.

Figure 1.2 Jean-Baptiste Pigalle, Denis Diderot, 1777, bronze, 52 x 34.5 x 25.5, Louvre, Paris. Photo: © RMN/G.Blot/C. Jean.

the world is ultimately both rational and beneficent, that nature, including humanity, is essentially good or at least not innately depraved, and that people have the potential to improve themselves and their environment and to make the world a better place.

Among the factors that gave particular credibility to this belief one ranks high: the epoch-making discoveries of Sir Isaac Newton (1642–1727) at the end of the seventeenth century regarding the motion of the planets and gravitational force. Newton's achievements had a profound and lasting impact that spread far beyond the sphere of physics. They suggested that the natural world could be explored and understood, and that nature and everything in it was governed by underlying 'laws'; that there were rational, universally valid answers to the questions asked by an enquiring mind; that for every effect there was an identifiable cause, for every natural phenomenon an explanation, a category and a definition, if only we try hard enough to find it. This confidence in reason or intellect lies at the heart of the Enlightenment.

The text that best exemplifies and embodies this outlook is the French *Encyclopédie, ou dictionnaire raisonné des sciences, des arts et des métiers* (*Encyclopedia, or an Analytical Dictionary of the Sciences, Arts and Trades*), published in Paris between 1751 and 1772 in 28 volumes and accompanied by 11 volumes of illustrative plates. (Further supplementary volumes were published almost up to the French Revolution in 1789.) The main editor of the work was Denis Diderot (1713–84, pronounced Dee-der-oh), assisted in the early stages by Jean d'Alembert (1717–83). The *Encyclopédie* certainly took seriously its remit of collating and communicating all available knowledge in the interests of progress. The following statement from one of Diderot's many articles in the *Encyclopédie,* the one entitled 'Encyclopedia', sets out the basic manifesto of the Enlightenment:

> The aim of an encyclopedia is to bring together the knowledge scattered over the surface of the earth, to present its overall structure to our contemporaries and to hand it on to those who will come after us, so that our children, by becoming more knowledgeable, will become more virtuous and happier; and so that we shall not die without earning the gratitude of the human race.

> (Diderot, 1755, p.635; trans. S. Clennell)

In that one brief statement we find the essence of the Enlightenment credo: that increase of knowledge will produce happier, more virtuous people. The message is one of universal application, appropriate to the entire human race. It was self-evidently better to be right than to be wrong: that is, to have a correct understanding of things, the relationship between them, and the 'laws' that governed those relationships. To be informed was manifestly better, more virtuous, than to be ignorant or prejudiced. Hence, as Diderot continued, all knowledge was good in itself; the discovery of truth in any field of human activity was a contribution to the advancement of human knowledge, and therefore to the advantage and ultimate happiness of humanity; the *Encyclopédie,* whose purpose was to spread that knowledge, was a worthy instrument of the Enlightenment. 'Enlightenment' itself (and its variants in other languages) signified the emergence of light and the dispersion of the clouds, particularly the clouds of ignorance, superstition, prejudice, oppression, dogma or myth. As Diderot insists later in the same article:

> All things must be examined, debated, investigated, without exception and without regard for anyone's feelings ... We must ride roughshod over all these ancient puerilities, overturn the barriers that reason never erected.

> (Gendzier, 1967, p.93)

Many of the authors who contributed to the work – the encyclopedists – were known as *philosophes*. These were not philosophers in our modern sense of the word, but a loose-knit group of like-minded intellectuals and cultivated, sociable and lively writers. Sharing a common view of the *Encyclopédie* and its mission, they were immensely knowledgeable in an age when it was still possible to have a good grasp of most branches of learning. Of all the encyclopedists, it was perhaps François Arouet de

Voltaire (1694–1778) who best personified the French Enlightenment: not only in his enormous and varied literary *oeuvre,* ranging from neoclassical tragedy to modern history and from Newtonian science to literary criticism, but also in his passionate, energetic, highly charged and publicized commitment to Enlightenment values, a commitment which seemed to intensify as he grew older. As 'the patriarch of Ferney' in the 1760s and 1770s, he settled in semi-exile at Ferney, near the Swiss border; he also kept a house in Geneva as a bolt-hole in case of trouble from the French authorities. Voltaire was known throughout Europe for his active intervention in humanitarian causes and his incessant attacks on abuses of every kind, particularly abuse of power by the Catholic Church and associated miscarriages of justice. All this was given sensational coverage by his flair for publicity, his Europe-wide contacts among influential people, including crowned heads – notably Frederick the Great of Prussia and Empress Catherine the Great of Russia – and above all by his inimitable style, pointedly ironic, forceful, mischievous, malicious and funny. Voltaire never missed his target. He made the authorities, the ecclesiastical perpetrators of superstition and cruelty, smart. He made them look not merely wrongheaded, wicked and unjust, but more – he made them look ridiculous. Voltaire's style also reflects another Enlightenment characteristic: its even, moderate temper, urbane, measured and witty. Passionately as Voltaire felt about fanaticism, cruelty and injustice, his strength of feeling was the more effective for its control, the rippling, amusing surface elegance beneath which a biting wit and irony fizzed, flashed and exploded. Voltaire's best-known work, which best reflects his character and style, is his 'philosophical tale' *Candide* (1759). Here, for example, is a statement by one of its main characters, a part-Spanish valet Cacambo, about the colonial impact of the Jesuit Fathers in Paraguay (the Jesuits were a body of Catholic missionaries):

> I know how the reverend fathers govern as well as I know the streets of Cadiz. It's a wonderful thing, their system of government. The kingdom is more than three hundred leagues across; it is divided into thirty provinces. The reverend fathers own everything, and the natives nothing. It is a masterpiece of reason and justice.
>
> (Voltaire, 1981, p.88; trans. Lentin)

This French Enlightenment tone and temper – detached, ironic and at times wickedly or darkly humorous – should be remembered when we come to discuss the very different Romantic temperament.

Although the term *philosophe* was French and applied mainly to thinkers from that country, it was also applied to intellectuals of any country who were sympathetic to an Enlightenment approach. Of the encyclopedists themselves, Baron d'Holbach (Paul Henri Dietrich) was a German expatriate and **Jean-Jacques Rousseau** (1712–78) was Swiss. 'My dear Davy,' Diderot wrote to the Scots philosopher **David Hume** (1711–76), 'you belong to all nations ... I flatter myself that I am, like you, [a] citizen of the great city of the world' (quoted in Gay, 1968, p.13). Diderot spoke for the thoroughly cosmopolitan spirit of the Enlightenment. French was the common language of the Enlightenment, as the Berlin Academy of Arts and Sciences acknowledged in 1783 when it set an essay competition on 'the universality of the French language'. The publications of the French *philosophes* were followed by an eager, albeit elite, readership across Europe. 'I see with pleasure', Voltaire wrote to a Russian in 1767, 'that an immense republic of cultivated minds is being formed in Europe' (quoted in Sorel, 1912, p.166; trans. Lentin). There were varieties of the Enlightenment in Spain, Italy, Germany, Austria and Russia; there was a distinct and distinguished Scottish Enlightenment (of which Hume was a leading figure), and in England there were even a Midlands Enlightenment and a Manchester Enlightenment. But it was in France that the rational, reformist agenda of the Enlightenment found its most forceful expression (see Figure 1.3).

Figure 1.3   Anicet Charles Gabriel Lemonnier, A Reading in the Salon of Mme Geoffrin, *1755, oil on canvas, 129 x 196 cm, Châteaux de Malmaison et Bois-Préeau, Paris. Photo:* © *RMN/Arnaudet.*

The actor Lekain is reading Voltaire's play L'Orphelin de la Chine (The Chinese Orphan) *before a bust of the then exiled author.*

The *philosophes* saw themselves as engaged in a battle for minds; they appealed to something which they saw and cultivated as a new factor in European society: public opinion. It was with public opinion in mind that they criticized existing institutions in France and what they saw as a corrupt and ineffective absolute monarchy in alliance with a corrupt and repressive Catholic Church. While they had friends in high places who assisted the project, the *Encyclopédie* had a stormy publication history, since its content and tone went far beyond the conventional remit of summarizing and categorizing knowledge. Its social and political polemic often operated through a subversive system of cross-referencing and ironic word play in an attempt to circumvent strict censorship laws, but this did not prevent several serious delays to publication of the work and determined opposition from powerful quarters.

EXERCISE   So far in this section you have been introduced to the main mission of the Enlightenment. Try now to stand back from the detail of the section, and summarize in about 50 words what you see as the main characteristics of that mission.

DISCUSSION   The main characteristics of the Enlightenment's mission were: (1) a confidence in reason or intellectual enquiry to bring greater happiness and progress to humanity; (2) a belief that all aspects of the human and natural worlds are susceptible of rational explanation; and (3) the desire to battle against ignorance, dogma, superstition, injustice and oppression.

How did you fare in this exercise? Did you write much more than the summary discussion set out in the discussion above? If so, it may be that you need further practice in the skill of extracting key points and summing them up concisely. You have encountered so far in this section a general exposition of the main characteristics of the Enlightenment mission, followed by some more detailed discussion of historical examples: the *Encyclopédie* and the writings of Voltaire. This combination of main points interwoven with or succeeded by illustrative detail is commonplace in academic writing. Detail has a useful function and is essential in academic study. It both illustrates and validates general claims. But its overuse can bring the risk of obscuring the main points of an analysis: 'not seeing the wood for the trees'. In the various assignments (TMAs) for this course and in the examination, you will be asked to support all major claims with detailed evidence drawn from a text or number of texts. The required balance between analysis (the ordering and identification of a number of interrelated points relevant to a set question) and illustrative detail or textual evidence will vary. In assignments covering more than one text, for example, there will be slightly less room for detailed references to texts and a greater need for strong points binding those texts together.

Try to keep in your mind this distinction between detail and argument as you read the rest of this unit. Often the main point being made will be highlighted in some way – perhaps by being stated at the opening of the section or at the beginning or climax of a paragraph, although some paragraphs (such as the paragraph above on Voltaire – p.11) will be devoted almost exclusively to the exploration or discussion of particular cases. Try to read the unit so that you track the main points carefully and read through the examples more quickly. Once you have begun work on the course texts (starting with Unit 2), the detail here will begin to make more sense, as and when you return to it. In order to help you develop this skill of prioritizing your attention as you read, we have highlighted summary points in bold in each section of this unit. We have also followed a procedure of including in each section the following elements, which appear in different combinations, proportions and sequences: (1) a brief statement on one or more main points relating to the Enlightenment; (2) some specific historical examples (including some on the introductory video); and (3) some indication of the ways in which the set texts of the course are located in the general 'landscape' of the Enlightenment. The latter component is intended to serve as a useful orientation tool as you prepare for specific assessment tasks. In the case of the present section, this kind of orientation is offered in the paragraph opening 'You will find in this course', below. Such overviews are intended for a relatively quick read at this introductory stage and are not intended to be in any way prescriptive.

EXERCISE   Turn now to your Audio-Visual Notes for the introductory video, *Aspects of Enlightenment*. After you have viewed section 1 of the video ('The *Encyclopédie*') and attempted the exercise relating to it in the notes, return to this unit.

Summary point: the main mission of the Enlightenment was to increase human happiness and progress by the application of reason. Enlightenment thinkers used reason or intellect to fight against dogma, superstition, injustice, prejudice and oppression. They saw all areas of human enquiry as susceptible to reasoned understanding of cause and effect, ultimately expressible in terms of universal laws or principles.

You will find in this course in one form or another the pervasive influence of the Enlightenment. Sometimes this influence is buried in deeply ambiguous texts such as **Wolfgang Amadeus Mozart**'s (1756–91) opera *Don Giovanni* (1787), which includes a famous toast to 'liberty'. The opera is seen by some as an attempt to subject to critical scrutiny the behaviour of at least one member of a corrupt eighteenth-century aristocracy and the social or class structure that facilitated his egoism. The **French Revolution** also unleashed a tremendous blast of energy which inspired its leaders with a sense of missionary zeal. Those involved in the Revolution believed, initially at least, that the Enlightenment had pointed the way towards political reform and the kind of system in which its principles could be put into practice. Many across Europe shared this enthusiastic belief. The German philosopher Immanuel Kant (1724–1804) hailed the opening stages of the Revolution as 'the enthronement of reason in public affairs' (quoted in Barzun, 2000, p.430).

Many aspects of **Napoleon**'s (1769–1821) regime – and certainly the image he sought to project of it – exemplify the intellectual and moral appeal of the Enlightenment. During the Revolution and on an even greater scale under Napoleon, the French not only prided themselves on being what they called *la grande nation* (the great nation) but also spilled across their frontiers and expanded France by force of arms. In the process they introduced across most of Europe systems of rational administration and modern laws and institutions owing much to the Enlightenment. The French saw themselves as bringing freedom, light, reason and modernity to Europe, and it is significant that their belief was long shared by many who came under French rule. This was perhaps an intense magnification of the general self-perception of enlightened Europe as a whole as the cultural centre of the world. Not that Europe was inward-looking: when Napoleon was sent to conquer Egypt from the Turks in 1798, he took with him 167 scholars, scientists, archaeologists and artists to map, survey, explore and describe the country; to investigate the antiquities of the land of the Pharaohs; and to publish their findings in 20 massive volumes. They were as fascinated by the civilization of ancient Egypt as they were contemptuous of the backwardness of modern Egypt, and Napoleon briefly ruled the country with a rod of iron. The whole enterprise was an example of 'the Enlightenment in action' (Barzun, 2000, p.445). Of course, this willingness to look beyond Europe was often motivated by commercial colonial interest. The East India Company, founded in London in 1600 and extremely active in the eighteenth century, was a classic example of a commercial enterprise established by the British to maximize profits.

The Enlightenment mission is evident in *Travels in the Interior Districts of Africa* (1799) by the Scot **Mungo Park** (1771–*c*.1805); the author, sponsored by the African Association on a voyage of exploration, built on the tradition of the knowledge-extending expeditions to the Pacific of Captain Cook. He wrote about his travels in order to increase his readers' knowledge of African geography and societies. To stereotypical European perceptions of Africans as 'barbaric', Park brought corrective insights based on his own first-hand observation and experience. This was one of many examples of reason correcting prejudice. Even as Romanticism was gaining pace in literature and art, the Enlightenment's concern for accurate facts and sound reasoning persisted in many areas of intellectual enquiry. The Evangelical Christian and anti-slavery campaigner **William Wilberforce** (1759–1833), in his thoughts on religion and slavery, adopted the archetypal Enlightenment procedure of structured, rational 'enquiry', seeking out the relationship of cause and effect in society's responses to these burning issues. *Thoughts and Sentiments on the Evil of Slavery* (1787) by **Quobna Ottobah Cugoano** (1757–c.1800) followed the *Encyclopédie* in applying rational, critical understanding to the practice of slavery in order to support the abolitionist cause, while other Enlightenment thinkers were using reasoned argument to support its retention.

Robert Owen (1771–1858) applied the critical reformist spirit of the Enlightenment in *A New View of Society* (1813–16), in which he set out his views on the management of industry and its workers based on his experience at the mill in New Lanark. He shared the Enlightenment's faith in the improvement, through the application of reasoned principle, of the individual and of society at large, and he used these beliefs to shape the work and the domestic environment of the mill-workers. Among the progressive Enlightenment thinkers of Manchester who debated topics as diverse as population growth, poverty, health, education, commerce and philosophy, Owen had gained knowledge which he saw as 'useful' in educating and reforming the character of these workers, thus ensuring their productivity and, he believed, their happiness. For Owen, as for most Enlightenment thinkers, the creation of happiness was a rational business, with identifiable causes and effects that could be formulated as universally applicable principles. The world did not have to be a vale of tears or a preparation for other states of existence. The very object of government, indeed, was held to be the maximization of pleasure, the greatest happiness of the greatest number, or – in the words of the Declaration of Independence with which the American revolutionaries set Europe the example of deliberate, purposeful, rational political change – 'life, liberty and the pursuit of happiness'. Owen identified himself explicitly with the Enlightenment cause by taking a stance against the 'ignorance and consequent prejudices that have accumulated through all preceding ages' (Owen, 1991, p.70), and was representative of that branch of the Enlightenment concerned with *practical* reform.

The application of reason and knowledge to practical reform was also the concern of the British **Royal Institution**, founded in 1799, which promoted the study and popularization of science in the interests of practical improvements in, for example, agriculture, industries such as leather tanning, and, more broadly, the condition of the poor and the prosperity of society in general. The scientist **Humphry Davy** (1778–1829) expressed his commitment to the discovery of universal principles or laws in chemistry. Napoleon drew up his Civil Code and introduced it across much of Europe, inspired by the Enlightenment idea of laws and principles of universal application. Beneath all of these spheres of enquiry covered in the course, there lay a terrific confidence in all-embracing explanations.

This desire to extend and increase knowledge was evident in concerns of a less overtly practical nature. **Edmund Burke** (1729–97), in his *A Philosophical Enquiry into the Origin of our Ideas of the Sublime and the Beautiful* (1757), set out to define, categorize and explain the nature and causes of the responses to art experienced and discussed by his contemporaries. Burke sought, in relation to aesthetics, to identify the properties of 'the beautiful', to distinguish the merely beautiful from 'the sublime', and to pinpoint their effects on the beholder. **Sir John Soane**'s (1753–1837) museum, given to the nation in 1833, can also be seen as an example of this classificatory and educational impulse, this time in relation to physical artefacts. This desire to classify, demystify and explain aesthetic experience had a profound effect on theorists, writers and painters, who felt that art itself was susceptible of rational explanation and control. In every art, craft and field of learning, knowledge was power and the key to progress. The Enlightenment mission penetrated all aspects of human thought and activity.

Enlightenment, science and empiricism

The Enlightenment's dedication to reason and knowledge did not come out of the blue. After all, scholars had for centuries been adding to humanity's stock of knowledge. The new emphasis, however, was on *empirical* knowledge: that is, knowledge or opinion grounded in experience. This experience might include scientific experiments or first-hand observation or experience of people, behaviour, politics, society or anything else touching the natural and the human. For any proposition to be accepted as true, it must be verifiable, capable of practical demonstration. If it was not so verifiable, then it was an error, a fable, an outright lie or simply a hypothesis. Although Enlightenment thinkers retained a role for theoretical or speculative thought (in mathematics, for example, or in the formulation of scientific hypotheses), they took their lead from seventeenth-century thinkers and scientists, notably Francis Bacon (1561–1626), Sir Isaac Newton and John Locke (1632–1704), in prioritizing claims about the truth that were backed by demonstration and evidence. In his 'Preliminary discourse' to the *Encyclopédie,* d'Alembert hailed Bacon, Newton and Locke as the forefathers and guiding spirits of empiricism and the scientific method. To any claim, proposition or theory unsubstantiated by evidence, the automatic Enlightenment response was: 'Prove it!' That is, provide the evidence, show that what you allege is true, or otherwise suspend judgement.

It would be difficult to exaggerate the prestige which Newton's discoveries gave to the *method* whereby he arrived at them. Empiricism worked and was seen to work. It was verifiable; the experiments could be repeated time and again, always with the same result and revealing the same connection between cause and effect, the same immutable underlying 'laws' of nature in operation. In the well-known epigram of Alexander Pope, Newton's elevated status is clear:

> Nature, and Nature's Laws lay hid in Night,
> God said, *Let Newton be!* and All was Light.

(Dobree, 1959, p.122)

Both the philosophical and practical advantages of Newtonianism and the scientific method were further and vividly brought out in the second half of the eighteenth century with startling advances in industrial technology. The *Encyclopédie* was explicitly inclusive of 'the arts', and in the eighteenth century these included technology and the mechanical arts. In his article 'Stocking-machine' in the *Encyclopédie,* lavishly illustrated in one of the supplements, Diderot showed how mechanization ingeniously multiplied human efforts and thus facilitated human comfort and convenience. In Britain, improving on James Hargreaves's spinning-jenny (1764), Richard Arkwright with his water-frame (1768) and Samuel Crompton with his mule (1779) applied technology to the mass production of cloth by steam-driven machines. Such labour-saving devices, so manifestly advantageous, illustrated the triumph of scientific method and Enlightenment rationalism. Empiricism was thus central to the Enlightenment's desire to establish knowledge on firm foundations rather than blindly following authority, convention, tradition and prejudice. Where such foundations were lacking, where the speaker or writer could not satisfactorily respond to the challenge to 'prove it', it was clear that their claims should be met with a strong measure of scepticism.

EXERCISE Try to formulate in roughly one sentence (and by covering up the answer below!) the summary point for the argument starting with the subheading 'Enlightenment, science and empiricism'.

DISCUSSION **Summary point: Enlightenment thinkers placed particular emphasis on empirical knowledge and what they described as scientific method: that is, knowledge verifiable by reference to experiment, experience or first-hand observation.**

Empiricism was applied to every aspect of human thought and activity. This is evident in many of the texts you will study in this course. The Scottish philosopher David Hume's approach to the issues of suicide and the immortality of the soul is suffused by a respect for the demands of empirical reasoning and the related question, 'Is such-and-such a factual claim probable in the light of common human experience?' Hume dismissed with evident relish all speculative reasoning not based on verifiable fact. By speculative reasoning he meant, above all, that based on religious revelation, private intuition, theological dogma and the authority of the churches. The explorer Mungo Park and his close associate, the scientist and botanist Joseph Banks (1743–1820), shared this concern with close observation as the basis of our knowledge of the world, though Park was a believing and practising Christian. The scientific method was happily applied in the eighteenth century by many believers and men of the cloth, who, unlike Hume, felt that science reinforced rather than undermined the reasonableness of religious belief. Cugoano's arguments against slavery were also based on appeals to observation and experience, inviting the reader to judge for himself. Landscape artists and theorists both amateur and professional, such as **William Gilpin** (1724–1804) and **John Constable** (1776–1837), paid greater attention to direct observation and sketching of their subject rather than simply the careful imitation of revered masterpieces of the past. This practice was not an eighteenth-century invention, but first-hand studies of the landscape assumed greater importance in relation to studio work as the century progressed. Seeing and thinking for yourself and drawing on the evidence of the five senses were central to the Enlightenment mindset.

Specialization of knowledge was less common in the eighteenth century than it is today, and the boundaries of what we now call 'science' were defined relatively late in the nineteenth century. For the *philosophes* and Enlightenment men and women generally, an interest in botany or chemistry might sit happily alongside intellectual enquiry into politics, art, literature and economics. As well as being an explorer, Mungo Park, who had qualified as a surgeon, had a keen interest in natural history and in the system of the Swedish naturalist Carl von Linnaeus (1707–78) for the classification of plants. It was common to speculate on connections between science and other subjects such as human nature, religion and morality. There were many debates, for example, on the workings of the nervous system in relation to the question of how far we are responsible for our actions, or on the physical laws of the natural world in relation to the nature or indeed the existence of God.

The Royal Institution in London played a large part in making science a fashionable concern of the educated elite. In the Midlands the Unitarian minister, radical thinker, chemist and inventor of soda water Joseph Priestley (1733–1804) conducted experiments that spread knowledge of experimental science throughout society. A supporter of the French Revolution, he saw the potential of science to contribute to political and religious change. The French scientist Antoine Lavoisier (1743–94) set in motion a development known as the 'chemical revolution', which changed the way in which chemical elements were classified, as well as recognizing the key role of oxygen in chemical processes. Both the French Revolution and Napoleon's regime perpetuated the Enlightenment emphasis on science as a means of acquiring mastery over the natural world: intellectual power was harnessed in the service of the state. By affording access to the general laws governing the physical universe, science was the strong arm, as well as the foundation, of reason. As Romanticism gained ground in the wider culture, science was sometimes perceived as an antidote (or a salutary, sobering, cold shower) to the feverish ravings of feeling or the imagination. To Enlightenment thinkers, science was much more than a set of topics to be studied. It represented the unshakeable triumph of the empirical method, the crucial testing of hypotheses against evidence, that could be applicable to all aspects of human enquiry, including questions of morality and religion.

EXERCISE   Now turn to your AV Notes, focusing on the section on science, which will direct you to watch section 2 ('Advances in medicine') of *Aspects of Enlightenment*, and attempt the exercise in the notes.

Enlightenment, religion and morality

Just as with other natural phenomena, Enlightenment thinkers came to the conclusion as a result of observation that human nature itself was a basic constant. In other words, it possessed common characteristics and was subject to universal, verifiable laws of cause and effect. As Hume put it:

> Mankind are so much the same, in all times and places, that history informs us of nothing new or strange in this particular. Its chief use is only to discover the constant and universal principles of human nature ...

> (Hume, 1975, p.83)

Hume was not consistent on this point, and his later writings suggest an essential difference between western and 'other' varieties of human nature. Nor did he view female nature in the same light as male. It was also widely accepted that human behaviour and the human condition were susceptible to environmental and educational influence. The desire for moral reform was supported by a belief in universally valid moral standards. The *philosophes* were confident that it was possible to identify virtue and vice, right and wrong, in a way that may seem alien to us today. If it was possible to discover universal laws that governed the physical workings of the universe, the same, they concluded, applied to the world of morality. In his *Enquiry Concerning the Principles of Morals* (1751), Hume confidently declared:

> The end of all moral speculation is to teach us our duty; and, by proper representations of the deformity of vice and beauty of

virtue, beget corresponding habits, and engage us to avoid the one, and embrace the other.

(Hume, n.d., p.409)

Summary point: Enlightenment thinkers believed that the basic principles underlying human nature were constant; they also believed that the human condition was susceptible of improvement. They felt it possible to formulate clear moral absolutes or universal standards.

This is one of the main sources of distinction between the Enlightenment and post-Enlightenment eras: later thinkers would be less confident about identifying a uniform human nature or clear moral absolutes. Mungo Park followed Hume in demonstrating, on the basis of his own experience as an explorer, that Africans conformed to a universal human nature rather than being fundamentally different from Europeans, as was contended by many of those engaged in the highly lucrative slave trade. Park's exploration of 'the dark continent' achieved much in changing attitudes on this subject. In general, there was a pervasive faith in the potential to discover the laws governing human behaviour and morality. It is possible to see the Enlightenment mindset at work even in works such as Mozart's *Don Giovanni*, which is open to several interpretations. This opera was influenced by a high art tradition of serious opera or *opera seria* in which characters overcome their flaws and achieve moral greatness. Commonly in tragedy the theme was the triumph of duty over love or passion. The chief character in *Don Giovanni* (Don Giovanni himself) does not even attempt this exercise, and is finally punished in a way that suggests the existence of moral absolutes. The opera's alternative title is *The Rake Punished*.

Increasingly, particularly in late Enlightenment texts, this confidence in our ability to discover and apply clear moral distinctions came into conflict with an alternative view of human nature and morality derived from philosophical materialism, which was particularly influential in France. To a materialist everything, from our nervous system and reflex actions to our innermost thoughts and most 'mystical' beliefs, was susceptible to examination by the physical sciences; our thoughts and actions were explicable in purely physical terms. If the universe was a kind of great machine in which everything was subject to unalterable laws, might not the same be true of human beings? Building on the foundations laid by ancient philosophers such as the Roman poet Lucretius (*c*.98–55 BCE) and bolstered by the Enlightenment's commitment to the physical sciences, many eighteenth-century thinkers, including Diderot, pursued the consequences of this philosophy. Materialism was based on the belief that everything we can know or experience has causes and explanations rooted in physical matter. Such ideas were seen as a threat to traditional religion with its belief in an immaterial or non-corporeal, spiritual soul able to survive the body after death, and also to the concept of free will and the capacity to choose between good and evil.

Materialism, then, had disturbing implications for Christianity and for morality conceived of as obedience to a set of divine injunctions. First, it seemed to leave little scope for God, except as a possible prime mover or great architect of the universe who, having set the universe in motion, thereafter sat back without intervening further, leaving it – and humanity – to operate like automata in accordance with the unalterable laws of nature. From this perspective divine providence, after its initial intervention, was redundant. Second, if everything is reducible to physical phenomena and processes, then physical sensations assume great importance in moral matters. Building on the well-established premise that the seeking of pleasure and the avoidance of pain are central to human happiness and well-being, eighteenth-century materialists rejected the fundamental Christian concept of original sin (humankind's innate depravity) and other guilt-inducing moral dictates in order to focus on human sensations and the relationship between physical and moral health. One consequence of this was a new legitimization of hedonism, or the conscious pursuit of pleasure.

Summary point: in Enlightenment France philosophical materialism, the belief that everything (including the apparently spiritual) can be explained in terms of physical matter and the laws governing it, became increasingly influential. It encouraged in some thinkers a tendency to argue that all moral matters might be reduced to the maximizing of physical pleasure.

The **Marquis de Sade** (1740–1814) twisted such ideas into perversity by rejecting as a moral criterion everything except that which conduces to the gratification of our physical desires and by defining human nature in terms of the 'natural' influences of physiology, environment and climate. This is an approach conducive to amoralism rather than to moral guidelines. Sade's *Dialogue between a Priest and a Dying Man* (1782) dramatizes the encounter of such a credo with the priest's conventional but ultimately assailable Catholic beliefs. The dying man's self-seeking hedonism conflicts with the Enlightenment requirement for a clearly defined, socially controlled moral code.

Materialism was one of many threats to the status of religion. Enlightenment thinkers analysed and criticized religious beliefs in the same way as they subjected to rational scrutiny secular topics such as geological or economic theories. By refusing to treat religion as sacrosanct or the source of its own authority, they threw down a challenge to ecclesiastical institutions, especially in France, where there was a strong alliance of church and state, and the former was seen both as a support and as a beneficiary (for example, through tax exemptions) of an inherently despotic system of government. The perceived corruption and grip on privilege of the Catholic Church, as well as its role in state censorship and its overall hostility to Enlightenment ideas, provoked in the French *philosophes* much anti-religious and anti-clerical criticism as well as the kind of sparkling irony and provocative wit that characterized Voltaire's *Candide* or his *Philosophical Dictionary* (1764). In *Candide,* James Boswell noted, 'Voltaire, I am afraid, meant only by wanton profaneness to obtain a sportive victory over religion, and to discredit our belief of a superintending Providence' (Boswell, 1951, p.210). In 1762 the Archbishop of Paris similarly complained about both the Enlightenment message and its tone:

> Disbelief has in our time adopted a light, pleasant, frivolous style, with the aim of diverting the imagination, seducing the mind, and corrupting the heart. It puts on an air of profundity and sublimity and professes to rise to the first principles of knowledge so as to throw off a yoke it considers shameful to mankind and to the Deity itself. Now it declaims with fury against religious zeal yet preaches toleration for all; now it offers a brew of seditious ideas with badinage, of pure moral advice with obscenities, of great truths with great errors, of faith with blasphemy.
>
> (Barzun, 2000, p.368)

The archbishop was right: the *philosophes* were implying that while the morality preached by Jesus was unexceptionable, educated people would be better off if they jettisoned the age-old lumber of theology, metaphysics, rituals, priests and monks. One of the alternatives frequently recommended to the enlightened was the natural, universal religion of deism, a pure and rational system of ethics uncluttered by dubious miracles, dubious science and dubious history. The authorities took action. In 1766 two young French nobles were sentenced to death for failing to remove their hats and singing ribald songs in the presence of a religious procession honouring the Virgin Mary. Sentence was confirmed by the supreme court in Paris, which noted that irreligion was rife and blamed Voltaire's *Philosophical Dictionary*. One of the young men escaped, and obtained a commission in the Prussian army through Voltaire's intervention with Frederick the Great. The other, the Chevalier de la Barre, was put to death, his tongue excised and his body burned at the stake together with a copy of the *Philosophical Dictionary*.

Summary point: the French Enlightenment subjected religion and its institutions to rational, secular analysis and was often disrespectful, sceptical and subversive in its attitude to the Catholic Church.

Even Rousseau, a fervent though unorthodox believer, did not escape censure. Both the Catholic Church in France and the Calvinist Church in Geneva were outraged by his suggestion that people were naturally good and that an emotional communion with nature was as sound a basis for faith as the formal teachings of the Church. Rousseau's *Émile* (1762), in which he advanced these views in a section called the 'Profession of faith of a Savoyard vicar', was formally condemned by the authorities at

Geneva and publicly burned together with his political tract *Du contrat social* (*Of the Social Contract*, 1762). The Archbishop of Paris, the Sorbonne and the high court in Paris likewise condemned *Émile* to be burned. Rousseau fled to asylum in Prussian territory.

Reasoned responses to religion could take many forms. It was rare for writers to profess outright atheism; even in those cases where we may suspect authors of holding this view, censorship laws made their public expression unlawful. These laws were particularly stringent in France. In many cases reasoned critique was applied to the practices of institutional religion, such as the corruption of the clergy or the rituals of worship, rather than to more fundamental matters of doctrine or faith. Wilberforce, a devout Christian, argued that Sunday might be spent more cheerfully than was customary in England, and Robert Owen's attacks on Scottish sectarianism also included complaints about the dour Calvinist sabbath. It was extremely common for those with specific church allegiances to adopt the rationalizing approaches popularized in more secular contexts. Mungo Park's Scottish Nonconformity (Park was a 'Secessionist', a sect of Protestant Calvinism) was coloured by the deist argument from design, discussed below. In England the Protestantism of the relatively tolerant Anglican Church accommodated a wide range and variety of approach to matters of belief. In both France and Britain there was a wealth of parsons, priests and lay preachers engaged in studying all the topics of interest to the average *philosophe*. Gilbert White, a country parson, was a naturalist, author of the still popular *Natural History of Selborne* (1789). One of the most prominent figures of the British Enlightenment, Samuel Johnson (1709–84), was a devout Anglican. In our period, Christianity itself was often orientated towards Enlightenment and reform (Aston, 1990, pp.81–99). In 1790, when the fiercely controversial reform of the French Church was introduced in revolutionary France, it had supporters as well as opponents among the clergy.

Natural religion was a form of religious belief founded on the observation of nature rather than on revelation or scriptural authority. Often associated with this approach was deism, a particular religious belief which holds that God designed and created the world, but so effectively that there would be no further need for his intervention. Deist views were expressed by those who questioned conventional Christianity and who believed in a universal rather than a sectarian God. They often used reason and argument together with their observation of nature: the existence of a benevolent, intelligent creator or supreme being was inferred from observation of the complex but well-ordered and indeed marvellous universe explored, revealed and explained by Newton. (This was called the 'argument from design'.) The notion of God as a necessary creator, first cause, supreme architect, or a kind of celestial clockmaker who devised and set the universe in motion, was well expressed by writers such as Voltaire. In 1774, at the age of 80 and moved by the spectacle of a magnificent sunrise, he prostrated himself on the ground, exclaiming: 'I believe! I believe in you! Powerful God, I believe!' Clambering to his feet, he added dryly: 'As for Monsieur the son and Madame his mother, that's a different story' (quoted in Gay, 1968, p.122). While philosophers such as David Hume questioned the logic behind such professions of faith, others were keen to embrace a belief in God apparently grounded in empiricism. The Catholic Church in France tended to regard deism as located on the slippery slope leading to atheism, while sections of the Anglican Church tolerated and even encouraged deist sentiments as a support to religion. Many Anglicans cited natural religion or deism alongside arguments drawn from the Bible. Cugoano was among those who adopted this eclectic approach in his views on slavery, and Rousseau saw God in nature as well as in the morality of the Gospels. William Gilpin, English parson and writer of travel guides, likewise saw God's presence in the beauty of the landscape while remaining attached to broad-church Anglicanism.

Summary point: deism, a reasoned form of belief in God based on the methods of natural religion – that is, observation of the natural world – often deployed the argument from design. This was the view that the intelligence and goodness of God, as designer of the world, could be inferred from the workings and beauties of nature. Deist arguments were used by those who embraced more traditional forms of worship, as well as by those who wished to challenge them.

When you study the *Olney Hymns* written by **John Newton** (1725–1807) and **William Cowper** (1731–1800), you will see how religious worship adapted to embrace a more intense, closely circumscribed system of belief and worship accessible to the uneducated working classes. Evangelical Christianity in Britain adopted the Enlightenment's concern with empirical investigation and applied it to its thinking on both the natural world and the Scriptures, albeit within the framework of particular religious beliefs, in order to produce a more reasoned form of worship better adapted to modern times. There were many attempts such as these to challenge forms of belief based on an unthinking acceptance of tradition and authority. The intellectual refinement of faith was prevalent. William Wilberforce, in his *A Practical View of the Prevailing Religious System of Professed Christians* (1797), subjected the state of contemporary religion to rational scrutiny and connected the decline of faith with increased industrialization and mechanization. His method of analysis drew on an enlightened secular approach in order to signal the need for a more intensely experienced form of faith. His personal commitment to religion continued to embrace a non-demonstrable belief in the afterlife. Enlightened rational scrutiny could assist in religious reform without destroying faith.

Setting aside these various shades of response to religious issues, one of the major developments of the Enlightenment was an increasingly secular approach to morality. It became more common for writers of all types of religious persuasion, as well as sceptics and non-believers, to discuss virtue and vice in terms that had little to do with religion or the spiritual and more to do with notions of individual or social well-being. Sade's sensualism rejected conventional Christian morality and social norms in order to take individual self-interest to excessive lengths.

Summary point: the Enlightenment's spirit of rational enquiry was deployed even by those who adhered to an intense spirituality. However, moral debates were increasingly decoupled from matters of religious belief and doctrine.

Enlightenment and the classics

The civilizations of ancient Greece and Rome formed both a common background and a major source of inspiration to Enlightenment thinkers and artists (see Figure 1.4). The dominant culture of the Enlightenment was rooted in the classics, and its art was consciously imitative and neoclassical. English literature of the first half of the century was known as 'Augustan' – that is, comparable to the classic works of the age of the Roman emperor Augustus (27 BCE–CE 14), notably Virgil and Horace and, from the late republican period, Cicero. Augustan literature was characterized by moderation, decorum and a sense of order. The Augustan poet would use classical allusion, authority and satire to

Figure 1.4 Henry Fuseli (Johann Heinrich Fussli), The Artist Moved by the Grandeur of Antique Fragments *(right hand and left foot of the Colossus of Constantine), 1778–80, red chalk and sepia wash on paper, 42 x 35.5 cm, Kunsthaus, Zurich. Photo: Lauros/Giraudon/Bridgeman Art Library.*

convey a deeply reasoned wisdom. The verse of Alexander Pope (see above, p.18) was quintessentially Augustan in its compressed insights into mankind, expressed in controlled, balanced verse. In his *Imitations of Horace*, Pope paid tribute to his admired classical model. Horace, he wrote,

> Will, like a friend, familiarly convey
> The truest notions in the easiest way.

(Quoted in Lentin, 1997, p.xxxvii)

From the grounding in Latin and Greek which formed the basis of their education, the wealthy and well connected of the eighteenth century were at home with the poetry, history and philosophy of the ancient world. In the words of Samuel Johnson, 'classical quotation is the *parole* [password] of literary men all over the world' (Boswell, 1951, vol.2, p.386). When Johnson dined in company with the disreputable politician John Wilkes, neither thought it out of place to discuss a disputed passage in Horace. James Boswell, Johnson's companion and biographer, and son of a Scottish law lord, the Laird of Auchinleck, recalled how in his youth he had associated well-known passages from classical verse with the natural, indeed 'romantic' beauties of the estate:

> The family seat was rich in natural romantic beauties of rock, wood, and water; and ... in my 'morn of life' I had appropriated the finest descriptions in the ancient Classicks, to certain scenes there, which were thus associated in my mind.

(Boswell, 1951, vol.2, p.131)

Across Europe the social elite studied antique statuary, either by viewing originals or copies close to home or by going on the 'Grand Tour' to Italy, to view original sculptures and buildings in Rome itself. To participate in such a tour, to be well versed in the ancient languages and to commission buildings and paintings in the antique style – a portrait by Sir Joshua Reynolds, a mansion by Robert Adam – signalled membership of a class that felt itself to represent the very best of western civilization and that surrounded itself with classical statuary or neoclassical artefacts as emblems of wealth, status and power (see Figure 1.5).

Men and women of the Enlightenment related to, empathized and identified with the ancient world, more particularly with the world of classical Rome, believing that eighteenth-century Europe had achieved a similar peak of cultural excellence. In the words of Edward Gibbon (1737–94 – see Figure 1.6), author of *The History of the Decline and Fall of the Roman Empire* (1776–88), contemporary Europe was 'one great republic, whose various inhabitants have attained almost the same level of politeness and cultivation' (Gibbon, 1954, p.107). By contrast, eighteenth-century Europe tended to reject as 'barbarous' or 'Gothic' the Middle Ages, which it called the Dark Ages, the entire millennium from the fall of Rome in the fifth century CE to the Renaissance in the fifteenth.

*Figure 1.5   F.G. Adam, marble statues of Apollo and Venus, 1740,
Frederick the Great's palace, Sans-Souci. Photo: Paul Kafno.*

*Figure 1.6   Lady Diana
Beauclerk, caricature of Edward
Gibbon, c.1770, pen drawing,
British Museum, London. Photo:
by courtesy of the Trustees of the
British Museum.*

Contrasting the perceived uncongeniality of the Middle Ages with the perfection of republican and imperial Rome, Gibbon looked back as the inspiration for his *Decline and Fall* to the moment in his Grand Tour when he sat musing in the ruins of the Forum at Rome, 'whilst the barefooted friars were singing vespers in the Temple of Jupiter' (quoted in Lentin and Norman, 1998, p.viii). The contrast between the noble ruins of pagan antiquity and the 'barefooted friars' suggested a tension between classical values and the Christian: Gibbon blamed the forces of 'barbarism and religion' for their contribution to the fall of the Roman empire (Lentin and Norman, p.1074).

The German philosopher Kant summed up the Enlightenment view of the Dark Ages as 'an incomprehensible aberration of the human mind' (quoted in Anderson, 1987, p.415). In 1784, defining Enlightenment as 'man's emergence from his self-incurred immaturity', Kant argued that people should cease to rely unthinkingly on authority and on received wisdom; they should have the courage to think for themselves. 'The motto of enlightenment', he declared, 'is therefore *Sapere aude!* Have the courage to use your own understanding' (Eliot and Whitlock, 1992, p.305). The motto was taken from Horace.

The classics, then, provided for Enlightenment thinkers not just a standard of artistic perfection for emulation (evident in the architectural projects of Sir John Soane, which you will study in Block 5) but also an independent set of criteria against which to measure, compare and contrast the past and contemporary world, and a spur to thought and action. To the particular delight of the anti-clerical *philosophes*, the classics suggested a secular alternative to Christian modes of thought and expression. In their constant assaults on conventional religion, they found in the ancient philosophies of Stoicism and Epicureanism, or an eclectic mix of both, an attraction and a pedigree that predated Christianity and suggested rational or at least dignified alternatives for people to live by – and indeed to die by. In the deaths of Socrates and Seneca, the classics offered a noble tradition of suicide, a mortal sin in the eyes of the Church. The dying Hume, as you will see in Block 1, claimed with apparent equanimity and very much in the spirit of the Romans that he had neither fear of death nor belief in a future life. The classics were also used to legitimize modern ideas on society and culture in a way that suggested Enlightenment ideas had universal force and relevance, being rooted in the oldest and greatest of civilizations.

Summary point: for Enlightenment artists and thinkers, classical antiquity provided a standard of greatness, a symbol of power and a secular legitimization of their own forward thinking.

EXERCISE   Turn now to your AV Notes, which will direct you to watch section 3 ('The classics') of *Aspects of Enlightenment*. When you have worked through this section of the video and attempted the exercise in the notes, return to this unit.

The Enlightenment on art, genius and the sublime

Enlightenment ideas on art and the creative process were deeply influenced by the contemporary veneration for reason, empiricism and the classics. The business of the artist was conceived of as the imitation of nature, and as far as high art was concerned, this process of imitation should be informed by an intelligent grasp of the processes used to produce classical art. The ancients and their art were seen as models in the judicious selection of the most beautiful elements observed in nature, creating forms of ideal or 'beautiful' nature that were derived from a distillation of the very best and a filtering out of physical flaws. The leading art critic Johann Joachim Winckelmann (1717–68) held up Greek statuary for imitation as the embodiment of perfection. Transmitted to the eighteenth century via a robust Renaissance artistic tradition based on the antique, Enlightenment Neoclassicism in its broadest sense attempted not only direct borrowings from the antique (the imitation of architectural motifs, the use of classical drapes to clothe figures, idealized treatment of the human figure based on antique sculpture, reference to sculptural poses), but also an emulation of the order, unity, proportion and harmony felt to underpin all classical art. The principles of classical composition were based on the notion of a clear focus on a central motif (a hero, martyr or saint); grand, unifying (as opposed to sparkling, dappled or disjointed) effects of light and shade that wouldn't distract the eye to the detriment of mental focus on an elevating subject; noble simplicity, balance and symmetry (see Figure 1.7). You will find in the art of **Jacques-Louis David** (1748–1825) the expression of a particularly pure form of classical composition.

As the century progressed, the dangers of servile imitation, or a formulaic approach to art, were increasingly recognized as the claims for more 'natural' art were asserted. A significant body of opinion developed that was critical of artists who simply imitated the art of the past in a way that degenerated into artifice and mannerism. In the 1760s Diderot, who also wrote as an art critic, was among those who insisted that artists should pay more respect to nature. Study of idealized antique statuary and the principles of anatomy and proportion that had informed it remained important to artists, but it was stressed increasingly that respect for these must not exclude or diminish first-hand observation of the human body. Life drawing classes at the academies of art allowed male artists to study the nude, but the human models were normally posed in highly artificial ways that complied with the conventions of antique sculpture; their poses and the positions of their limbs were fixed in the drawing studio

Figure 1.7 Nicolas Poussin, The Holy Family in Egypt, *1655–7, 105 x 145.5 cm, The State Hermitage Museum, Saint Petersburg.*

The principles of classical composition demonstrated in this painting – balance, symmetry, broad, unified light effects and a prominent, hierarchical positioning of the main figures – influenced generations of eighteenth-century painters. Poussin was greatly influenced by antique friezes and statuary.

by a complex arrangement of ropes, pulleys and blocks (see Figure 1.8). Theorists called increasingly for less artificial poses and methods of observation.

This growing quest for the 'natural' extended to changing views on the status of different genres or subjects in art. While high art, inspired by classical or religious subjects, retained its position at the top of the hierarchies perpetuated by the academies of Europe, there was a growing appreciation of the lower genres of landscape, still life and scenes of everyday life, which required more direct observation of a more natural reality. In landscape art, as you will see, the idealized classical landscapes of the seventeenth-century French artist Claude Lorrain (1600–82) remained extremely influential. But there was also an increasing tendency to place more emphasis on directly observed sketches of the landscape that, while still beautifying nature, allowed for

Figure 1.8   Michel-Ange Houasse, The Drawing Academy, *c.1725, 61 x 72.5 cm, oil on canvas, Royal Palace, Madrid. Photo: © Patrimonio Nacional.*

imitation of a greater variety of natural effects. Enlightenment artists and critics were emboldened to demand greater naturalism or realism in art, in both style and subject matter, as a result of the popularity of Dutch and Flemish paintings, which had generated a northern tradition increasingly seen as a real alternative to the classical. In England William Gilpin and other artists and writers interested in what they called the 'picturesque' advocated travel as a means of viewing real landscapes and directly observed sketches as part of the process of producing views 'fit for a picture'. The quest for greater naturalism was seen in France as an antidote to the early eighteenth-century excesses of the Rococo, a specific adaptation or 'debasement' of the grand classical style characterized by serpentine curves and asymmetric forms applied mainly to portraiture and to erotic and playful mythological subjects (see Figure 1.9). In the second half of the eighteenth century, a greater respect for nature was seen as a moral solution to the luxury and corruption of the Rococo's aristocratic patrons.

Given the emphasis on imitation, it is perhaps unsurprising that the Enlightenment concept of the imagination was essentially that of

Figure 1.9   François Boucher, The Triumph of Venus, *1740, oil on canvas, 130 x 162 cm, National Museum of Fine Arts, Stockholm. Photo: National Museum of Fine Arts.*

Boucher's frivolous and erotic Rococo style and treatment of mythological subjects exerted a large influence on mid-eighteenth-century taste. Associated with aristocratic decadence, they led to calls later in the century for art that was both more natural and more moral.

producing new variations on old themes. The imagination was held to combine impressions observed in nature and previous art, but was generally not understood or required to include any great flights of fancy. The pleasure of art lay in the recognition of the familiar reprocessed in ways adapted to modern times. While the *Encyclopédie* article on 'Genius', written by Jean François de Saint-Lambert, defined genius as consisting of extraordinary powers of mind, intuition and inspiration transcending mere intelligence, most Enlightenment commentators on aesthetic matters saw such qualities as appropriate to a specific stage of the artistic process (the initial moment of inspiration, the preliminary sketch) rather than as qualities that should dominate or overwhelm. Genius was a quality of mind to be welcomed, but the creative process must also involve reflection, study and observation.

Indeed, many Enlightenment thinkers shared the conviction that good art was largely, though not exclusively, the product of compliance with well-established rules derived from the classics and empirical reason. As Voltaire observed in 1753, 'I value poetry only insofar as it is the ornament of reason' (quoted in Furst, 1969, p.19). Voltaire's aesthetics, like those of most French writers of the eighteenth century, were based on the neoclassical canons of literature laid down in the reign of Louis XIV by such critics as Nicolas Boileau in his *Art of Poetry* (1674). So while Voltaire was a pioneer in introducing Shakespeare to the European public, he did so with profound reservations and, as it were, holding his nose, arguing that Shakespeare's plays included 'gold nuggets in a dung-heap'. He presented Shakespeare as a unique genius who succeeded despite such lamentable violations of the neoclassical rules as mixing comic and tragic elements in the same play. Voltaire was in good company in defending the accepted literary canons and explaining 'genius' as the exception that proved the rule. Sir Joshua Reynolds (1723–92), President of the Royal Academy in London, adopted the same view in relation to art:

> Could we teach taste or genius by rules, they would no longer be taste and genius. But though there neither are, nor can be, any precise invariable rules for the exercise, or the acquisition, of these great qualities, yet we may truly say that they always operate in proportion to our attention in observing the works of nature, to our skill in selecting, and to our care in digesting, methodizing, and comparing our observations. There are many beauties in our art, that seem, at first, to lie without [outside] the reach of precept, and yet may easily be reduced to practical principles.
>
> (Reynolds, 1975, p.44)

The artist, in other words, should not let his imagination run away with him. Hume, too, warned of this danger:

> The *imagination* of man is naturally sublime, delighted with whatever is remote and extraordinary, and running without control into the most distant parts of space and time in order to avoid the objects which custom has rendered too familiar to it.
>
> (Quoted in Hampson, 1968, p.158)

The deeper irony for today's reader is that it was precisely this unconstrained escapism into long ago and far away, the 'remote and extraordinary', that was to captivate and characterize the Romantics.

Summary point: Enlightenment ideas on art and the artist were dominated by reason, moderation, classicism and control. However, there was recognition of the elusive quality of original 'genius'.

If most aesthetic ideas of the Enlightenment emphasized reason and experience, and classified 'genius' as something outside the rules, there was one further concept mentioned by Hume, 'the sublime', that seemed to strain Enlightenment rationality to its limits. Theorized by Edmund Burke in his *Philosophical Enquiry* (see above, p.17), a sublime aesthetic experience was one that inspired awe and terror in the spectator or reader. The sublime was something literally overwhelming, either because of its enormity (a high mountain, a deep chasm, a blinding light), its infinity (the spiritual or timeless) or its obscurity (a cloud-capped mountain, a floating mist, night, intense darkness) – all, significantly, the opposite of the precise, measured, penetrating 'light' of the Enlightenment. When faced with the sublime, the viewer, listener or reader felt a kind of paralysis of the will and of the powers of understanding and imagination. At the same time, as an *aesthetic* experience (grounded in art rather than reality) the sublime allowed for the thrill of danger without its real consequences. Immensely popular in this context across Europe were the 'works' of Ossian, ostensibly a poetic cycle by a Gaelic bard of the third century CE, but in fact the invention of James MacPherson (1736–96), who published his prose 'translations' in 1760. Napoleon was among the many devotees of Ossian, as much moved by the tales of legendary heroes in a wild, rugged and primitive northern setting as by Homer's more familiar Greeks and Trojans. This kind of exalted experience was increasingly sought in art and by the late Enlightenment was a dominant aesthetic mode:

> It is night. I am alone, forlorn on the hill of storms. The wind is heard in the mountain. The torrent pours down the rock. No hut receives me from the rain, forlorn on the hill of winds. Rise o moon from behind the clouds. Stars of the night, arise!

(MacPherson, Colma's lament from *Ossian*, quoted in Barzun, 2000, p.409)

In Mozart's *Don Giovanni* the sublime emerges in the infernal forces that swallow the main character at the end of the opera, and perhaps in the sublime courage of the man who defies them. The image of Prometheus, the demi-god punished for his defiance of the king of the gods, began to haunt the poetic imagination when **Goethe** (1749–1832) devoted to it a dramatic fragment and ode (1773). In Unit 28 you will study a setting by **Schubert** (1797–1828) of part of this work. For the philosopher Jean-Jacques Rousseau, it was the possession of a non-material soul that allowed people to seize the infinity of the sublime. This sensation of phenomena straining or exceeding the limits of human understanding was later to form the basis of a fully-fledged Romantic aesthetic.

Summary point: in the Enlightenment the theorization and popularization of the sublime began to undermine the eighteenth century's otherwise clear emphasis on the knowable, the rational and controllable.

The Enlightenment and nature

The sublime was potentially subversive of the Enlightenment mindset, which focused mainly on the power of human intelligence to grasp and explain the natural world, and indeed to discover natural causes of phenomena previously considered supernatural. There were, for example, frequent attempts to demystify the 'miracles' narrated in the Bible, since the violation of the laws of nature which a miracle implied was a physical impossibility and a contradiction in terms. The Marquis de Sade was appealing to an established Enlightenment mentality when he declared that there was no need to look beyond the physical world of nature (including human physiological needs), to the spiritual, in order to explain human behaviour. Hume had already popularized the notion that human beings can be understood purely as creations of nature. Enlightenment science and technology sought to open up to scrutiny and harness the power of all aspects of the natural world, while landscape painters and garden designers attempted to prune, beautify and frame nature in ways that emphasized the human capacity to control it. Nature was regarded as an object of investigation rather than a force or attraction in its own right.

When Samuel Johnson visited Scotland with his companion and biographer James Boswell in 1773, he recorded his impressions in *A Journey to the Western Islands of Scotland*.

EXERCISE Read the following passage on the Highland mountains from Johnson's *Journey*. How would you describe his attitude towards mountainous regions? In answering this question, it will be helpful to identify key words that betray the emotional colour of Johnson's response.

> Of the hills many may be called, with Homer's Ida, *abundant in springs*, but few can deserve the epithet which he bestows upon Pelion, by *waving their leaves*. They exhibit very little variety, being almost wholly covered with dark heath, and even that seems to be checked in its growth. What is not heath is nakedness, a little diversified by now and then a stream rushing down the steep. An eye accustomed to flowery pastures and waving harvests, is astonished and repelled by this wide extent of hopeless sterility. The appearance is that of matter incapable of form or usefulness, dismissed by Nature from her care, and disinherited of her favours, left in its original elemental state, or quickened only with one sullen power of useless vegetation.
>
> It will very readily occur, that this uniformity of barrenness can afford very little amusement to the traveller; that it is easy to sit at home and conceive rocks, and heath, and waterfalls; and that these journeys are useless labours, which neither impregnate the imagination, nor enlarge the understanding. It is true, that of far

the greater part of things, we must content ourselves with such knowledge as description may exhibit, or analogy supply; but it is true, likewise, that these ideas are always incomplete, and that, at least, till we have compared them with realities, we do not know them to be just. As we see more, we become possessed of more certainties, and consequently gain more principles of reasoning, and found a wider basis of analogy.

Regions mountainous and wild, thinly inhabited, and little cultivated, make a great part of the earth, and he that has never seen them, must live unacquainted with much of the face of nature, and with one of the great scenes of human existence.

(Greene, 1986, pp.611–12)

DISCUSSION   'Hopeless sterility', 'repelled', 'disinherited', 'uniformity of barrenness': these terms betray Johnson's personal aversion to mountains, particularly those stripped bare of vegetation. Although he sees them as among the 'great scenes of human existence' (no doubt because of their significance and scale, which as dutiful empirical reasoners we need to see and confirm for ourselves), they emerge as natural features to be shunned by those seeking 'amusement' (objects of interest).

Let's pause a moment to consider what Johnson is saying and his mode of delivery, his style. Johnson is the archetypal voice of the Enlightenment. Note the prose: poised, balanced, eloquent, dignified, 'Augustan' indeed, combining classical learning (the italicized quotations from Homer) with close observation, and drawing broad, balanced conclusions. The mountains themselves, he says, are of inherently little interest to the thinking man, and from the aesthetic point of view the Scottish mountains, far from overwhelming by their 'sublimity', are particularly unattractive, arid and monotonous. The Highlands, not being amenable to agriculture, also lack 'usefulness'. Johnson's is the view of the city dweller, conscious of the interdependence of productive labour and civilized society (the word 'civilized' derives from 'city').

Summary point: to the enlightened, wild nature was often a source of discomfort rather than a stimulus to the imagination.

Wild nature, whether in the Highlands or the Alps (the passage of which was considered an unpleasant obstacle on the Grand Tour to Italy), was to be shunned or brought under control. (Napoleon, who crossed the Alps several times on his early campaigns, was as emperor to build mountain passes to facilitate communication with the Italian parts of his 'French empire'.) The late eighteenth-century fashion for picturesque landscape art and sketching discussed by William Gilpin in his *Observations on ... the Mountains and Lakes of Cumberland and*

Westmoreland (1786) and **Uvedale Price**'s (1747–1829) *Essays on the Picturesque, as compared with the Sublime and the Beautiful* (1794) recommended a judicious selection and arrangement of landscape motifs so that the viewer's eye would be led into the middle distance of a picture and encounter a painted scene in an ordered way. Mountains were often safely relegated to the background. Once again, the emphasis was on control of nature and on the pre-eminence of the *human* perspective or viewpoint.

In other respects, however, the Enlightenment placed nature in the foreground. In the last section we saw how nature or naturalism became increasingly important to artists. In the same way, nature became increasingly recognized as a guide or force in moral matters. Once thinkers were removed from contemplation of its raw or real state (in, for example, the form of wild landscapes), they elevated its virtues and often overlooked its defects. The most renowned advocate of natural simplicity was Rousseau, who in his *Discourse on the Sciences and the Arts* (1750) and his *Discourse on the Origin of Inequality* (1754), as well as in *Émile* (1762), promoted the idea of natural simplicity and the primitive as a corrective to corrupting wealth and sophistication. ('Discourses' were, like 'Enquiries' and 'Dialogues', an established type of Enlightenment rational enquiry.) Although Rousseau did not believe that human society should revert to a crude primitive state, he did attempt to promote the virtues of a simpler life close to nature, and used the idea of the 'primitive' to highlight the deficiencies of contemporary society and point the way to reform. Finding much contemporary culture morally corrupt, he advocated a regenerated culture very different from that of the Parisian *salons* frequented by the *philosophes* (see Figure 1.3). For most Enlightenment thinkers sociability was central to their mission to share ideas, extend knowledge and engage in debate. Rousseau was initially a part of these enlightened social circles, sharing a common background in *salon,* coffee house, club, academy or learned society, where conversation and ideas flowed freely. Later, however, and partly as the result of arguments born of his own sense of alienation, he distanced himself and began to feel that truth was more likely to emerge from solitary reflection or imaginative reverie, and from the country rather than the city. In his novels (and also in an opera which he composed called *Le Devin du village – The Village Soothsayer*) he highlighted the virtues of simple people in communion with nature and their own hearts.

If the interest in nature expressed by most Enlightenment thinkers was less intense than Rousseau's, it is nevertheless true that all of them used the word 'nature' in a polemical sense, to highlight by contrasting with nature whatever they saw as unjust, unnatural and harmful in their own society and culture. Thus there was frequent appeal, in the *Encyclopédie* and elsewhere, to 'natural law', 'natural rights' and 'natural equality'. In many of these pronouncements use of the term 'nature' was highly questionable in that it was based on assumptions about how the world and its inhabitants might have been before the rot had set in, and before the establishment of specific social, moral and political structures. In moral, social and political matters, 'nature' represented an ideal state of affairs towards which we should strive.

Summary point: Enlightenment thinkers regarded nature (in the sense of the physical, observable world) as an object of study and wild nature as a force to be controlled. However, in many theoretical contexts (for example, aesthetic and moral matters) they often saw it as an authoritative guide or ideal, and deferred to it in a polemical, reformist spirit intended to highlight contemporary injustices and errors.

3   The forces of change: towards Romanticism

The relationship between the Enlightenment and the movement known as Romanticism, which dominated early nineteenth-century culture, is the subject of intense debate among scholars. There is no single correct way of defining this relationship, and one of the main challenges you will face in this course is in forming your own conclusions on the subject. It is possible, for example, to see the French Revolution as a cataclysmic event that tumbled the old order and ruptured faith in the Enlightenment and its reformist ambitions, thus stimulating the intense inwardness and doubt symptomatic of much Romantic thought. (This dimension of the Revolution is explored further below.) Equally, the growth in our period of a new class benefiting from the profits of industry and agrarian reform is often seen as a transforming influence in the wider culture. Freed from the conventional allegiances of the hereditary noble and genteel sections of society to the classical and the decorous, this emergent capitalist elite ('new money') expressed different priorities in art, literature and music as it attempted to assert its new status and identity. After the Revolution, these priorities included a new fear of the great mass of the population untouched by the Enlightenment, and a search for ways of controlling it. The reforms to factory conditions proposed by Robert Owen, for example, might be seen as a combination of enlightened humanitarianism and social control.

It can also be argued, however, that the seeds of Romanticism were sown by the Enlightenment itself. It was, after all, the Enlightenment that stimulated vigorous discussion and criticism of the status quo as part of an impulse towards the creation of a more modern culture. Certainly, the quest for rebellion and modernity intensified in the Romantic era. In the following section we'll be looking at some of the developments of the eighteenth century that are now often called 'pre-Romantic'. It is unwise to apply hindsight in such a way as to suggest that certain cultural developments took place in anticipation of others. Most large-scale cultural changes involve a complex web of factors. Nevertheless, Romanticism can be seen to have had gradual as well as more sudden causes, some of which, particularly the growing status of emotion and more personal responses to the human and natural worlds, we outline briefly below. We will then examine other agents of change.

The increasing status of feeling

Although the Enlightenment advocated the rigorous use of reason as the main means of achieving progress, some of its major thinkers also recognized the role of feeling or emotion, particularly in moral matters. Chief among these was Rousseau. He felt that 'inner sentiment' played an important part in matters of conscience and of religious faith, as well as in human relations. By 'sentiment' he meant everything embracing intuition (a word rarely used in the eighteenth century) and emotion *except* extreme emotion, which was normally referred to as 'passion'. As his career developed, Rousseau became obsessive about sentiment. He had begun, like the rest of the *philosophes,* as a model rationalist, contributing articles on music to the *Encyclopédie* and writing works such as *Émile* that focused on a reasoned analysis of society's defects and proposed rational solutions. As a result of various quarrels, temperamental difficulties and growing paranoia (outlined in Video 1, band 3 and Unit 5), he increasingly saw himself as the enemy of other Enlightenment thinkers, whose excessive reliance on reason alone had, he believed, led them astray. If only they listened to their heart and conscience as much as to their reason, he believed, they would see things his way. In his best-selling *La Nouvelle Héloïse* (1761) he wrote of the infallible promptings of individual conscience: 'Whatever I feel to be right, is right. Whatever I feel to be wrong, is wrong' (Hampson, 1968, p.195).

To Hume, Rousseau's 'sensibility' (propensity for feeling) impeded rather than assisted his common sense. It threatened the processes of sound, empirical reasoning in the formulation of his views on religion and morality, and it seemed inappropriate to use sentiment as a means of establishing facts. (You will encounter in Unit 5 a detailed discussion of the differences between Hume and Rousseau.) Rousseau advocated a natural religion based on 'feeling' God's power and goodness through the contemplation of nature, in addition to deploying some of the more conventional arguments of rational deism (see Figure 1.10).

Rousseau's emphasis on sentiment led, in his later career, to a period of intense introspection explored through his autobiographical *Confessions* (which he read informally to friends in 1771), *Reveries of the Solitary Walker* (on which he worked between 1776 and 1778, the year of his death) and *Rousseau, Judge of Jean Jacques* (completed in 1776), all of which were published posthumously. In these works he attempted to justify himself to those with whom he had quarrelled, to set the record straight, as he saw it. In the *Reveries* he described solitary walks in which he meditated on nature, and experienced by the lapping water of a lakeshore the delicious sensation of pure existence, while pouring scorn on his enemies, the *philosophes*, whom he increasingly classified as dogmatists. He indulged to an unprecedented degree in self-absorption, in an avowed conviction of and a delight in the consciousness of his own uniqueness, in posing and in answering the question: 'what am I myself?' (Furst, 1979, p.57). In the *Confessions* too he begins with the same fascination with self:

> I am undertaking a work which is wholly without precedent ... I wish to show my fellow-men a man in all his natural truth, and I myself will be that man. Myself alone. I feel my heart, and I know men. I am not made like any of those whom I have seen. I venture to believe that I am not made like any other men who exist. If I am no better than they, at least I am different.

> (Rousseau, 1847, p.25; trans. Lentin)

The *Confessions* are written in a way that suggests openness and sincerity with what appears to be a ruthless and unforgiving exposure of his own faults, disappointments in love and sexual obsessions. In fact, they construct very carefully the persona with which he wishes to be identified: ardent but just. In contrast with the mainstream Enlightenment (say, with Johnson's reflections, implicitly based on a view of man as a social creature, a thinking member of rational society), Rousseau's prime concern is with *himself* as an individual and the uniqueness of his identity in a society with which he finds himself at odds.

Figure 1.10 Anonymous, Rousseau 'Contemplating the Wild Beauties of Switzerland', *1797, engraving (frontispiece to R.B. Mowat,* The Age of Reason, *1934, London, Harrap).*

The Romantics were to draw inspiration from Rousseau's closeness to nature, including wild mountainous scenes.

Rousseau was not the first writer to engage in deep self-reflection or to be inspired by strong feeling. However, the nature and timing of Rousseau's writings had a profound impact on an eighteenth-century readership beginning to tire of pure reason and eager to explore aspects of their own identities. A conscious tinge of emotionalism counteracted Augustan common sense and the noonday clarity of the *Encyclopédie*. Poems such as Young's *Night Thoughts* (1742) and Thomas Gray's *Elegy written in a Country Churchyard* (1742–51) set a fashion for melancholic verse set in 'gothic' surroundings, typically a moonlit graveyard. Such verse foregrounded the emotion of the narrator's voice as he reflected on the inevitability of death, allowing his imagination freer range by relating to the evocative environment, the poet communing with himself and his own thoughts. Night settings were to become an important source of inspiration for Romantic writers, musicians and artists. In England the best-selling novels of Samuel Richardson (1689–1761), *Pamela or Virtue Rewarded* (1740) and *Clarissa* (1747–8), told deeply emotional tales, detailing the subjective reactions of innocent women deceived by rakes, and were very influential for later Enlightenment writers such as Diderot. For these writers the aim was to stir the readers' emotions to the core, to the point of making them weep. From the 1760s onwards there was throughout Europe a cult of intense sensibility inspired in great part by figures such as Richardson and Rousseau. Rousseau's *La Nouvelle Héloïse*, which ran to 70 editions in France by 1789, told the story of two lovers torn between their love and duty to a third member of a love triangle. Translated into many languages, the novel inspired writers well into the nineteenth century.

Summary point: in the second half of the eighteenth century, a growing number of writers, artists and thinkers, many inspired by Rousseau, became preoccupied with the expression of emotions. Self-absorption and a concern with one's unique identity became more central.

This was paralleled in the emotionalism of the *Olney Hymns*, in which the Evangelicals Newton and Cowper sought to move their congregation with a sense that open-hearted receptivity to Christ's sacrifice and redeeming love could purge and revolutionize their own lives. The purpose and indeed the effect of the Evangelical mission within the Anglican Church was literally to move and stir the suppliant: to induce tears, fainting, speaking in tongues, profound emotional disturbance and spiritual regeneration. Religious 'enthusiasm' – the conviction of direct personal communion with God, a personal zeal for Christ, empathy with his sacrifice on the cross (a quality discouraged by traditional Anglicans and deplored by Dr Johnson as akin to fanaticism) – was the motive force of Evangelicalism. The rapid growth in our period of Methodism, originally a variant of, and then an alternative to, Anglicanism, also intensified emotional worship. Of John Wesley (1703–91), the founder of Methodism, it has been said: 'No single eighteenth-century figure influenced so many minds' (Dorn, 1940, p.241). His preaching began in the 1730s, and therefore constituted one of the earlier stimuli to the cult of feeling. Wesley had experienced, preached and encouraged the soul-shaking emotionalism associated with conversion, in reaction to the worldly and tepid decorum approved by the mainstream Anglican Church. There were many manifestations of such emotionalism outside the context of religion. Sentimental (in the sense of 'full of sentiment') plays became popular at the theatre, and weeping in the galleries was taken as a sign of an audience's healthy moral conscience. This new emphasis on feeling in art and literature (see Figure 1.11) may have been, in part, a result of the increasing secularization of the life of many of the privileged and educated; emotional fulfilment from art and literature was perhaps particularly important to those who felt that religion no longer answered their needs.

Figure 1.11 Etienne Aubry, Paternal Love, *1775, oil on canvas, 78.7 x 101.5 cm, Barber Institute of Fine Arts, University of Birmingham. Photo: Bridgeman Art Library.*

Aubry's painting exemplifies the cult of feeling that swept through European culture from the 1760s onwards. Sentiment was harnessed as a didactic, moral force.

As an art critic, Diderot was among those who encouraged artists to paint emotive, moral anecdotes calculated to make the virtuous shed tears. Like many others, he argued that all good people would weep at the same misfortunes and would draw universal lessons from highly personal responses. This unprecedented emphasis on emotion drew greater attention to the personal responses of the individual, one of the central concerns of an emergent Romanticism.

In Germany from the 1770s there was a similar shift towards emotion in the form of the *Sturm und Drang* movement, normally translated as 'storm and stress'. The 'stress' was a form of reaching or striving forward that embraced a creative rebellion against convention in the cause of freedom, whether artistic, emotional or even political. Friedrich Schiller's *The Robbers* (1781) is a play about idealistic, self-assertive young anarchists who emulate Robin Hood. Their leader, the 'hero', Karl Moor, takes revenge on a hateful hide-bound society by committing a series of atrocious murders. He denounces authority in heady language:

> The law has never yet formed a great man. It is freedom that has bred colossuses ... Put me in charge of a band of men like me, and I will make of Germany a republic beside which Rome and Sparta will seem like nunneries.

(Sorel, 1912, p.162; trans. Lentin)

The unprecedented appeal of 'storm and stress' is shown by the reception of *The Robbers* on the opening night, which, as the commentator observed, marked a crucial literary and psychological threshold:

> The theatre was like a lunatic asylum, with rolling eyes, clenched fists, hoarse uproar among the audience. Strangers fell sobbing into each other's arms, women tottered, half-fainting, to the door. It was a universal disruption into chaos, out of whose mists a new creation is emerging.

(Hampson, 1968, pp.201–2)

The movement also emphasized the eccentricities of individual character, as opposed to the Enlightenment's focus on a universal human nature. The outlook projected by *Sturm und Drang* was that of the alienated outsider, the socially excluded, the outlaw. Alienation, self-expression and the sublime were also prominent in an early novel by Goethe, *The Sorrows of Young Werther* (1774). This novel, one of the most popular of the late eighteenth century, was close in its plot and tone to Rousseau's *La Nouvelle Héloïse*, but pushed the despair of impossible love to even more tragic extremes (see Figure 1.12). Life followed art when young men imitated Werther not only in the clothes they wore, but even to the point of committing suicide. Among the thousands of adolescent readers of *Werther* harbouring dark thoughts was a lonely 16-year-old officer

Figure 1.12   Thomas Rowlandson, The Triumph of Sentiment (Butcher Weeping over Werther), *1787, Goethe Museum, Düsseldorf.*

cadet from Corsica training at the royal military academy at Paris, Napoleon Bonaparte.

Rousseau's new emphasis on sensibility or feeling stimulated an interest in forces that posed a threat to the centrality of Enlightenment reason. Equally, his view of nature as a site of meditation and spiritual contemplation challenged the pre-eminence of nature as something to be categorized, controlled and exploited. Nothing could be further from the Augustan common sense and sociability of Johnson, a city dweller addressing other city dwellers in his observations on the Highlands, than the introspective, fanciful and self-indulgent reflections typical of Rousseau's 'sensibility'. Yet for the generations that grew up on Rousseau, nothing was more attractive:

> Emerging from a long and happy reverie, seeing myself surrounded by greenery, flowers and birds, and letting my eyes wander over the picturesque far-off shores which enclosed a vast stretch of crystalline water, I fused my imaginings with these charming sights, and finding myself in the end gradually brought back to myself and my surroundings, I could not draw a line between fiction and reality; so much did everything conspire equally to make me love the contemplative and solitary life I led in that beautiful place.
>
> (*Reveries of the Solitary Walker,* 'Fifth Walk', 1782, in Rousseau, 1979, pp.90–1)

For Rousseau nature was a part of, rather than separate from, his own thoughts, feelings and imaginings. This attitude, together with his emphasis on personal feeling, exerted a powerful influence on the Romantics.

Enlightenment, humanity and revolution

We have seen from Diderot's article 'Encyclopedia' that the *philosophes* were convinced that their mission was for the benefit of their fellow human beings. For all of them, concern for humanity was the mainspring of their ideas and activities. The article on 'Fanaticism' (by Alexandre Deleyre) in the *Encyclopédie* sums up what they most bitterly opposed:

> *Fanaticism* is blind and passionate zeal born of superstitious opinions, causing people to commit ridiculous, unjust, and cruel actions, not only without any shame or remorse, but even with a kind of joy and comfort. *Fanaticism,* therefore, is only superstition put into practice.
>
> (Gendzier, 1967, p.104)

At the heart of the fight against fanaticism was Voltaire. His plea for religious toleration – *Écrasez l'infâme!* (crush the infamous thing) – was the slogan with which he branded fanaticism and its attendant ills. But his protests combined prolific and eloquent criticism in print with the personal championing of individual cases. The most famous instance of *l'infâme* was the case of Jean Calas in 1762. Calas, a Protestant from Toulouse, was wrongfully convicted of having murdered his son for converting to Catholicism. (The young man had committed suicide.) Calas was condemned to death by the high court at Toulouse. The horrible sentence of breaking on the wheel was carried out. After a long and energetic campaign by Voltaire, the verdict was quashed. The triumph for Voltaire and Enlightenment – the Europe-wide publicity for the cause of reason, justice, penal reform and religious toleration – was spectacular.

The Enlightenment's concern for humanitarian reform fuelled the ambitions of the generation that came to maturity on the eve of the Revolution. The *Encyclopédie* popularized notions of equality and natural rights which had become commonplace by 1789. This concept of the rights that should come to us at birth was not, however, normally related to more modern notions of equality of wealth and power. The Enlightenment was always conscious of what Boswell called 'the superiority of cultivated minds over the gross and illiterate' (Boswell, 1951, vol.2, p.133) and of the fragility of civilization in the face of riot and disorder. It was not until *after* the period covered by our course, in the middle decades of the nineteenth century, that there was any real extension of political rights to the masses. But there was a common conviction, propagated by the *philosophes,* that everyone had the right to equal justice before the law and the right not to be exploited by those enjoying power and privilege. Once again the cries for political reform were particularly strident in France, where injustice and inequality, long subject to Enlightenment criticism, were no longer felt to be tolerable.

In a broader sense, a concern for humanity manifested itself in a conviction of universal rights: everyone was entitled to be treated in a way fitting their dignity as a human being. In his poem *The Task* (1785) Cowper expressed his sorrow at man's inhumanity to man:

> There is no flesh in man's obdúrate[1] heart,
> It does not feel for man; the natural bond
> Of brotherhood is severed as the flax
> That falls asunder at the touch of fire.
> He finds his fellow guilty of a skin
> Not coloured like his own, and having power
> To enforce the wrong, for such a worthy cause
> Dooms and devotes him as his lawful prey.

> (Benham, 1902, pp.198–9)

The *philosophes* spoke out with a united voice against the slave trade. Voltaire and Diderot were among many who protested against it in the name of man's common humanity. Cugoano, in his *Thoughts and Sentiments on the Evils of Slavery*, used the term 'enlightened' to denote a humane code of conduct opposed to slavery, although not all Enlightenment thinkers expressed such opposition, so deeply entrenched was the practice in contemporary economic and political thought and activity. Boswell defended slavery, while Johnson opposed it. The ex-slave **Robert Wedderburn** (1762–1835), author of *The Horrors of Slavery* (1824), cited the Enlightenment authorities of truth, justice and the ancients in his vehement critique of the practice.

Summary point: humanitarianism and a concern with common human rights were central to the Enlightenment mission. In some, if not all, thinkers this led to an impulse to attack common inhumane practices such as religious oppression and slavery.

EXERCISE   Turn now to your AV Notes, which will direct you to watch section 4 ('Humanity and the noble savage') of *Aspects of Enlightenment*. When you have worked through this section of the video and attempted the exercise in the notes, return to this unit.

As a young man, Voltaire had had two spells in the Bastille for impertinence towards members of the nobility, and the injustice and

[1] The accent shows where the stress falls in this line.

indignity rankled. Yet Voltaire, who later became immensely rich, was no social radical. The *philosophes* in general contributed little to political thought as such; they hardly troubled about which might be the best form of government for implementing their cherished reforms. Montesquieu, in his erudite and influential *De l'esprit des lois* (*On the Spirit of the Laws*, 1748), advocated a system of institutional checks and balances, and the separation or balancing of executive (governing) power, legislative (lawmaking) power and judicial power (the power of the judges) in order to counter the unlimited exercise of state power by the executive (the king). Montesquieu and Voltaire were much impressed by Britain's constitutional or 'limited' monarchy, in which the monarch's powers were curbed by a partly representative assembly (Parliament) and an independent judiciary. Britain was often compared favourably with absolute monarchy in France. But Voltaire, who had long since popularized British values in his *Philosophical Letters or Letters on the English* (1734), was also attracted by enlightened models of absolute monarchy, such as those practised in the second half of the eighteenth century by Frederick the Great of Prussia, Catherine the Great of Russia, Joseph II of Austria (Mozart's patron), Gustav III of Sweden and Charles III of Spain. Voltaire, who was for a time historiographer royal to Louis XV until his independence and propensity for mischief-making made the court too hot to hold him, was moderate, pragmatic, undogmatic, flexible, and politically and socially conservative. Europe's traditional social structure being, so it was thought, fixed and immutable, it mattered little *how* enlightenment was implemented as long as it *was* implemented.

EXERCISE   Turn now to your AV Notes, which will direct you to watch section 5 ('Frederick the Great and enlightened absolutism') of *Aspects of Enlightenment*. When you have worked through this section of the video and attempted the exercise in the notes, return to this unit.

The *philosophes* and enlightened opinion generally believed that the *Encyclopédie* was proving its worth and that Enlightenment ideas were slowly but surely gaining ground among the educated across Europe. Voltaire himself, no starry-eyed optimist, thought so. His *Candide* (1759) is a mercilessly witty attack on facile optimism in the face of every kind of disaster: war, earthquakes and man's inhumanity to man. Nevertheless he wrote to a friend in 1764:

> Everything I observe is sowing the seeds of a revolution that will inevitably come to pass, which I shall not have the pleasure of witnessing ... By degrees enlightenment has spread so widely that it will burst forth at the first opportunity, and then there will be a

grand commotion. The younger generation are lucky: they will
see some great things.

(Bruun, 1967, p.102)

But it cannot be emphasized enough that neither Voltaire nor Rousseau
nor anyone before 1789 anticipated the revolution that actually took
place in France or the violent and bloody course that it took. What
Voltaire looked forward to was an enlightened, humane and orderly
society of moderate property owners, a society whose members were
guaranteed freedom to worship (or not to worship), to read, publish and
discuss whatever they wished, a humane penal system, the rule of law,
freedom from arbitrary arrest, and impartial justice for all. These rights
were duly proclaimed by the revolutionary National Assembly in 1789 in
the Declaration of the Rights of Man and Citizen.

Rousseau, while not disdaining these rights, went much further in his
insistence on linking freedom with morality. In *The Social Contract* he
argued that society was a moral entity, not simply the aggregate of selfish
individual preferences. The 'general will' or consensus of the people
constituted a moral imperative binding on all members of society, and
which, if they listened to the voice of conscience as well as to reason, all
individuals truly desired in their heart. The good society should prescribe
the strict morality, frugality and civic-mindedness conventionally
attributed to ancient Sparta, republican Rome and Rousseau's native
Calvinist Geneva. The state should enforce education and a religion that
inculcated these virtues, and in the final analysis it should *compel* people
to be good for, according to Rousseau, only the morally good individual
could be truly free. The influence of Rousseau's ideas on the later course
of the French Revolution can hardly be doubted. *The Social Contract*
appeared in 32 editions across the decade 1789–99. Revolutionary leaders
like **Maximilien de Robespierre** (1758–94), who came to power in
1793–4 and instigated the Terror, were fired by Rousseau's vision of the
good society and cited his works to justify terror and coercion (see
Figure 1.13). Rousseau himself had envisaged much gentler means of
effecting change: consensual politics and (in his educational treatise
Émile) good parenting lay at the heart of his agenda, rather than the
bloodshed of the Terror and the enforcement of revolutionary norms by
a minority of visionary fanatics assisted by a politically motivated street
crowd.

**Summary point: although the Enlightenment helped to prepare a
climate of opinion which welcomed the French Revolution, the
philosophes themselves did not foresee the Revolution or the way
it developed.**

It may be questioned whether Rousseau, who had drafted conventional
constitutions intended for Corsica and Poland, had not in his *Social
Contract* produced a piece of utopian thinking rather than a blueprint for
practical implementation. At any rate, for most *philosophes* enlightenment

was for the educated upper echelons of society. They wrote for the nobility and educated clergy, administrators, lawyers, academics, doctors and journalists, for the good bourgeois, the 'enlightened', 'judicious' and 'philosophic' reader of the *Encyclopédie,* not for the labouring poor or the unlettered masses. There were only 4,000 subscribers to the *Encyclopédie* – it was an expensive purchase (Gendzier, 1967, p.xx) – and those in France in sympathy with the Enlightenment numbered perhaps 50,000 out of a population of 20 million. The benefits of enlightenment would, it was hoped, trickle down in due course to the lower classes, but the potential of the masses for unrest was recognized and feared as a constant in history and a positive obstacle. For the

Figure 1.13   Anonymous, Supreme Being, Sovereign People, French Republic, *1794, Musée Carnavalet, Paris. Photo: Photothèque des musées de la ville de Paris/Philippe Ladet.*

Voltaire and Rousseau (who died in 1778) seen by the French revolutionaries in 1794 as harbingers of the Revolution. The words read: 'Supreme Being. Sovereign People. French Republic.' From behind the spreading rays of the sun appears the all-seeing eye of Providence observing the beneficent influence of Voltaire and Rousseau. To Voltaire's right is a bust of Brutus, the patriotic assassin of Julius Caesar. Rousseau is depicted as the author of Émile, *in which he preached the regeneration of society through a more 'natural' education. Relations between Voltaire and Rousseau were more distant than suggested by this idealized portrayal.*

masses, therefore, conventional religion remained a useful form of social control: 'Natural religion for the magistrates,' Voltaire wrote (in English), 'damn'd stuff [conventional religion] for the mob' (quoted in Dorn, 1940, p.211).

The works of the Enlightenment, then, were produced by and for a cultivated elite. Its culture was that of coffee house, *salon*, theatre, chateau, academy and club. Its characteristics were sociability, reasonability, wit, learning, style, badinage and civilized discourse. The aristocratic audiences who heard Figaro's reproach to his master Count Almaviva in Beaumarchais's *Marriage of Figaro,* the Paris 'hit' of 1784, or in its operatic version by Mozart (1786), enjoyed the raillery at their own expense:

> Because you are a *grand seigneur* you think yourself a great genius! Nobility, wealth, rank, offices: all this makes you high and mighty! What did you ever do to deserve all that? You took the trouble to be born, that's all!

> (Lagarde and Michard, 1962, p.400; trans. Lentin)

Likewise Mozart's *Don Giovanni* (1787) opens with Leporello's grumbles about his aristocratic master:

> I want to be a gentleman, and I don't want to serve any longer, no, no, no, no, no, no.

> (Bleiler, 1964, p.85)

But reading these works as 'revolutionary' may be reading too much into them. In the first place clever and cheeky servants were the staple of comedy and comic opera, and *Don Giovanni* was described on the title page as just that: a comic opera (*dramma giocoso*).

At any rate, even though someone in the pit on the first night of Beaumarchais's *Figaro* is said to have thrown an apple core at a duchess in a box, the aristocratic audiences had no inkling that their status and whole way of life were under threat. The traditional concept of society throughout Europe was a static one based on monarchy and a privileged nobility. If they thought about political revolution at all, it was in terms of a move to a more accountable, constitutional system on the British or perhaps the American model. No one dreamed of social upheaval. Marie Jean Antoine Nicholas de Caritat, Marquis de Condorcet (1743–94), one of the most radical *philosophes,* ardent for rights for women and blacks, was sure of one thing in 1789: monarchy was impregnable. Mme de la Tour du Pin, a young Frenchwoman in 1789, recalled that she and her aristocratic friends were 'laughing and dancing our way to the precipice. Thinking people were content to talk of abolishing all the abuses. France, they said, was about to be reborn. The word "revolution" was never uttered' (quoted in Davies, 1997, p.674).

If the Enlightenment was elitist it was also male-driven, and you will detect in this course a male bias in the choice of text authors. To some extent this is to misrepresent the period we are studying. Engaging women authors included Mary Wollstonecraft (1759–97) and the novelist Jane Austen. **Mme de Staël** (1766–1817), one of the most influential women of the period, who formed a bridge between the Enlightenment and Romanticism, does feature in Units 7–8 and in Video 2, band 2. In other respects, however, you may begin to appreciate the very real male bias of the culture when you view this video and consider the challenges faced even by women with connections of wealth and power like Staël. How much greater, then, must have been the difficulties faced by women like **Mary Prince** (1788–*c*.1834), a former slave, in finding a voice with which to express their own views and experiences. It was widely accepted that more educated women might become involved in amateur study such as drawing, music or botany. However, women who, like **Jane Marcet** (1769–1858), wished to become involved in the study of science, either required influential connections (for example, entrance to a high society *salon*) or were forced to engage in their study in private, domestic settings such as the drawing room; grand public settings were overwhelmingly a male domain. It is true that French women in particular became much more politically active during the Revolution, and that in Britain women intellectuals such as Wollstonecraft reinforced such efforts. But society generally was not ready to establish or endorse this growing female militancy in any sustained way.

Summary point: Enlightenment culture was mainly by and for the privileged elite. This elite was fearful of the potentially disruptive power of the uneducated masses. Nor was it ready to embrace equality of the sexes.

In every sense the French Revolution came as an appalling shock to the system, and it marks the great watershed in the period covered by this course (see Figure 1.14). When, at Valmy in 1792, an army of French revolutionaries put to flight a regular Prussian force intent on stamping out the Revolution in the name of the Old Regime, Goethe, who was present, declared: 'Here today a new epoch of world history begins' (quoted in Mowat, 1934, p.328). Condorcet wrote an optimistic *Sketch of a Historical Tableau of the Progress of the Human Mind* (1793), a noble statement of his faith in the future and a summation of Enlightenment expectations; but he wrote in the shadow of the guillotine, and he committed suicide to avoid execution. The clear-headed confidence, perhaps over-confidence, of the *philosophes* in the possibility of progress and human potential for good received its comeuppance after 1789. Many began to have second thoughts about their mission, and in their doubts, as well as in the work of those who continued in the mainstream Enlightenment tradition, lie some of the seeds of Romanticism.

Edmund Burke voiced these reservations eloquently in his *Reflections on the Revolution in France* (1790), which became the bible of those who opposed the Revolution and who took what henceforth was to become known as a 'conservative' stance. To those in Britain who expressed admiration for the Revolution and saw it as a model for imitation, Burke argued that the British constitution, far from being (as British radicals argued), a mere political convenience to be rewritten or torn up at will, was an organic entity to be nurtured and venerated like some ancient oak. It was the fruit of tradition, it distilled the collective wisdom of bygone ages, it was a bond between past and present, a trust from history, binding on the living. Sympathisers who applauded Burke included Catherine the Great, on whom Voltaire had lavished praise for her support of Enlightenment causes and as a paragon of 'enlightened absolutism', and the historian Edward Gibbon. Gibbon, who in his *Decline and Fall of the Roman Empire* had exercised much wit and learning at the expense of Christianity, now drew back in fear of the wider, and alarming, social implications of the Enlightenment. Of the French Revolution, Gibbon wrote to his patron Lord Sheffield in 1792, 'If

1.14 Anonymous, Exercise of the Rights of Man and French Citizen, *1792, engraving, Bibliothèque nationale de France, Paris.*

The French Revolution as seen by its royalist critics.

Exercice des Droits de l'Homme
et du Citoyen Français.

this tremendous warning has no effect on the men of property in England, ... you will deserve your fate' (Morley, 1891, p.253). When, the same year, the House of Commons voted against the abolition of slavery, Gibbon declaimed against Wilberforce and his followers: 'in this rage against slavery, in the numerous petitions against the slave trade, was there no leaven of new democratical principles? No wild ideas of the rights and natural equality of man? It is these I fear' (Hampson, 1968, p.153). For in Britain, to be radical meant to aim at reform of an ineffective and corrupt monarchy and electoral system; to be extremely radical meant sharing the views of Mary Wollstonecraft, Thomas Paine (1737–1809), Joseph Priestley, Thomas Beddoes (1760–1808), William Godwin (1756–1836) and others (including the poet **William Wordsworth**, 1770–1850), who all, at least initially, expressed enthusiasm for the French Revolution and called for far-reaching democratic reform at home, thus intensifying the vehement conservative backlash.

Summary point: the French Revolution strongly divided educated opinion in Europe. To be against the Revolution was to adopt a 'conservative' philosophy, which cast doubts on the reformist ambitions of the Enlightenment.

The Enlightenment and modernity

In its desire to replace outmoded, irrational ways of thinking by the rational, the sensible and the progressive, the Enlightenment was self-consciously modern. A manifestly scientific age and the visible advancement of knowledge in the eighteenth century required, it was felt, an overhaul – or at least a careful critical and radical scrutiny – of culture, society and their institutions. This was the implicit message of the *Encyclopédie*. Its contributors were convinced that they were motivated by feelings of beneficent humanity, that they were on the side of the future and that the future was on their side. In spite of its allegiance to the classical tradition, the Enlightenment was a modernizing force, keen to review and regenerate culture and society. The classics themselves were often used as authorities to support change. When Diderot argued in the *Encyclopédie* article 'Epicureanism' for a moral code that legitimized the pursuit of pleasure, he appealed to the authority of the ancient philosopher Epicurus. Napoleon was described by Stendhal as 'imbued with Roman ideas' (Stendhal, 2004, p.53), though the Roman style and emblems of his rule moved rapidly from republican to imperial. When William Gilpin set out his new aesthetic of the picturesque, he cited the poets Ovid and Virgil to exemplify the evocative landscape effects he sought in art. Excavations of ancient sites such as Pompeii and Herculaneum and new scholarship on antiquity brought fresh models and inspiration to architects and their patrons. Architects such as Soane invigorated their architecture by drawing on such scholarship. More broadly, the Enlightenment's mission of rational scrutiny and reform opened the way for changes of attitude and values among the educated sections of society. Diderot described the purpose of the *Encyclopédie* as being 'to change people's way of thinking'. As we have seen, moral codes were secularized; deism was promoted as a more rational, acceptable version of religion. Authority of all kinds – monarchical and ecclesiastical as well as noble privilege – was challenged. These changes were accelerated and converted to action in France by the Revolution, which swept away within a few years what it called the Old Regime, the old social and political order and the privileges of nobles and clergy.

In 1790 the French first adopted a form of constitutional monarchy on the British model, guided and restricted by a legislative assembly representative of a wider, though by no means completely inclusive, constituency. Respect for noble birth was replaced by respect for men of property regardless of their lineage. The relatively moderate reforms of the early years of the Revolution then gave way to more violent upheavals, as resentment stirred against the new aristocracy of the rich. The monarchy was replaced by a republic (see Figure 1.15), which in turn, under pressure of war and civil war, soon fell under the sway of a ruthless dictatorship. When the violence had abated and political power was once more restored to a property-owning elite, there was scope for a large new meritocracy with equal citizenship and equal treatment before the law. While under the Old Regime no one had been admitted to the French court since 1760 unless he could trace his noble ancestry back to the fourteenth century, Napoleon's declared maxim was *la carrière ouverte aux talents* (careers open to talent). His claim that every foot-soldier carried in his knapsack the baton of a marshal of France was not literally true; nevertheless his marshals and administrators included men of humble origin brought to positions of authority by the needs of the Revolution and the Napoleonic empire, and even raised to Napoleon's imperial nobility. These were spectacular changes on an unprecedented scale. When Napoleon rose to power, the changes were seen as gleaming signs of France's modernity, a model to be imposed on the rest of Europe. Napoleon could be seen as the 'son of the Revolution' who guaranteed its positive achievements while protecting its beneficiaries from the former anarchy and violence of the urban crowd.

Napoleon's image as 'son of the Revolution', restorer of order, product of the Enlightenment, bearer of civilization and 'great man' often masked a brutal political cynicism. The painting by the French artist **Antoine-Jean Gros** (1771–1835), *Bonaparte Visiting the Plague-Stricken of Jaffa* (1804), shows Napoleon as compassionate hero when he had in fact just authorized a number of violent atrocities during the Egyptian campaign. From the first, he suppressed freedom of expression and the press, reintroduced slavery in the French colonies, and came to be seen by many as another brand of tyrant. But it was some years before Europe lost faith in the positive, modernizing energy he seemed to represent, and after his fall he was missed as a vigorous, inspiring and enlightened

Figure 1.15   Anonymous, La Chûte en masse (They all fall down)*, caricature print, Musée Carnavalet, Paris. Photo: © RMN/Bulloz.*

Enlightenment and modernity combine in this depiction of the electric spark of liberty overturning the thrones of the crowned heads of Europe and the Pope.

alternative to the reactionary restored Bourbon monarchy. Spain, attached to its Catholic and social traditions, resisted his modernity as it fought his invading armies, and Napoleon's imperial ambition to complete his domination over the whole of Europe stimulated national self-consciousness as a counteracting force in Spain, Russia and Germany.

Another modernizing force in the period covered by our course was the growing pace of industrialization, as the methods of cottage outworkers were gradually replaced by mass factory production of goods. As people moved increasingly to work in towns, old social communities and values were under threat, and it was in such a climate that Evangelical Christianity, which you will study in Block 3, began to thrive. The concept of 'modernity' is often associated with the secular, rational and progressive aspects of the Enlightenment, more specifically with the growing status of secular public opinion (Porter, 2000, p.23). The process of 'modernizing' permeated culture in all kinds of ways, however, and was certainly not restricted to the secular. Evangelicals defined a new kind of faith in response to growing concerns about the ability of traditional Anglicanism to meet the needs of a swiftly changing society. The poet William Cowper and the Evangelical Christian John Newton collaborated on the production of new hymns for the parish of Olney. Together with the anti-slavery campaigner William Wilberforce, they turned their backs on the growing pursuit of material prosperity that came with industrialization in order to define more exacting or rewarding routes to salvation. Reacting against what he saw as a detrimental decline in faith, Wilberforce proposed an alternative, spiritually inspired modernity in the form of a religion that built on personal experience while rejecting superstition. The modernizing forces of the Enlightenment could, then, take the form of regeneration rather than the violent break with tradition produced by the Revolution.

The modernity of the Enlightenment also had aesthetic consequences. Whig landowners in Britain wishing to assert their independence from conservative royalist politics 'modernized' the landscape by sweeping away rambling, picturesque gardens associated with nostalgia and replacing them with the extensive lawns and artificial water courses made fashionable by the landscape designer Capability Brown (see Figure 1.16). They built obtrusive, gleaming white Palladian mansions in a grand classical style in dominating positions within 'wild' landscapes such as the Lake District in order to assert their modern taste and their will for change. And yet such impulses towards modernity did not remain unchallenged. The Enlightenment's own respect for nature stimulated lively debate among thinkers such as William Wordsworth, Uvedale Price and William Gilpin about the extent to which art and artifice should alter the natural appearance of the landscape. The scene was set for a man versus nature dialectic that would lie at the heart of Romantic concerns.

Summary point: the Enlightenment was characterized by an impulse towards modernity in matters of government, politics, religion and aesthetics. There were those, however, who questioned the rapid momentum and effects of change.

4   Conclusion

EXERCISE   Try to note down as many of the key characteristics of the Enlightenment as you can remember.

DISCUSSION   How did you manage this? Did you remind yourself of some of the main characteristics by checking the summary points? The exercise you have just carried out is one of *consolidation* and *revision*. We recommend that you carry out a similar exercise as you work through all subsequent

Figure 1.16   B.T. Pouncy, after T. Hearne, engravings from R. Payne Knight, The Landscape: A Didactic Poem, *1794. Photo: by permission of the British Library.*

The methods of Kent and Capability Brown as parodied by R. Payne Knight. The upper of the two engravings shows the 'nature' of the 'Improvers' with its shaven lawns, 'nude waters', monotonous 'clumps' and serpentine walks. The lower shows the return to nature advocated by Knight and other champions of the picturesque school.

units. In most cases you will not have the assistance of summary points, so it is important that you try to express and note these yourself as you work through the material. If you follow this advice, you will find that your examination preparation at the end of the course is much more manageable.

EXERCISE Read the anonymous article from the *Encyclopédie*, 'Philosophe' (1765), in the appendix to this unit (pp.61–3). What characteristics of the enlightened thinker are identified in it? How useful or significant do you find this description of a typical *philosophe*?

DISCUSSION Rational action, following the 'torch' or light of reason, empirical verification of knowledge ('bases his principles on an infinite number of particular observations') and a focus on useful knowledge ('he knows its true value'), scepticism ('he can suspend judgement'), sociability ('sociable qualities'), contributing to civilized society ('who wants to give pleasure and make himself useful'), 'full of humanity', 'honour and integrity', 'kneaded with the yeast of order and rules': these are some of the qualities you may have found, or you may have noted different ones. The description in the article seems to offer an ideal, with which actual *philosophes* would have complied to varying degrees. But it does appear to sum up nicely the guiding spirit of the Enlightenment. There is even, at the end, a characteristic note of reformist propaganda as a plea is made for enlightened rulers.

As you turn now to study in detail the set texts of the course, you will be able to track the appearance of some of the characteristics of the Enlightenment outlined in this unit. You will also be able to challenge and refine some of the generalizations made, and begin to appreciate how these ideas changed in nature and emphasis as they were embodied in actual texts produced by individual minds. It can be useful to reconstruct the cultural history of the past in such a way that trends, conflicts and developments emerge more clearly, and it is certainly valuable when assessing our own responses to consider the larger picture. We hope that our attempts at definitions will offer you a window into the period.

The process of producing culture is complex. The texts you will study are the products of differing and fluctuating cross-currents of cultural, social and historical forces. In our period these cross-currents included the emergence and establishment of Romanticism. It may not be possible, in many cases, to classify the texts you encounter straightforwardly as 'enlightened' or 'Romantic'. Nevertheless, it may be helpful to signal at this stage some of the main shifts or cultural changes that characterized or accompanied the transition from a European culture greatly influenced by Enlightenment thought to one in which Romanticism acquired growing importance. We summarize these shifts below and will reconsider in the Course Conclusion their importance in your course texts. We shall also offer there a more detailed outline of the main characteristics of Romanticism, which you should consult before you reach the end of the course if you feel it might be useful. Both this unit and the Course Conclusion are intended as useful reference points and resources for the entire course. In the meantime, test your reading of the course texts as you come to them against the points made in the following list by noting under these headings the titles of those texts that seem relevant to them. How accurate are these summary points?

Cultural shifts: from Enlightenment to Romanticism, c.1780–1830

1   A growing impulse towards revolution, rupture, transformation and radicalism.

2   A growing scepticism about the potential to identify objective, empirically validated and universally valid truths, and an increased emphasis on subjectivity.

3   An increasing emphasis on the self, introspection, identity and individualism.

4   A growing exploitation and intensification of an aesthetic of the sublime.

5   A growing adaptation of classical sources to a modern psyche, heightened by a concern to identify, respect and differentiate 'authentic' classical practices; alongside this, a growing attraction towards non-classical sources of inspiration, such as the Gothic, the Oriental and the 'exotic'.

6   An increasing incorporation of the personal and private into public culture and an increasing use of public culture for self-promotion.

7   A shift from reason to sentiment and passion.

8   An increasingly subjective and relativist approach to morality and a growing emphasis on individual liberty.

9   A growing appreciation of both the dynamism and restorative powers of nature and of its intimate connection with human thought, morality and feelings.

10   The triumph of the notion of genius and self-expression; a growing emphasis on the autonomous creativity of the imagination.

11   A growing preoccupation with death and an impulse towards melancholy, immortality, the divine, the unintelligible, the unseen, mystical and supernatural.

a thrust towards
...e hero and of the

...g rise of a

...increasing
...a cultural and
...tum in the movement

...nce and cultural

...or knowing the causes
...the contrary works out the
...pates them, and accepts
...which, you might say,
...ects which can arouse in him
...being or to being a reasonable
...e rise to reactions on his part
...Reason is, for the *philosophe*, what
...ce which impels the Christian to act; it is
...*osophe*.

...ng by their passions without reflecting before
...are men who walk in darkness; on the other hand
...in his passions, acts only after reflecting; he is
..., but there is a torch in front of him.

...*pe* bases his principles on an infinite number of particular
...ns. The people adopt the principle without thinking about the
...tions which have led to it: they think that the maxim exists as it
...e on its own, but the *philosophe* goes back to the sources of the
...maxim; he examines its origins, he knows its true value, and uses as
much of it as suits him.

[From this knowledge that principles are derived only from particular
observations the *philosophe* derives a respect for the science of facts; he
likes to learn about details and about all that is not guesswork; so he
considers that a mind which concentrates on meditation alone and which
holds that man arrives at the truth from within himself is a fundamentally
unenlightened mind.][2]

---

[2] Square brackets here indicate a summary of a passage that has been omitted.

For the *philosophe* truth is
and which he believes he c
able to distinguish it when h
with probability; he takes as t
doubtful what is doubtful and
does more, in that a great streng
no reason to judge, he can suspe

So the philosophic mind concentrat
which take everything back to its fu
only the mind which the *philosophe*
concerns go further than this.

Man is not a monster who must live onl
the depths of a forest. The needs of every
associate with other people; and whatever
own needs and well-being commit him to li
reason requires him to know, study and wor
qualities.

Our *philosophe* does not think he is in exile in
think he is in a hostile country; as a sensible ma
the benefits which nature offers him; he wants to
company of others; and to find this he has to give
with those among whom he lives by chance or by h
the same time he finds what suits himself: he is a civi
wants to give pleasure and make himself useful.

Most people of high rank, whose many activities do not
enough time for meditation, are ferocious to those who in
not their equals. Ordinary philosophers who meditate too
rather who are bad at meditation, are ferocious to everyone
from men and men avoid them. But our *philosophe*, who is a
his time between solitude and human society, is full of humar
like Terence's[3] Chremes who feels that he is a man and that his
humanity makes him concerned with the bad or good fortunes o
neighbour. *Homo sum humani a me nihil alienum puto.*[4]

It should be unnecessary to point out here how much concern the
philosophe has for everything called honour and integrity. Civil socie
in a sense a divinity on earth to him; he praises it warmly, honours it
with integrity, with exact attention to his duties and by a sincere desire
not to be a useless or tiresome member of it. Feeling for integrity plays
as great a part in the mechanical constitution of the *philosophe* as the
enlightenment of the mind. The more reason you find in a man, the
more integrity you find. On the other hand, where fanaticism and

[3] Publius Terentius Afer (Terence c.190–159 BCE), a Roman playwright. Chremes was
a character in his play *Heauton timoroumenos* (*The self-tormentor*).

[4] I am a man and nothing which is human is foreign to me.

superstition dominate, passions and anger dominate. The *philosophe*'s temperament is to act according to a sense of order or to reason; as he is strongly attached to society, it is much more important for him than for other men to do everything that he can to produce only effects which fit in with the idea of a civilized man. There is no fear that, because no one is keeping an eye on him, he will embark on an action which betrays his integrity. No. Such an action in no way fits the mechanism of a civilized man; you might say he is kneaded with the yeast of order and rules; he is filled with the idea of the good of civil society; he knows the principles of it better than other men. Crime would be too much against his nature, he would have to destroy too many natural and too many acquired ideas. His capacity to act is, as it were, turned to a certain note like a string of a musical instrument; it cannot produce a different one. He is afraid of being out of tune, of not being in harmony with himself; and that reminds me of what Velleius said of Cato of Utica:[5] 'He never', he said, 'did good actions in order to be seen to be doing them, but because it was not in his nature to act otherwise.'

This love of society, which is so essential to the *philosophe*, shows how true the Emperor Antoninus'[6] remark was: 'How happy peoples will be when kings are philosophers or when philosophers are kings!'

The true *philosophe*, then, is a civilized man who acts in all things according to reason, and who combines a spirit of reflection and precision with social manners and qualities. Graft a sovereign on to a philosopher of like quality and you will have a perfect sovereign.

Source: Anonymous (1765) 'Philosophe', in D. Diderot (ed.) *Encyclopédie*, vol.xii, Paris, pp.509–11; trans. S. Clennell.

References

Anderson, M.S. (1987) *Europe in the Eighteenth Century 1713–1783,* 3rd edn, Harlow, Longman.

Aston, N. (1990) *Religion and Revolution in France 1780–1804,* Basingstoke, Macmillan.

Barzun, J. (2000) *From Dawn to Decadence: 500 Years of Western Cultural Life,* New York, Harper Collins.

Benham, W. (1902) *The Poetical Works of William Cowper,* London, Macmillan.

---

[5] Velleius was a character in a work by the Roman orator, Cicero. Cato of Utica, 'the conscience of Rome', was a Roman statesman.

[6] Titus Aurelius Fulius Antoninus Pius (CE 86–161), Roman emperor.

Berlin, I. (1999) *The Roots of Romanticism*, ed. H. Hardy, London, Chatto & Windus.

Bleiler, E.H. (ed.) (1964) *Don Giovanni by Wolfgang Amadeus Mozart*, Dover Opera Guide and Libretto Series, New York, Dover Publications.

Boswell, J. (1951) *The Life of Samuel Johnson,* 2 vols, London, Dent (first published 1791).

Bruun, G. (1967) *The Enlightened Despots,* 2nd edn, New York, Holt, Rinehart and Winston.

Davies, N. (1997) *Europe: A History,* London, Pimlico.

Diderot, D. (1755) 'Encyclopedia', in D. Diderot (ed.) *Encyclopédie*, vol.V, Paris.

Dobree, B. (ed.) (1959) *Alexander Pope's Collected Poems,* London, Dent (first published 1924).

Dorn, W.L. (1940) *Competition for Empire 1740–1763,* New York, Harper & Brothers.

Eliot, S. and Whitlock, K. (eds) (1992), *The Enlightenment: Texts, II,* Milton Keynes, The Open University.

Furst, L. (1969) *Romanticism,* London, Methuen.

Furst, L. (1979) *Romanticism in Perspective,* 2nd edn, London, Macmillan.

Gay, P. (1968) *The Enlightenment: An Interpretation,* New York, Vintage Books.

Gendzier, S.J. (ed. and trans.) (1967) *Denis Diderot's 'The Encyclopedia': Selections,* New York, Harper Torchbooks.

Gershoy, L. (1963) *From Despotism to Revolution,* New York, Harper Torchbooks (first published 1944).

Gibbon, E. (1954) *Decline and Fall of the Roman Empire,* vol.4, London, Dent (first published 1787).

Greene, D. (ed.) (1986) *Samuel Johnson,* Oxford, Oxford University Press.

Hampson, N. (1968) *The Enlightenment,* Harmondsworth, Penguin.

Hume, D. (1975) *Enquiries Concerning Human Understanding and Concerning the Principles of Morals*, ed. L.A. Selby-Bigge and P.H. Nidditch, 3rd edn, Oxford, Clarendon Press.

Hume, D. (n.d.) *Essays Literary, Moral and Political,* London, Routledge.

Lagarde, A. and Michard, L. (eds) (1962) *XVIIIe Siècle: Collection textes et littérature*, Paris, Bordas.

Lentin, A. (ed.) (1997) Horace: *The Odes in English Verse,* Ware, Wordsworth Classics.

Lentin, A. and Norman, B. (eds) (1998) Edward Gibbon: *The History of the Decline and Fall of the Roman Empire: 28 Selected Chapters,* Ware, Wordsworth Classics.

Morley, H. (ed.) (1891) *Memoirs of Edward Gibbon Written by Himself and a Selection from his Letters,* London, Routledge.

Mowat, R.B. (1934) *The Age of Reason: The Continent of Europe in the Eighteenth Century,* London, Harrap.

Owen, R. (1991) *A New View of Society and Other Writings,* ed. G. Claeys, Harmondsworth, Penguin.

Porter, R. (2000) *Enlightenment Britain and the Creation of the Modern World,* Harmondsworth, Penguin.

Reynolds, Sir J. (1975) *Discourses on Art,* ed. R.R. Wark, 2nd edn, New Haven and London, Yale University Press.

Rousseau, J.-J. (1847) *Les Confessions,* Paris, Charpentier.

Rousseau, J.-J. (1979) *Reveries of the Solitary Walker,* trans. P. France, Harmondsworth, Penguin (first published 1782).

Sorel, A. (1912) *L'Europe et la Révolution Française,* vol.1, Paris, Plon.

Stendhal (1962) *Racine and Shakespeare,* trans. G. Daniels, New York, Crowell-Collier Press.

Stendhal (2004) *A Life of Napoleon,* trans. R. Gant, ed. A. Lentin, Milton Keynes, The Open University.

Voltaire, F.A. de (1981) *Candide,* ed. J.H. Brumfitt, Oxford, Oxford University Press (this edition first published 1968).

Block 1 Death of the Old Regime?

Introduction to Block 1

Prepared for the course team by Alex Barber and Antony Lentin

The half century from *c.*1780 to 1830 was one of unprecedented change – complex, turbulent and often radical and fundamental, nowhere more so than in the cultural shifts leading from Enlightenment to Romanticism. Assumptions moulded at that time still largely dictate the way we think about the role of culture and the creative artist in society.

The period produced a very rich variety of texts of every kind: musical, artistic, philosophical, historical, religious and scientific. Our selection from among these has been made in the hope that you will find each of them absorbing and enjoyable in its own right. But beyond this we also anticipate that close study of these texts in all their diversity will prompt you to recognize some of the main characteristics of the culture of the period, and to appreciate the shared and changing values, consciousness, and perceptions of the men and women of that time.

In this opening block you will study (a) Mozart's opera *Don Giovanni* (2 units), (b) texts relating to changing attitudes to religion, evidence and death in the late Enlightenment (2 units), and (c) – in broad outline – the French Revolution (1 unit). A number of themes common to this seemingly random and eclectic group of topics give it a surprising coherence. You will find specific cross-references in the units, and we expect that you will notice other affinities as you work through the units and texts.

In this introduction we provide no more than an overview of the block's three main components by reflecting on the possible usefulness of taking the 1789 Revolution as a reference point when thinking about texts produced before that date. (This suggestion is offered simply as one way of thinking about the significance of the texts as you study them and, later, as you revise them.)

The title of this block, *Death of the Old Regime?,* uses a translation of the French expression *ancien régime,* first used by French revolutionaries as a label for the social and political structure they had just overthrown. This structure was traditional and hierarchical, headed by a hereditary monarchy and a privileged nobility and church; its basic essentials had underlain European culture for centuries and had seldom been seriously questioned, let alone physically attacked. The shock caused by the assault on this structure spread far beyond France, though it was there that the changes were most dramatic and far-reaching. Unit 6 summarizes the main events of the French Revolution and suggests something of their consequences.

It would be crude to think of the texts preceding Unit 6 entirely in terms of their leading up to the Revolution, an event that occurred later in time and which few people anticipated. Still, the Revolution did not spring out of nothing; there was a climate of opinion throughout Europe that welcomed it, at least in its opening stages. And there are curious respects in which the Revolution does seem occasionally to have been, if not heralded, then prefigured. An example of this can be found in *Don Giovanni,* the text for Units 2 and 3.

The opera closes with a lustful aristocrat being dragged to hell as punishment for his sins, while the remaining cast sings a chorus to the effect that evil-doers always receive their just deserts. In case you are silently cursing us for having just given away the plot, bear in mind that seeing or hearing the opera while *not* knowing the ending would be inauthentic. The story of Don Juan[1] was familiar, even hackneyed, by 1787, when Mozart's operatic version (with its libretto by Lorenzo da Ponte) was first performed in Prague, two years before the outbreak of the French Revolution. What distinguished this new setting was a concern with social divisions and interactions. Mozart and da Ponte were not overtly advocating the overthrow of the Old Regime in Europe, but they were certainly raising questions about its character. As a nobleman born to privilege without responsibility, Don Giovanni is immune to the sanctions that would apply to all non-aristocrats, and only a supernatural power is in a position to mete out the justice which the chorus, at great length, insists that he richly deserves. At the end of the opera, the original audiences were left to consider what should or could be done about this inability of society to control the excesses of some of its members. Should we really have to rely on supernatural powers? Could terrestrial power be arranged otherwise? No attempt is made to settle the issue in the opera. Don Giovanni's refrain of *'Viva la libertà!'* (long live liberty!) was prophetic, perhaps, but not in ways his real-life counterparts in the aristocratic audience of a courtly opera house would in any sense have appreciated.[2]

Another example of the *apparent* foreshadowing of the French Revolution may be found in the Marquis de Sade's descriptions of scenes of imaginary torture in *120 Days of Sodom* (*c.*1785, mentioned briefly in the audio recording on Sade and its accompanying notes). Sade is a marginal figure in this course, but a scene from one of his novels may suggest how easy it can be to draw simplistic conclusions from superficial similarities. Sade's descriptions of imaginary instruments of torture have some affinity with the horrendous violence of the Terror that followed the Revolution of 1789, and in particular with the guillotine

[1] Don Giovanni is simply Don Juan in Italian.

[2] *Viva la libertà!* was also the revolutionary slogan James Boswell had emblazoned on his cap. Boswell (whom you met in Unit 1 as the biographer of Dr Johnson) sported this cap, part of a Corsican costume, as a champion of the cause of Corsican independence from Genoa and (after its annexation in 1768) from France. See Quennell, P. (1947) *Four Portraits: Studies of the Eighteenth Century,* London, The Reprint Society, p.45.

(which Sade himself only narrowly escaped a few years later). Yet closer inspection also reveals important differences.

The decision in 1792 to retain the death penalty in France was reached by a narrow majority of those who suddenly found themselves elected and called upon to shape the country's future. They were moderate, educated men who shared the ideals of the Enlightenment and entertained high hopes of human nature. The full potential of human nature could, they thought, at last be realized once society was liberated from the shackles of the Old Regime. They welcomed the invention urged on them by one of their number – a distinguished physician who had contributed to the *Encyclopédie,* one Dr Guillotin – not only as a marvel of rational, scientific ingenuity, but also as a device with a positive, practical and indeed *humanitarian* function. For it proved an efficient and pain-free instrument of execution for the few (they hoped) anti-social individuals in any society who, having forfeited by their heinous wrongdoing the right to participate in that society, must regrettably be made an example of. The horrors came later: the guillotining of the anointed king and his queen, the adoption of guillotining as an instrument of mass execution, the attempted extermination of sections of society, including aristocrats and priests but mostly ordinary people, who were denounced as 'enemies of the people' by a fanatical minority and its militant followers, and condemned to death in the interests of a supposedly new, purified and better society. None of these developments were anticipated in the heady, optimistic, early days of the Revolution, when it was felt that men, being naturally good, would act towards each other as brothers. The madness of indiscriminate massacre took hold in France in reaction to counter-revolution and foreign invasion and under a ruthless dictatorship between 1792 and 1794. In the words of the *Marseillaise* (the French national anthem to this day), the revolutionaries called for the impure blood of the enemies of the Revolution at home and abroad to water the fields of republican France. But those who sang these words felt themselves to be inspired not by the novels of the Marquis de Sade, which were read by only a tiny number of people, but by the stirring ideals of liberty, equality and fraternity.

The block title ends with a question mark. Shattering, indeed epoch-making though it was, it is possible to overstate the significance of the Revolution to our period. Few foresaw it or its ferocious climax, and not everything was changed by it. Most strikingly, the Old Regime survived – shaken, reformed or at least affected by the Revolution – in the three great land powers of Europe – Prussia, Austria and Russia – as well as in Britain, the world's greatest naval, commercial and (increasingly) industrial power. These powers fought with revolutionary and later Napoleonic France on and off between 1792 and 1815, and in the end they won.

Nor was the Revolution the main or only agent for all developments taking place at the time. This is clear from changes in what many were prepared to consider as acceptable evidence for 'matters of fact'. The received Enlightenment view was that science, or more generally sensory experience, is the only reliable pathway to truth and that scientific methodology should be emulated in every sphere of enquiry, not only in fields where it had been successfully deployed already such as astronomy or medicine. Attempts were made to apply scientific thinking to test the claims of religion, for example, or to study the human mind. The texts for Unit 4, two short essays by Hume on suicide (is it ever morally permissible?) and on the afterlife (is there likely to be one?), follow this agenda exactly. But later in the century Rousseau among others began to question the adequacy of conclusions reached exclusively through the five senses using scientific principles. The protagonist in Rousseau's 'Profession of faith of a Savoyard vicar' (to be studied in Unit 5) seeks religious enlightenment not only through the five senses but also through inner conviction, sentiment, the inspirational power of nature, and the believer's direct communion with God. Many of Rousseau's intellectual peers, like Hume, regarded such sources as fallacious, utterly irrelevant to truth, even to religious truth. Optimism about the scope of science was certainly not universally or permanently undermined, and with the explosion of industry in the nineteenth century science came to dominate as never before. But Rousseau's assertion that there were other means of arriving at the truth about a particular topic did grow into a significant and influential alternative.

The emergence of this personal and subjective alternative, which is broadly classed as 'Romantic', cannot be straightforwardly linked with the drift towards revolution and the breakdown of rigid structures. Rousseau rejected not only the old regime of church and state, but also the Enlightenment obsession with experiment and science as the definitive source of knowledge. Leading revolutionary figures, on the other hand, paid homage to scientific principles as a route to social progress – from streamlined visions of a new society to the efficient killing machine successfully advocated by Dr Guillotin. It is a grim irony that one of France's leading scientists, Antoine Lavoisier, was among the victims of the guillotine. No one before 1789 would have predicted such a thing. Or would they? Lavoisier's elimination was no less incredible than the elimination of the fictitious Don Giovanni at the end of the opera. Explaining the Don's painful descent into hell, his servant Leporello insists: *'Vero è l'evento'* (it really happened).

Unit 2
Mozart's *Don Giovanni*: composition and context

Prepared for the course team by Donald Burrows

Contents

Study components (Units 2 and 3)

Weeks of study	Supplementary material	Audio-visual	Anthologies and set books
2	AV Notes Illustrations Book	Audio 1 and 2 Video 1 *Don Giovanni* (video)	Anthology I

Although Units 2 and 3 are of approximately equal word length, the listening exercises in Unit 3 will require additional time and concentration. If you find that your work on Unit 2 goes fairly easily, press on to Unit 3 immediately.

Objectives

By the end of your work on Units 2 and 3 you should be able:
- to relate Mozart's setting of *Don Giovanni* to previous treatments of the story;
- to describe the circumstances of the opera's first productions in Prague and Vienna;
- to explain the use that the librettist and the composer made of the particular opportunities provided by the genres of opera (i.e. a musical setting), drawing on particular examples from *Don Giovanni*;
- to describe the story and its treatment in terms of contemporary political and social events, and in terms of 'Enlightenment' or 'Romantic' ideas.

1   Introduction

The following two units are devoted to the study of *Don Giovanni*, an opera by Wolfgang Amadeus Mozart (1756–91) (Figure 2.1), which was first performed in Prague in 1787. It is a rich and complex dramatic work, and I hope that you will find it a stimulating and enjoyable 'text' to study. From the point of view of the course, it is clearly an Enlightenment-period text, and therefore it is chronologically appropriate for the early study units. It also raises, by virtue of its subject matter and the way this is treated, several important issues concerning social relationships, gender relationships and the freedom of the individual; these relate directly to themes that will recur throughout the course. You need to bear in mind throughout, however, that the object of the creators of the opera was to provide an engaging and powerful theatrical entertainment involving the interaction of individual human characters, not a treatise on intellectual, social and political issues. The powerful portrayal of human relationships within the opera does indeed lead us to reflect on broader issues, as it must also have done for the original audience, but the experience does not lead to tidy or simplistic conclusions.

Figure 2.1   Joseph Lange, Wolfgang Amadeus Mozart, *1789, oil on canvas, International Stiftung Mozarteum, Salzburg.*

The object of these units is therefore simply stated: to get to know Mozart's *Don Giovanni* in its original context, with some appreciation of the way that it was presented as an opera in 1787. Within this there are a number of aspects that are particular subjects for study:

1   The circumstances of the opera's first performances, and the versions of the opera that were performed under Mozart's direction.

2   The treatment of the story, particularly in relation to previous stage versions.

3   The nature of opera as a musical and dramatic genre, and the relationship of *Don Giovanni* to the types of opera that were composed and performed in eighteenth-century Europe.

4   The techniques used by the librettist and composer in presenting the plot and delineating characters.

5   The specific musical techniques and forms that were used by Mozart in the opera.

6   The treatment of class, gender relationships and issues of individual freedom in the opera.

Unit 2 will mainly be concerned with locating *Don Giovanni* in the place and time that it was created. To understand the context, it is necessary to know something not only about the composer and the librettist, but also about the background history of other theatrical treatments of the story, about contemporary theatrical practices in eighteenth-century Prague and Vienna, about the musical genre(s) of opera on which the composer drew, and about the circumstances of the original productions under Mozart's musical direction. This contextual material alternates with a number of practical exercises that will introduce you to the opera in performance and to various technical matters. These exercises will prepare you for the more detailed study of sections of the opera that are the subject of Unit 3.

The units include occasional examples in musical notation, largely for the purposes of illustration or to show you how the music is written down. You will not be expected to become fluent in reading music. (You may nevertheless, I hope, come to understand the way that musical notation provides a visual representation for the sounds.) The units do, however, encourage you to develop your listening skills, by guiding you through the audio extracts from the opera that we have provided. In many cases I shall describe the musical 'events' of a particular extract and then invite you to listen in order to check, and to experience for yourself, the various points that I cover; these may relate to the musical structure of complete movements or sections, as well as particular incidents. It's important that you treat these tasks as exercises in recognition and understanding, as much as if I had asked you to make the identifications for yourself. It is inevitable that musical descriptions will make reference to technical features such as melodies, chords and keys, but if you have little previous experience of music you should not be deterred by this, because you should find that you can recognize the most important features when you listen, following my preparatory descriptions. Chords and keys are such fundamental parts of Mozart's musical technique that I cannot avoid references to them, and at the end of section 5 of this unit, before you begin more intensive listening to the music, I set out what you may be expected to hear for yourself. On such matters as keys you can work within whatever you find to be your own level of understanding: for the purpose of assignments you will not be expected to make any references to, or identifications of, keys beyond those that are stated in the units as specific examples – though you may, of course, look beyond these examples if you feel able to do so.

You have two complementary resources for *Don Giovanni*: the video to give you a sense of the opera as a dramatic experience and the audio extracts for more intensive study of particular sequences. Your principal guide to the detailed study of the opera will be through its verbal text – the words that Mozart set to music – which is available at two levels in the course material: a synopsis (plot summary) for the complete opera (Anthology I, pp.5–16) and the complete texts for the audio extracts, which are given in the original Italian accompanied by an English translation (in the AV Notes). Although I hope that you will gain some sense of the literary style of the libretto (and its musical treatment), you do not need to understand Italian beyond the sense that is apparent from the English translation, which tells you what is happening from moment to moment. Your video performance of the opera may also have English subtitles, though these usually give a summary of the meaning of the text rather than a translation of each word. When following the audio extracts you have some additional help from the CD track numbers: cue numbers for the tracks are given next to the texts in the AV Notes, and these should help you to know where you are as you follow the text while the music is playing. (The track numbers also help you to locate reference points in the text.) Even when you look at the notated music for the opera, the text will still be your essential guide: you can follow the words while listening to the music examples.

Until you are experienced in the techniques of keeping up with the musical events and are used to the sound of the sung Italian language, you will need to do a little preparation before listening to an extract from the opera. This usually means checking the synopsis first (to see what happens in the extract, and to understand its context), and then reading through the text of the audio extract before you listen. Although detailed work on movements from the opera will primarily be undertaken through the audio extracts, you may wish to follow examples from the video as well: this is all to the good but is not essential. (It would also require you to find the extracts on the video, which is time-consuming unless you have a note of the track numbers or counter-readings for each movement.) However, it is important to remember when you listen to the audio extracts that the music was designed to carry stage action.

Although this unit is primarily concerned with *Don Giovanni* as a work created at a particular time and place, you need to be aware of the fact that the opera has a complex 'prehistory' and 'posthistory'. On the one hand, it was composed against the background of a long and diverse tradition of literary and dramatic works on the subject of the Don Juan legend; the most relevant of these will be considered in section 2 of this unit. On the other hand, Mozart's opera was immensely influential on subsequent generations of Europeans who took an interest in music or literature: *Don Giovanni* became a 'classic' or 'canonical' work in European culture. The popularity of the opera brought the story into the consciousness of many people who otherwise would have disregarded it, and it was Mozart's version of the story which became the standard point of reference in European experience.

That last sentence needs a considerable qualification, however, because the integrity of the original opera was soon lost; within a few years of Mozart's death versions were being given that, although they used parts of the original music, had diverged considerably from the original conception of the librettist and the composer. Furthermore, successive generations saw different things in, and drew different messages from, the opera and treated it according to their own interests or preoccupations. Theatrical practice, always flexible in adopting new interpretations and in adapting texts to new circumstances (including the strengths and weaknesses of particular performers), had no respect in these matters, and the opera was sometimes given in forms so distorted as to be scarcely recognizable. Very early on the opera attracted new stage 'traditions', and in the early nineteenth century the emphasis of its presentation had altered to become a 'Romantic' style opera. (One of the major changes that this involved will be described in section 8 of Unit 3.)

Literary figures took a lively interest in *Don Giovanni*. Goethe declared that Mozart was the only composer who could have dealt with the subject of his *Faust*, for which 'the music should be in the manner of *Don Giovanni*' (Rushton, 1981, p.127); the German writer E.T.A. Hoffmann (1776–1822) wrote a short story around one aspect of the opera.[3] *Don Giovanni* was also the principal topic of one chapter in Stendhal's *De l'amour* (1822). The German lyric poet Eduard Mörike wrote a *novelle* on the subject of the journey of Mozart and his wife to Prague before the first performance of *Don Giovanni* (*Mozart auf der Reise nach Prag*, 1856), which gives an extravagant picture of Mozart's personality that reflects the hold both the opera and the composer had gained on the 'Romantic' imagination.

Not surprisingly the intermediate, and often very powerful, conceptions of the opera that have been staged during the last 200 years still have an influence today. We cannot experience precisely or completely the

[3] About 1813 Hoffmann even changed his third baptismal name from Wilhelm to Amadeus in homage to the composer.

original effect of the opera as it was given in the original theatre, even in such technical details as the sound of the singers and the orchestra, let alone the stage setting and the gestures of the performers. (When you get to section 9 of this unit you will see on Video 1 a theatre comparable to the original one.) Nevertheless, by going back to the original text of the opera (including the stage directions), by learning something of the theatres of the time, the context of the original audiences, and the way that the composer and librettist worked, we can make some imaginative contact with the opera as it would have been experienced. Given this approach, you may find that any modern performance, whether as recorded sound, video or live performance, does not measure up to the ideal performance you imagine. You should be prepared for this, and in fact it is a good sign, because it will sharpen your critical awareness of what the 'work' may be and the possible alternative interpretations. To return to the original form of the opera sometimes involves actively cancelling out aspects that derived from later stage traditions; you should be aware of the importance of this subsequent history when listening to and watching modern performances, and aware also of the fact that the opera has been seen to carry different messages. Furthermore, the treatment of the story in *Don Giovanni* is in many respects ambiguous; as you come to know the work, you may well form your own judgements as to the 'messages' that were explicit or implied in the 1780s.

For the moment, however, these considerations need not inhibit you from experiencing the opera in a modern performance. Before proceeding further, therefore, you should watch the complete opera video.

EXERCISE First, read through the complete synopsis (Anthology I, pp.5–16). Remember to read the list of characters carefully before beginning the story itself. Do not worry about the details of the action, most of which will become explicit as you watch the performance; rather, try to gain a general sense of the plot and the characters. Keep the synopsis to hand in case you want to refer to it during the video, but if possible try not to distract the flow of the opera by stopping the video to check particular details.

Then play the video. The performance lasts nearly three hours, and the opera is in two parts (acts). It is preferable to arrange your time so that you can see the complete video at a single sitting or, better still, in a single sitting for each act with a short break for refreshments between, as the original audience did. Remember that the object is to gain a sense of the opera as a whole. The AV Notes provide an introduction to features of the particular production that is presented on the video, and I suggest that you refer to the notes before you start watching.

Having seen a complete performance of the opera, you now need also to practise the techniques involved with listening to the audio extracts, in particular by using the libretto to follow what is going on. You should not become so immersed in following the words that you hardly listen to the music! Rather, the text should become a way that helps your listening by locating you accurately in the performance; in fact, the most important thing to grasp is the way that the music carries, paces and enhances the words. This enhancement can often occur through what happens in the orchestra, as well as in the delivery of the singers.

For this exercise I've chosen the most famous scene in the opera, the denouement when Giovanni finally has to face judgement. This is the aspect of the story which is featured in the opera's original title: *Il dissoluto punito; o sia il Don Giovanni (The Libertine Punished, or Don Giovanni* – see Figure 2.2).

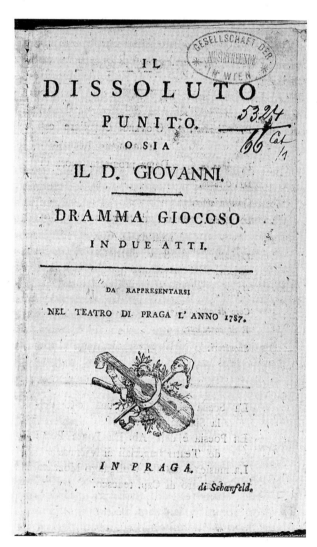

Figure 2.2   Title page from printed libretto of Don Giovanni, *Prague, 1787, Gesellschaft der Musikfreunde, Vienna.*

EXERCISE   First of all read the synopsis of Act Two, Scene 8–15 (Anthology I,
pp.13–16). Then read through the text of the audio extract (AV Notes,
extract 8: Act Two finale – stop when you reach 'Scena ultima'). When
you feel that you have a basic understanding of the text, listen to the
extract (Audio 2, track 1 to the beginning of track 16). I suggest that you
listen at least twice, following the Italian text during one or more
playings, and using the track numbers to check that you are in the right
place in the text as the scene proceeds.

There are no questions for this exercise: as I said, it is a practice in
techniques for listening to audio extracts, which will also give you some
familiarity with the sound world of the opera. (Many of the subsequent
listening exercises are similarly devoted solely to increasing your aural
experience of the opera.) The scene itself will be studied in more detail
in Unit 3. You may well find at first that it is rather bewildering trying to
match up the text with what you hear. In opera the words sometimes
pass quickly, never to return, while at other times the words are repeated
extensively, holding the mood or one moment in the action. There's an
additional snag here because in some places the characters sing their
words simultaneously, particularly during the argument between
Giovanni and Elvira. On the other hand, the entry of the statue is
unmissable, and it is easy to follow his words in the solemn delivery.

When you feel that you have made sense of this scene (and, I hope, also
appreciated its dramatic excitement), proceed to the next section.

2   The librettist

I have so far referred to *Don Giovanni* as 'Mozart's opera', but of course
this is an over-simplification: Mozart composed the music, but to an
Italian text that had been provided by someone else, the librettist
Lorenzo da Ponte (1749–1838) (Figure 2.3).[4] Da Ponte led a life as
remarkable, and almost as colourful, as that of the famous adventurer
and libertine Giacomo Casanova (1725–98), with whom he had an
intermittent friendship. He was born at Ceneda (now Vittorio Veneto) in
north-eastern Italy as Emmanuele Conegliano, the eldest son of a Jewish
tanner. The family converted to Christianity in 1763 when his widowed
father married a Roman Catholic, and adopted the name of the local
bishop. Da Ponte trained at two local seminaries in his home area and
took orders as a priest; in 1773 he celebrated mass for the first time, and
also moved to Venice as tutor to two sons of a noble lady. The next year

[4] The complete text of an opera is the **libretto** (plural: librettos or libretti). The
printed texts are sometimes also referred to by the same term, or are distinguished as
'word-books'. Remember that terms highlighted in bold (at their first mention) can be
found in the glossary at the end of the block.

Figure 2.3   Anonymous, Lorenzo da Ponte*, oil on canvas, 22.4 x 17.6 cm, Casa Italiana, Columbia University in the City of New York.*

he and one of his brothers were appointed professors in the seminary of Treviso, but a controversy erupted over verses written by Da Ponte on the subject of whether people are happier living in organized social systems or in a 'state of nature' (a topic that we now particularly associate with Rousseau), and by then his personal life was also becoming the subject of scandal. He continued in Venice as private tutor to various households, but eventually a court case was brought against him concerning his relationship with the daughter-in-law of one of his landladies. Over 60 witnesses testified against him, but Da Ponte slipped beyond Venetian jurisdiction before judgement could be served on him. He fled first to Gorizia (which was part of the Austrian territories in the Italian region), where his first stage works – Italian versions of German and French plays – were produced, and then in 1781 he went on to Dresden in the hope of securing a post at the Saxon court. Finding no success there (and also wishing to escape the consequences of another new amorous involvement with two sisters), he proceeded to Vienna where he had better fortune. In 1783 Emperor Joseph II engaged a company for the production of Italian opera and, through the influence of the principal court composer Antonio Salieri (1750–1825), Da Ponte was appointed Theatre Poet. The following years saw the zenith of Da Ponte's career. He is best remembered for his association with Mozart in three Italian operas – *Le nozze di Figaro* (after the play *Le Mariage de Figaro* by Pierre-Augustin Caron de Beaumarchais), *Don Giovanni* and *Così fan tutte* – but he was kept very busy preparing opera libretti for several composers, including Salieri and Vicente Martín y Soler (1754–1806).

EXERCISE   *Don Giovanni*, although first performed in Prague, was initially prepared in Vienna. Read now the extract from Da Ponte's memoirs (Anthology I, pp.3–5), in which he gives his own account of his work on the opera, and the opera's reception at the performances in Vienna which followed the original Prague production. What are the principal factual points that Da Ponte conveys?

DISCUSSION   As often happens, the memoirs do not tell us many of the things that we would dearly like to know, such as the chronology and nature of his collaboration with Mozart in this case. The memoirs do, however, tell us that Da Ponte was very busy in his duties as Theatre Poet, working with several composers; indeed, the demands were such that he had to leave Prague before the first performance of *Don Giovanni* because of other commitments in Vienna. Nevertheless, he was actively involved in the preparation of the Prague performances. (In the eighteenth century the 'poet' also often fulfilled the functions of a modern producer.) The opera did not receive such an enthusiastic reception in Vienna when it was performed there as it had done in Prague.

In his memoirs Da Ponte presented a carefully constructed image of his life, and we should not place too much reliance on his presentation of the factual details, not only because they were written at a much later period but also because Da Ponte gave rather a vainglorious statement of his achievements (and, we may guess, of his amorous adventures). It is improbable that he simultaneously prepared three completely different original librettos, though it is likely that he often had several projects in prospect at the same time. In his memoirs Da Ponte also presents himself as the unfortunate victim of intrigues and malice, and it is difficult to separate fact from fiction: some of his problems were clearly created by his own actions. Nevertheless, the operatic world in which he worked was highly competitive; the amount of talent around exceeded the opportunities provided by performances and productions, and this applied to librettists as well as to composers.

Following the death of Joseph II in 1790, Da Ponte failed to find favour with his successors, and he was dismissed from his Austrian post. He thought of going to Paris but was deterred by the revolutionary unrest there and, partly on the advice of Casanova, went to London instead. (By now he had a permanent companion whom he had acquired in Trieste; she was said to be the daughter of an English merchant, and it is uncertain whether they were ever married.) He sustained a career in London for more than ten years, supplementing his work as a librettist for the opera house in the Haymarket by setting up a printing press and a bookshop for Italian poetry, and collaborating in a venture to publish music. By 1804, however, he was in serious difficulties on account of debts, and he escaped by shipping his wife and children off to America, following them in April 1805. He became a grocer and general merchant in New York, then in Sunbury and Philadelphia (Pennsylvania), supplementing his income by dealing in Italian books and teaching Italian. In 1819 he returned to New York, now an American citizen, where he maintained his Italian activities; in 1825 he even encouraged the visiting opera company led by the famous singers Manuel García and María Malibrán to perform *Don Giovanni*. Unlike Giovanni, Da Ponte died of natural causes at the age of 89. (Mozart had died, at the age of 36, nearly 47 years previously.)

3   The libretto and the *Don Giovanni* story

One of the things that Da Ponte did not mention in his memoirs is that he worked up his libretto from another recent Italian opera text by Giovanni Bertati (1735–1815) for an opera composed by Giuseppe Gazzaniga (1743–1818), which had been performed at the Teatro San Moisè in Venice in February 1787 (see Figure 2.4). Neither Da Ponte nor Mozart saw that opera production, nor probably did they see the musical score, but the details of the libretto leave no doubt that Da Ponte used a copy of the printed word-book from the performances. It was not an unusual practice for opera librettists to work from a previous libretto, and indeed much of Da Ponte's work in Vienna was concerned with adapting pre-existing libretti to new productions. Da Ponte's use of Bertati's text was, however, far beyond an adaptation; he rearranged the previous material and added much of his own, in such a way that the treatment of the subject received new emphases and cancelled some of the features that had been present in the earlier version.

Da Ponte also adopted a different literary style – see Figures 2.5 and 2.6, which show the same scene in the texts by Bertati and Da Ponte. Even without a knowledge of Italian, you will see that Da Ponte uses few of Bertati's phrases, and (when the diction becomes more regular towards the end of the scene) uses a verse form with shorter lines. Bertati's libretto was in any case not sufficient to carry a complete full-length opera. His Venetian entertainment, *Il capriccio drammatico,* was in two acts, of which the second, entitled separately 'Don Giovanni o sia il convitato di pietra' ('Don Giovanni, or the Stone Guest'), was effectively an opera within an opera, which had been set up by the performers in

Figure 2.4 Title page from printed libretto of Don Giovanni, *Venice, 1787, Biblioteca Nazionale Marciana, Venice.*

the first act. Bertati, in turn, had been influenced by the French comedy, *Don Juan* by Molière, produced in Paris in 1665. Molière's play subsequently became best known through a rather weaker French verse transcription by Thomas Corneille dating from 1677, but Molière's original text had been published, and incidents and phrases from the Italian librettos show that this version was known to both Bertati and Da Ponte.

The 'prehistory' does not end there, however, because the Don Giovanni (or Don Juan) story had a rich previous tradition in literary works and dramatic productions. The formal dramatic foundation seems to have been a play by Spanish monk Tirso de Molina, *El burlador de Sevilla y convidado de piedra (The Trickster of Seville, or the Stone Guest)*, published in 1630 but probably written about 15 years previously. This was a three-act drama, in which the moralistic message about the punishment of evil-doers was presented in a fairly heavy-handed way.

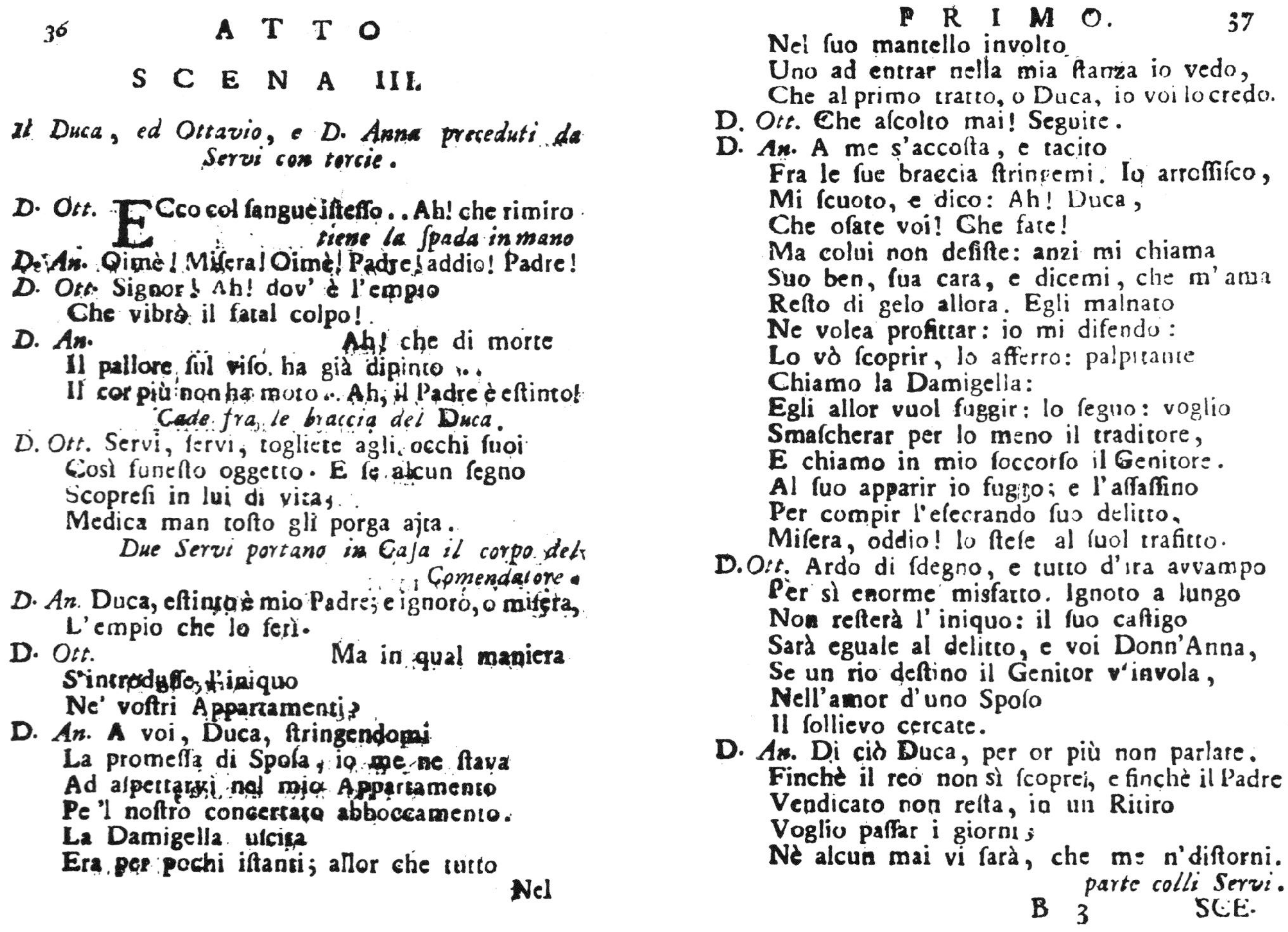

P R I M O. 37

Nel fuo mantello involto.
Uno ad entrar nella mia ftanza io vedo,
Che al primo tratto, o Duca, io voi lo credo.
D. Ott. Che afcolto mai! Seguite.
D. An. A me s'accofta, e tacito
Fra le fue braccia ftringemi. Io arroffifco,
Mi fcuoto, e dico: Ah! Duca,
Che ofate voi? Che fate!
Ma colui non defifte: anzi mi chiama
Suo ben, fua cara, e dicemi, che m'ama
Refto di gelo allora. Egli malnato
Ne volea profittar: io mi difendo:
Lo vò fcoprir, lo afferro: palpitante
Chiamo la Damigella:
Egli allor vuol fuggir: lo fegno: voglio
Smafcherar per lo meno il traditore,
E chiamo in mio foccorfo il Genitore.
Al fuo apparir io fuggo; e l'affaffino
Per compir l'efecrando fuo delitto,
Mifera, oddio! lo ftefe al fuol trafitto.
D.Ott. Ardo di fdegno, e tutto d'ira avvampo
Per sì enorme misfatto. Ignoto a lungo
Non refterà l'iniquo: il fuo caftigo
Sarà eguale al delitto, e voi Donn'Anna,
Se un rio deftino il Genitor v'invola,
Nell'amor d'uno Spofo
Il follievo cercate.
D. An. Di ciò Duca, per or più non parlare.
Finchè il reo non sì fcoprei, e finchè il Padre
Vendicato non refta, in un Ritiro
Voglio paffar i giorni;
Nè alcun mai vi farà, che me n'diftorni.
parte colli Servi.

B 3 SCE-

36 A T T O

S C E N A III.

Il Duca, ed Ottavio, e D. Anna preceduti da
Servi con torcie.

D. Ott. Ecco col fangue iftelfo.. Ah! che rimiro
tiene la fpada in mano
D. An. Qimè! Mifera! Oimè! Padre, addio! Padre!
D. Ott. Signor! Ah! dov'è l'empio
Che vibrò il fatal colpo!
D. An. Ah! che di morte
Il pallore ful vifo ha già dipinto...
Il corpo più non ha moto. Ah, il Padre è eftinto!
Cade fra le braccia del Duca.
D. Ott. Servi, fervi, togliete agli occhi fuoi
Così funefto oggetto. E fe alcun fegno
Scoprefi in lui di vita,
Medica man tofto gli porga ajta.
Due Servi portano in Cafa il corpo del
Commendatore.
D. An. Duca, eftinto è mio Padre; e ignorò, o mifera,
L'empio che lo ferì.
D. Ott. Ma in qual maniera
S'introduffe l'iniquo
Ne' voftri Appartamenti?
D. An. A voi, Duca, ftringendopai
La promeffa di Spofa, io me ne ftava
Ad afpettarvi nel mio Appartamento
Pe'l noftro concertato abboccamento.
La Damigella ufcita
Era per pochi iftanti; allor che tutto
Nel

Figure 2.5 Act One, Scena 3 from Bertati's libretto Il capriccio drammatico (pp.36–7), Biblioteca Nazionale Marciana, Venice.

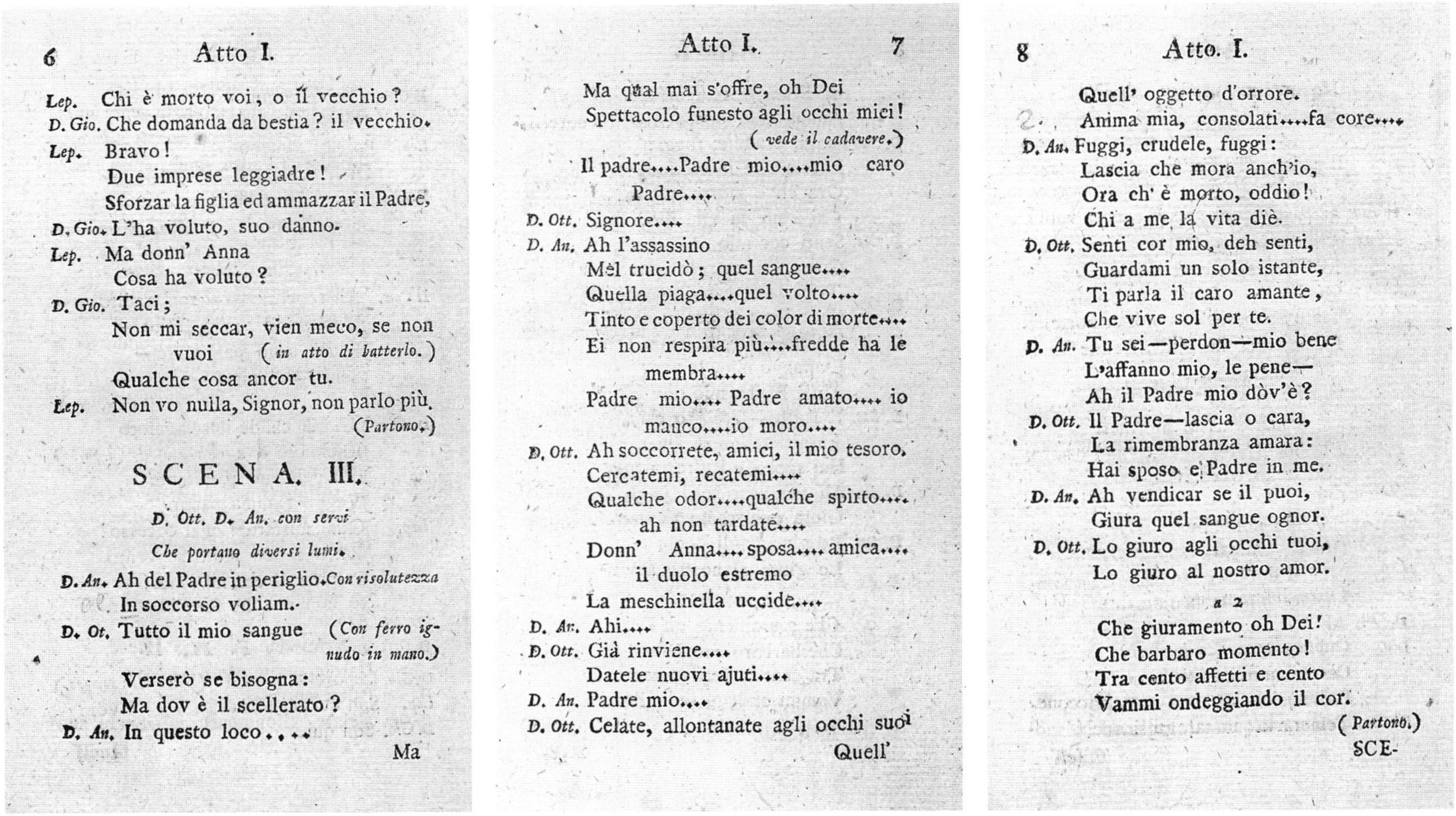

6   Atto I.

Lep. Chi è morto voi, o il vecchio?
D. Gio. Che domanda da bestia? il vecchio.
Lep. Bravo!
    Due imprese leggiadre!
    Sforzar la figlia ed ammazzar il Padre,
D. Gio. L'ha voluto, suo danno.
Lep. Ma donn' Anna
    Cosa ha voluto?
D. Gio. Taci;
    Non mi seccar, vien meco, se non
        vuoi   (*in atto di batterlo.*)
    Qualche cosa ancor tu.
Lep. Non vo nulla, Signor, non parlo più.
        (*Partono.*)

SCENA. III.

D. Ott. D. An. con servi
Che portano diversi lumi.
D. An. Ah del Padre in periglio. *Con risolutezza*
    In soccorso voliam.
D. Ot. Tutto il mio sangue   (*Con ferro ig-*
                                nudo in mano.)
    Verserò se bisogna:
    Ma dov' è il scellerato?
D. An. In questo loco....
                            Ma

Atto I.   7

Ma qual mai s'offre, oh Dei
Spettacolo funesto agli occhi miei!
        (*vede il cadavere.*)
    Il padre....Padre mio....mio caro
        Padre....
D. Ott. Signore....
D. An. Ah l'assassino
    Mel trucidò; quel sangue....
    Quella piaga....quel volto....
    Tinto e coperto dei color di morte....
    Ei non respira più....fredde ha le
        membra....
    Padre mio.... Padre amato.... io
        manco....io moro....
B. Ott. Ah soccorrete, amici, il mio tesoro,
    Cercatemi, recatemi....
    Qualche odor....qualche spirto....
        ah non tardate....
    Donn' Anna....sposa....amica....
        il duolo estremo
    La meschinella uccide....
D. An. Ahi....
D. Ott. Già rinviene....
    Datele nuovi ajuti....
D. An. Padre mio....
D. Ott. Celate, allontanate agli occhi suoi
                            Quell'

---

8   Atto. I.

Quell' oggetto d'orrore.
    Anima mia, consolati....fa core....
D. An. Fuggi, crudele, fuggi:
    Lascia che mora anch'io,
    Ora ch' è morto, oddio!
    Chi a me la vita diè.
D. Ott. Senti cor mio, deh senti,
    Guardami un solo istante,
    Ti parla il caro amante,
    Che vive sol per te.
D. An. Tu sei—perdon—mio bene
    L'affanno mio, le pene—
    Ah il Padre mio dov' è?
D. Ott. Il Padre—lascia o cara,
    La rimembranza amara:
    Hai sposo e; Padre in me.
D. An. Ah vendicar se il puoi,
    Giura quel sangue ognor.
D. Ott. Lo giuro agli occhi tuoi,
    Lo giuro al nostro amor.
                    a 2
    Che giuramento oh Dei!
    Che barbaro momento!
    Tra cento affetti e cento
    Vammi ondeggiando il cor.
                    (*Partonò.*)
                        SCE-

Figure 2.6   Act One, Scena 3 from Da Ponte's libretto Don Giovanni (pp.6–8), Gesellschaft der Musikfreunde, Vienna.

The play became known in Naples, then a Spanish territory, and from there it spread through Italy in versions of *Il convitato di pietra*, the earliest surviving text probably being that attributed to Giacinto Andrea Cicognini, published about 1650. Nearly a century later, another influential Italian version was the three-act play *Don Giovanni Tenorio, o sia il dissoluto (Don Giovanni Tenorio, or the Debauchee)* by Carlo Goldoni, produced in 1736. (Goldoni, known in the first part of his career primarily as a writer of comedies, was subsequently equally famous as an opera librettist.) In Vienna a ballet score on the subject of Don Juan composed by Christoph Willibald Gluck (1714–87) was performed in 1761, and in 1777 the full-length opera (described as a 'dramma tragicomico') *Il convitato di pietra, o sia il dissoluto*, composed by Vincenzo Righini to a libretto by Nunziato Porta, was performed in both Prague and Vienna.

Beyond the formal literary treatments lay also 'subliterary' traditions: the story was the subject for dramatic entertainments by travelling acting troupes for carnivals and fairs. Often these have left little documentary trace, even in the form of scenarios for improvised drama. The informality and buffoonery of the Italian *commedia dell'arte* tradition (in which simply drawn 'stock' characters featured) seem to have been incorporated in the versions that spread out from Naples. In 1713–14 a French version with songs (*comédie en chansons*) is documented from the Foire Saint-Germain and other Parisian fairs. Goldoni wrote his play with the intention of rescuing the story from what he considered to be the unworthy level of farce represented by the popular tradition; this in itself is testimony to the lively tenacity of the subject.

It is not known how far Da Ponte was aware of these earlier presentations of the story. Apart from Molière's play, it seems likely that he would also have known Goldoni's in view of his scholarly interest in Italian literature, and would have had an acquaintance with some of the Italian descendants from Tirso's play. He may also have had first-hand experience of the popular play tradition. Given that he was under considerable time pressure when he wrote his libretto for *Don Giovanni* on account of the simultaneous commissions, he may have adopted the story because he was already familiar with the subject matter, and was aware of the rich possibilities of additional motivations and incidents that might be used to elaborate Bertati's text. Da Ponte, like others before him, was perhaps influenced by the popular traditions in his portrayal of certain elements, such as the melodramatic treatment of Don Giovanni's end and the characterization of Zerlina, the village girl. The 'catalogue aria' in Act One also seems to relate to the traditions of popular drama, though Leporello's character is given much more depth by Da Ponte (and Mozart) than that of the comic servants in these traditions.

When it comes to Da Ponte's treatment of the structure of Bertati's libretto, three examples will show how radically he diverged from his source. In Bertati's version Donna Anna tells her tale immediately after her father has been killed and then leaves the action, taking no further part in the pursuit of Giovanni or a relationship with Ottavio. Although Da Ponte needed to elaborate and lengthen Bertati's text, he also concentrated the action by removing some of Bertati's characters, a second servant to Giovanni and one further lady (Donna Ximena). And among the things that Da Ponte created that owed little or nothing to Bertati was the elaborate and substantial structure of the first act's final scene.

It is not necessary for you to remember the titles and authors of all of the versions of the *Don Giovanni* story that I have mentioned. However, you should bear in mind the rich background against which Da Ponte and Mozart created the opera: the story had been treated many times before, and its essential features – the licentious principal character who eventually receives punishment, and the ghostly stone guest who acts as messenger – would have been well known to everyone, including the opera's original audience. (If anything, the story itself might have been thought rather vulgar on account of its associations with popular tradition.) The choices that Da Ponte and Mozart made in their treatment of the story are specific and individual, strengthening some aspects while reducing the significance of others. *Don Giovanni* is, in the end, a very different work from the plays by Tirso, Molière and Goldoni, and indeed from Bertati's operatic version.

4   Opera genres and characterization

If there was a rich background to Da Ponte's treatment of the Don Giovanni story, there was an equally interesting history behind Mozart's opera as a musical and dramatic work. The history of Italian opera is complex, not least because local conditions – in the taste and skills of composers, librettists, performers and audiences – resulted in much variety. 'Local' could refer to Venice, Florence, Rome or Naples, but it could also mean London, Vienna, Dresden or St Petersburg, because Italian opera had been adopted throughout most of Europe in the eighteenth century as a desirable cultural commodity. (The principal exception was France, where a different style of opera had developed in French.) In its origins, around the year 1600, the genre of opera had been associated with court entertainments, and many eighteenth-century Italian opera companies were court employees performing in court theatres. Although royal, noble and aristocratic patrons held the purse-strings, opera was nevertheless (as with other forms of dramatic entertainment) quite difficult to control. The closure of an opera company could cause considerable political unpopularity, and by the early eighteenth century Italian opera relied on a highly professional international circuit of composers, librettists, performers and scene-designers. Negotiations for leading singers were often conducted through diplomatic channels, almost as matters of foreign policy. Some Italian opera companies were relatively independent civic enterprises, following a pattern that had begun in Venice during the 1630s, but here again conditions and methods of management varied greatly. When Samuel Johnson, in the section on John Hughes from *Lives of the English Poets*, gave his famous description in the late 1770s of Italian opera as 'an exotic and irrational entertainment, which has always been combated, and always has prevailed' (Johnson, 1961, vol.1, p.370), it was based on his knowledge of the London opera house, a commercial venture that was in permanent difficulty throughout the eighteenth century in meeting the costs of 'exotic' foreign performers and stage settings.

Eighteenth-century Italian opera is sometimes portrayed as primarily a social plaything for the aristocracy, and certainly opera-going was an important social (and political) activity. However, there is also good evidence that audiences (as well as librettists and composers) had a lively interest in opera as a genre; the leading singers were treated in the manner of modern popular stars, and there was both public and private comment on the merits of different productions. The pattern of opera subscriptions, organized in annual seasons, often meant that members of the audience went to see the same opera several times during a run of performances. Furthermore, although opera was a musical medium, it also had wider significance, for Italian opera culture was literary as well as musical, as you may have gathered from Da Ponte's activities as librettist, Italian teacher and bookseller. For three centuries opera was the principal – arguably, virtually the only – form of Italian drama, and opera libretti were among the primary literary creations of Italian culture. Librettists regarded themselves as poets, using appropriate verse structures for their texts, with recognizable traditions of prosody and rhyme schemes.

While it is difficult to generalize about the various subtypes of Italian opera in the eighteenth century, there was nevertheless a generally perceived distinction between **opera seria** and **opera buffa** – between 'serious' and 'comic' genres of opera.[5] These were rather colloquial terms: on the opera librettos themselves authors were more likely to describe works as *dramma per musica* (drama in – or through – music) or, as in the case of *Don Giovanni, dramma giocoso* (jesting drama). In spite of its designation, *Don Giovanni* has a story that deals with serious topics. To see how far it might be described as a 'comic opera', it is necessary to know a little more about the characteristics of eighteenth-century *seria* and *buffa* genres.

The division between the two types was really created in the early eighteenth century as a result of changes that occurred around the year 1700; during the seventeenth century there had been little need for any

[5] The terms 'serious opera' and 'comic opera' were, as it happens, specifically used in London in the second half of the eighteenth century to describe different types of production by the Italian opera company.

such separation because 'serious' operas usually incorporated 'comic' scenes. *Opera seria* developed as a form which self-consciously followed dramatic ideals from Aristotle's *Poetics*[6] and the seventeenth-century French neoclassical dramatists Racine and Corneille. Its characteristics were first established as part of a reform movement led by a group of literary connoisseurs (the 'Arcadian Academy') in Rome, directed against librettos that were undisciplined, irrational and often licentious. *Opera buffa* developed initially in Naples and Venice, originally as comic *intermezzi* (short dramas that were played between the parts of serious operas, and unrelated to them in plot), but from 1740 onwards the *buffa* genre developed as full-length operas, especially in the hands of the librettist Goldoni and the composer Baldassare Galuppi (1706–85). *Opera buffa* was initially a less well-regarded genre, partly because *opera seria* dealt with characters of high social and political status,[7] but in the second half of the century it became as popular as *opera seria*. The following paragraphs, which necessarily simplify a complex subject, contrast the subject matter of the two types and their technical characteristics.

Opera seria dealt with 'serious' stories, preferably taken from ancient history, presented with dignity and according to formal conventions that were followed by librettists and composers. The political and amorous intrigues of the plots involved powerful public figures such as Julius Caesar and Alexander the Great (who could sometimes be identified with current rulers), and the plots were 'moral' in the sense of dealing with the proper behaviour of those in power. Tragic endings were rejected as being unworthy of the civilized state, and the plot concluded with a *lieto fine* (happy ending), often contrived through an act of generosity from a ruler who had hitherto behaved in an arbitrary manner. When characters of lesser social status appear (e.g. shepherds), they usually turn out to be princes in disguise or abandoned at birth. *Opera buffa* dealt with more 'ordinary' people, initially also incorporating some stock characters from Neapolitan comedy. The plots could be very varied in subject matter, but featured swift stage action involving frequent entrances and exits of different characters.

Opera seria had two basic musical forms: **recitative**, which moved the action forward, and **arias** (solo songs, in ***da capo*** form) which came at moments of reflection, reaction or summation. ('Recitative' will become comprehensible when you study examples from *Don Giovanni*; *da capo* form will be explained in section 5 of this unit.) The scenes were organized so that a principal singer would leave the stage after singing

---

[6] The fragmentary *Poetics* of Aristotle (384–322 BCE) is the earliest extant work of dramatic theory and reflects his views on Greek tragedy.

[7] As you will discover in Unit 9, there was a similar perceived hierarchy in the genres of painting.

his/her aria (the leading roles were played by *castrati*[8] and sopranos); the first two acts of a three-act drama would usually end with a single principal character on stage. *Opera buffa* also employed recitatives and arias, but developed simpler styles of arias and incorporated more ensembles in which the solo characters sang together; the acts usually built up to an ensemble in the final scene, with Goldoni developing the idea of the 'chain ensemble' from several successive incidents, carried by a series of linked musical movements.

While it does not seem to have been too difficult for a dramatist who had written comedies to move into *opera buffa* librettos, as Goldoni did, the writing of an *opera seria* libretto was a more specialized task that involved both meeting strict literary requirements and fulfilling the unyielding theatrical conventions of the 'exit aria'. The librettist had to contrive sufficient political and amorous intrigue to sustain dramatic tension and provide strategic excuses for about 25 arias, properly distributed among six or seven singers according to their rank. The writer who became most admired for his *opera seria* libretti was Metastasio (Pietro Trapassi, 1698–1782), an Italian who was resident in Vienna as court poet from 1730. Metastasio's libretti had complex but credible plots that were practical for musical setting, were cast in elegant and dignified verse, and had suitably elevating conclusions:

> They embodied Enlightenment ideals, portraying characters able to overcome selfish human desires in order to achieve greatness in thought and deed in a world where monarch and subject alike must adhere to the highest moral principles. In their universality his messages remained apolitical and so posed no threat to the nobility who supported the theatre in most Italian centres.
>
> (M.P. McClymonds, 'Opera seria', in Sadie, 2001, p.486)

EXERCISE   On the basis of the above descriptions, describe where *Don Giovanni* stands in relation to the genres of *opera seria* and *opera buffa*. Since your acquaintance with the opera has been limited, respond in general terms on the basis of your overall impression.

DISCUSSION   Mostly, *Don Giovanni* conforms more closely to the *buffa* genre: there are many scenes of fast-moving incidents, the range of characters includes villagers/peasants, and ensembles feature as prominently as solo arias (particularly in the finale sections of the acts). The principal character certainly does not 'adhere to the highest moral principles'. The voices used are also more typical of *opera buffa*, in that the leading men

---

[8] *Castrati* were male singers who had been castrated before puberty in order to preserve their 'unbroken' (high-register) voices; normal growth in other respects often resulted in voices of considerable power.

are played by tenors and baritones, not by *castrati*. Yet there are also some complications which mean that *Don Giovanni* is not simply a 'comic' opera. Don Ottavio and the Commendatore are high-status, 'moral' characters. If the behaviour of 'great ones' was a principal concern of *opera seria*, it is also the fundamental topic of *Don Giovanni* because Giovanni is an aristocratic figure – a 'cavalier'. The 'happy' ending is that he gets his just punishment. Both the punishment of Giovanni and the opening scene in which the Commendatore is murdered are presented in a 'serious' manner, and both Anna and Elvira exhibit the responses and attitudes of 'serious' characters.

In *Don Giovanni* there is a mixture of 'serious' and 'comic' characters, and even the latter are very far from the simple formulaic buffoons of popular comedy. (This is true of many operas from the later, developed forms of the *buffa* genre.) Da Ponte and Mozart use the serious/comic aspects of the story and the combination of high-status and low-status characters in their cast as motivating resources within the drama.

EXERCISE   Compare the arias on Audio 1, tracks 24 and 25 ('Or sai chi l'onore', 'Batti, batti'). Listen to them and describe briefly how the music is used to distinguish the two different female characters. Do not refer to the texts: this is an aural exercise in recognizing (and trying to describe) the way that 'high' and 'low' characters are distinguished by musical means, such as different types of melodies or the use of the orchestral accompaniment.

DISCUSSION   I don't think that there's much doubt as to which is the more 'serious' character! The first is clearly an impassioned, elaborate aria requiring great vocal agility from the singer; it lies high in the voice and has angular melodies which require forceful delivery over an energetic orchestral accompaniment. The second is more 'tuneful', beginning with regular short phrases in which the melody moves by simple pitch-steps over equally simple harmony; the orchestra either supports the voice unobtrusively or fills in with rather playful interludes. In the second half of the aria the music changes to a rather jig-like rhythm, but again with a tuneful theme beginning largely with simple steps.

I would not have expected you to be so precise in your technical description of the differences as in the answer that I gave, and you may well have been uncertain about the type of description that was appropriate; nevertheless, I hope that what I have described bore a recognizable relationship to what you heard. From the answer that I've just given, I'll sum up the various musical features in more detail now, as this may be useful in giving you pointers to listen for in other extracts. I'll do this under three simple headings, which may also suggest ways that you could organize your thoughts about other examples. However, remember that my three headings, though applicable to most examples, are not exclusive, and in other places you may be able to refer (for example) to chords, key changes or dynamic contrasts between loud and soft.

1   Pitch: the feature of register (Anna as a high voice), and the distinction between step-wise melodies (Zerlina) and wide-ranging melodies with wider leaps. Examples 2.1 and 2.2 show you the opening phrases of the two melodies, with steps and leaps marked as 'S' and 'L' respectively. As the musical phrases develop, the latter distinction is not continued so clearly, but the first phrases are particularly important for establishing characters and situations.

Example 2.1

Example 2.2

2   Rhythm: notes and phrases of regular lengths (Zerlina), in contrast to more jagged, pointed rhythms and complex phrases (Anna). In addition to the character of individual rhythms or phrases, there is also the feature of **metre**, the underlying beat-structure of the music. There is a noticeable change of metre in Zerlina's aria (at the words 'Pace, pace, o vita mia'), but retaining Zerlina-like characteristics such as step-wise pitch movement. Technically the change of metre is described as from **'simple' time** to **'compound' time**. In the former the beat is divided into two shorter notes, in the latter into three: see Examples 2.3 and 2.4. The 'compound' rhythms are particularly associated with the villagers in *Don Giovanni*.

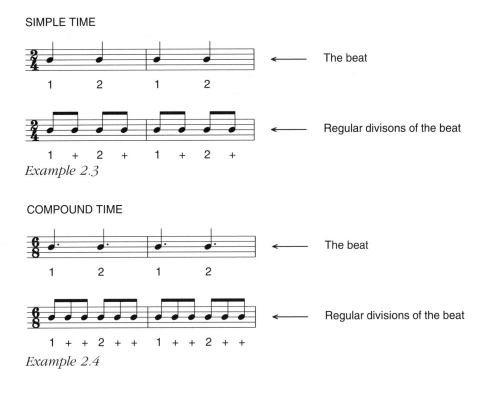

Example 2.3

Example 2.4

EXERCISE   Listen now to the demonstration of 'Simple and compound time' on
Audio 2, track 19.

---

3   Accompaniment: simple orchestral accompaniment, with occasional
links between the phrases (Zerlina), in contrast to the energetic
accompaniment to Anna's aria, which the singer then has to
dominate. As a result, the relationship between the singer and the
orchestra is more relaxed in Zerlina's aria, while the relationship
helps to generate tension in Anna's aria.

EXERCISE   Before proceeding, listen to the arias again with these descriptions in
mind.

Even though there is a pretty straightforward contrast between those
arias, the complexity of Mozart's approach is also apparent. The musical
language of 'Batti, batti' may be straightforward, but the aria becomes
elaborate (and technically more demanding) as it goes along: Zerlina is
not just a simple peasant. Also, the arias dramatize situations and

emotions as well as characters in their music. The first aria is not only sung by Donna Anna (a 'serious' character) but also carries her emotional turmoil as, having recalled how she was attacked, she now demands revenge, and thus the music needs a weighty style. The second aria is not only sung by Zerlina but it gives her the means to woo her husband-to-be into a reconciliation, and thus needs to have music that can be performed in a flirtatious manner.

In spite of this complication, a good way of approaching the music of *Don Giovanni* is through Mozart's presentation of his individuals on the basis of musical character-types. There are 'serious' characters – Donna Anna, Don Ottavio and the Commendatore are clearly in this category – and 'comic' characters, including Zerlina, Masetto and Leporello. The other principal woman, Donna Elvira, sits somewhere between and fits quite well with another category: *parti di mezzo carattere* or 'intermediate' characters, though her title indicates her high social status. She is developed as a particularly interesting linking character in the story. Perhaps rather surprisingly, it is remarkably difficult to place Don Giovanni himself on the serious/comic scale; in this, as in many things, he is ambiguous and eludes easy definition.

The cast line-up of *Don Giovanni* fulfils almost exactly the ideal that Mozart described when writing to his father in May 1783, when a new Italian opera company in Vienna had just opened:

> Well, the Italian opera buffa has started again here and is very popular ... Our poet here is now a certain Abbate Da Ponte. He has an enormous amount to do in revising pieces for the opera and he has to write *per obbligo* [as part of his duties] an entirely new libretto for Salieri, which will take him two months. He has promised after that to write a new libretto for me. But who knows whether he will be able to keep his word – or will want to? ... I should dearly love to show what I can do in an Italian opera! ... The most essential thing is that on the whole the story should be really comic; and, if possible, he [the librettist] ought to introduce two equally good female parts, one of these to be *seria*, the other *mezzo carattere*, but both parts equal in importance and excellence. The third female character, however, may be entirely buffa, and so may all the male ones, if necessary.

(Letter from WAM to LM, 7 May 1783, in Anderson, 1985, pp.847–80; underlining in original)

5   Prague and Vienna: the background to *Don Giovanni* and Mozart's career

You will probably have noticed that, although *Don Giovanni* was first performed in Prague, most of the relevant references to the careers of Da Ponte and Mozart that I quoted have concerned Vienna. In the Treaty of Westphalia (1648) which ended the Thirty Years War, the Crown of Bohemia was formally acknowledged as a hereditary possession of the Vienna-based Habsburg family. Thus Prague fell within their empire, whose territorial interests in the eighteenth century included not only Austria, Bohemia and Hungary, but areas of Italy and the Netherlands as well: see the map of Europe in 1789, p.4. (The Habsburg ruler of Austria also held the title of 'Holy Roman Emperor', giving him nominal authority over the 'German lands'.[9]) Prague (the principal city of Bohemia) was therefore a city under Austrian jurisdiction, but it was sufficiently distant from the centre to have retained a civic culture of its own: the journey from Prague to Vienna took three days by coach. It had therefore the simultaneous benefits of access to Viennese cultural resources and a certain degree of independence. The Austrian region, with a natural focus on Vienna, saw a remarkable concentration of musical talent in the years between 1760 and 1830: it was the period of Haydn, Mozart, Beethoven and Schubert. In some ways public music-making in Vienna, in concerts and opera, was less developed than in contemporary London or Paris, but a key factor seems to have been the presence of a group of musically-interested and educated aristocratic patrons: the names of members of the Lobkowitz, Lichnowsky and Schwarzenberg families, for example, recur as givers of private concerts and dedicatees of musical publications. Vienna also provided a generous raft of civil service posts (about 10,000) to back up the aristocratic system. The major families only spent part of their time in Vienna; most of them had a bewilderingly large number of palaces dotted through the Austrian lands, many of them even with their own private theatres. Prague was the second city of the Austrian kingdom, and so it is not surprising that from time to time it saw flourishing artistic and social activity, supported by Bohemian and Austrian families who had permanent palaces there (Figure 2.7).

Mozart had been brought up in Salzburg, an Austrian city about the same distance from Vienna as Prague is, where his father held office as a court

[9] The 'German lands' (or the 'Holy Roman Empire') was largely a geographical expression. It extended from the French border on the Rhine to the river Oder in the east, and consisted of some 400 German states ranging from sizeable kingdoms (like Prussia and the Habsburg kingdoms of Austria and Bohemia) to tiny principalities a few acres in size, all nominally independent. The ties of the Holy Roman Empire were mainly those of language and culture. Politically, it was fragmented and disunited.

Figure 2.7 J. Gregory, after L. Kohl, view of Prague from the right bank of the Vltava, 1835, engraving, 48.9 x 68.7 cm, Museum of the City of Prague, Czech Republic. Photo: reproduced by courtesy of the Museum of the City of Prague, Czech Republic.

musician to the prince-archbishop. In spite of European tours in which he had made a great impression as a youthful prodigy, and some reasonable success later on in various cities including Munich and Paris, Mozart found it difficult to secure an acceptable post elsewhere and for a time he also held a court post at Salzburg. Life there became increasingly irksome, however, and Mozart felt frustrated that it provided little outlet for his musical talents and ambitions. Matters came to a head in 1781, when he provoked his dismissal from the Salzburg court and moved to Vienna. He was then 25 years old and for the remaining ten years of his life he was based in Vienna, where he married Constanze Weber in 1782 and enjoyed a career of varying fortunes. For a few years he was successful as a concert artist (particularly in concerts featuring his piano concertos), but it would be wrong to interpret his career as a shift from court patronage to a modern commercial basis. Mozart relied on patronage in Vienna, remained there because the opportunities for such patronage were hopeful (from a broad range of contacts, not merely the landed aristocrats), and above all hoped for the security of commissions and a permanent post from the court.

Unfortunately, during his first years there Vienna was an unpropitious place for some of the genres of composition in which Mozart excelled. Emperor Joseph II, sole ruler since the death of his mother Maria Theresa in 1780, had instituted some wide-ranging reforms. These involved redirecting church finances (which had the effect of limiting the grand orchestrally-accompanied performances of the mass, which had been an important musical tradition in both Vienna and Salzburg) and making drastic economies in court spending, of which the Italian opera company was the first victim. The Viennese (and Prague) theatres were not specialist 'opera houses', but could host a variety of genres: French plays as well as Italian operas were popular throughout the European courts. Joseph had decided to give active encouragement to German-language drama, which in practice included German translations of French plays, and initially he also promoted *Singspiel*, a German form of opera with substantial musical movements but spoken dialogue. Of the new works which were commissioned for the court theatre under this policy, by far the most successful one was by Mozart, *Die Entführung aus dem Serail*, first performed at the (court) Burgtheater in July 1782.

A liberalization in Joseph's attitude, and probably some local pressure, resulted in the formation of a new Italian opera company the next year, already mentioned in connection with Da Ponte's employment. Thus a new phase began in Vienna's operatic history, which had seen important developments during the previous half-century. Da Ponte managed to meet Metastasio in Vienna just before the latter's death in 1782, but for some years Metastasio's style of *opera seria* had received little encouragement. From the 1750s onwards there was a fashion for French opera, ballet and plays, encouraged by Maria Theresa, and realized to good musical effect by Gluck after his appointment as court composer in 1755. In the 1760s Gluck's main interests were in a 'reform' style of serious Italian opera which was less formalized and more fluid in its musical construction, and incorporated French-style elements of dancing, spectacle and the use of the chorus. His opera *Orfeo ed Euridice* (1762) was a landmark in this new operatic genre. Perhaps not surprisingly, Gluck developed a career in Paris as well as Vienna (without incurring the loss of his Viennese court post), which sustained his creative endeavours when both Italian and French opera had little opportunity in Vienna. When Joseph took over the running of the theatres (through a manager, Count Rosenberg) in 1776, he initially declared that the Burgtheater would be a 'national theatre' where only German works were performed. When Italian opera was re-introduced to Vienna in 1783, the favoured genre was not *opera seria* with its past associations but *opera buffa*. Between 1786 and 1790 the Viennese Italian opera company was responsible for some remarkable productions from several composers, though no others achieved the level of the Mozart–Da Ponte collaborations *Le nozze di Figaro* (1786), *Don Giovanni* (1788), and *Così fan tutte* (1790). The golden period was, however, short-lived because of political and financial difficulties during Joseph II's last years.

Mozart's last two operas, *Die Zauberflöte* (*The Magic Flute*) and *La clemenza di Tito* (*The Generosity of Titus*), written and performed during the last months before his death in 1791, provide an interesting corrective to the temptation to draw general trends from local conditions. *La clemenza di Tito*, performed in Prague in celebration of the coronation of Joseph II's successor as King of Bohemia, was based on an adaptation of an old *opera seria* Metastasio libretto: in terms of subject matter, *opera seria* continued into the nineteenth century in parallel with *opera buffa. Die Zauberflöte* was a German *Singspiel* performed in a suburban theatre by an independent theatre company, and we might be tempted to identify this genre with a more independent bourgeois audience. But *Die Entführung aus dem Serail*, Mozart's previous *Singspiel*, had been written for the court theatre, and Mozart's father complained on one occasion that 'a gentleman, even a nobleman with decorations, will clap his hands and laugh so much over some ribald or naïve joke' at a German performance at one of the suburban theatres.[10]

It is important to realize, also, that although the old genre of *opera seria* continued, the musical style for the operas had changed. Musical historians distinguish between the high **Baroque** musical style of the first half of the eighteenth century (as in the music of J.S. Bach and Handel) and the **Classical** style of the last decades (as in the music of Haydn and Mozart). Many factors contributed to the change in musical style, but one of them was probably the influence of *opera buffa* itself. The fast-moving stage activity of the new genre required a different style of music: instead of conveying sentiment, the music had instead primarily to support the action. The change in musical style was absorbed by all musical genres, including those of instrumental music and indeed of *opera seria* itself. Mozart's *La clemenza di Tito* was composed in 1791 in a similar musical style to *Don Giovanni*, very different from the style of the music in the very first setting of Metastasio's libretto in 1734 by the composer Antonio Caldara.

In tandem with changes in style went changes in forms – that is, the organization of individual movements. I mentioned in section 4 that the standard form for the solo operatic song in the *opera seria* genre from the first half of the eighteenth century was the Baroque *da capo* aria. This comprised three sections: a first section (sometimes called the 'A' section) to one set of words, a second section (or 'B' section) to another text, and then a repeat of the 'A' section, except that the singer was expected to elaborate the melody with additional musical decoration (usually in faster notes) which demonstrated his/her technique and good taste.

The pattern therefore looked like this:

> A   B   A repeated.

---

[10] The sentence, in a letter from Leopold Mozart to Lorenz Hagenauer in January 1768, is not included in Anderson's edition of the Mozart letters, but is quoted in Badura-Skoda, 1973–4, p.196.

This looks nice and simple, and in general the scheme is not too difficult to recognize if you know what to listen for. The forms from the Classical period are not as easy to describe, but the fundamental principle was that they relied on the use of keys and key relationships.

This sounds very technical but, as I'll explain at the end of this section, you will probably be able to recognize at least some of the important points as you listen to the music, without having to know the 'theory' of the matter. Essentially, the Classical musical style was a tonal style in which a particular note functioned as the overall focus or 'home' note; if the chosen pitch was the note 'D' for example, we would describe the music as being 'in D', and the music would begin and end in that key. The Baroque *da capo* aria was itself a tonal form: the 'A' section would begin and end in the 'home' (or tonic) key, the 'B' section would be in a different key (that is, would have a different pitch as its 'home' note), and then the 'A' section would return the music to the original key. In Mozart's arias the sections are not so clearly separated as in the *da capo* aria, and so there is a more seamless movement from one key to another, but the background feature of a 'home' key in which the music begins and ends is still important.

The movement away from, and back to, the tonic key is basic to the way that Mozart's musical style 'works'. On a larger time-scale keys can be regarded as an extension of harmony, which means the use of chords (the combination of several different pitches at the same time). Harmony relies on changing the chords but still keeping a relationship to a tonic or 'home' chord. Although I described melodies and rhythms as separate entities earlier in this unit, in fact they are all tied together with the harmony: the chords are part and parcel with the 'tune' that they accompany. Just as, in the course of a melody, the chords change underneath (but end up by going back to the 'home' chord), so keys move away from the tonic and back again. The chords, and the key changes, are important to the pace of the action in opera: if you stay with the same chord or key, the music (and therefore the action) stands still, while changes of chord or key imply movement – either physical movement on the part of the singer or some emotional progression in the dramatic situation. Sudden changes of chord, and sudden changes of key, can have an arresting effect and delineate in music surprising events or sudden changes in the action.

EXERCISE   Another basic resource, while staying (for example) in the key of 'D', is to change the music from 'major' to 'minor'. You do not need to know about the theory of major and minor keys in order to hear the effect of this. Listen now to the audio demonstration of major and minor chords and keys on Audio 2, track 20.

As you work through the audio extracts from *Don Giovanni* in Unit 3, I'll be pointing out particular examples of Mozart's use of the resources of chords and keys. His technical brilliance in these matters is one of the principal contributing factors to the dramatic power of the opera. In terms of what you might be expected to hear without any technical training in music, there are three levels:

1   Sudden changes of key (or the use of remarkable individual chords) to interrupt or divert the music. In general you should not have any difficulty in recognizing these. Indeed, once I have pointed out the existence of this resource, you will probably notice examples for yourself independently.

2   Moments of return to the tonic key, usually accompanied by the return of the opening melody of an aria. I shall point some of these out, and the moments concerned will also sometimes be identified with CD track numbers. You would probably not have noticed these unless your attention had been drawn to them, but I hope you will be able to hear them for yourself when you know that they are there.

3   More long-term use of keys: for example the gradual move away from, or return to, the tonic key or the static effect caused by *not* moving away. (There are even some examples of long-term key relationships where a particular chord or key is apparently deliberately referred to much later in the opera.) These are more subtle, and you may have to take what I say on trust. However, you may be aware of the *effect* of these strategies, particularly in pacing the theatrical action, without being able to explain how this effect has been created. These matters are difficult to put into words without some technical knowledge of music, but you can be moved (or carried along) by Mozart's skilfully appropriate use of keys and harmony all the same!

6   The first performances of *Don Giovanni*

During 1781–3 a new theatre was built in Prague under the patronage of Count Franz Anton Nostitz-Rieneck (see Plate 2.1 in the Illustrations Book). Like the Burgtheater in Vienna, it was a fully equipped professional theatre with an audience capacity of about 1,000, and like the Burgtheater it was used for a variety of different dramatic productions. It opened in May 1783 with a German play (Lessing's *Emilia Galotti*), and in 1785 it saw the first performance of a play in Czech. Italian opera also came to feature in the theatre's programme, and Mozart was invited to come to Prague to direct *Le nozze di Figaro* a few months after its Viennese premiere in May 1786. *Figaro* had had a modest success in Vienna, but it became popular in Prague, where the theatre manager Pasquale Bondini introduced it into his programme in

December 1786, initially under the musical direction of one of his house musicians. Mozart arrived in Prague on 11 January 1787, and became aware of the popularity of his opera on his first evening there at a ball given by Baron Breitfeld, a wealthy member of the Bohemian aristocracy:

> At six o'clock I drove with Count Canal to the so-called Breitfeld ball, where the cream of the beauties of Prague is wont to gather. Why – *you* ought to have been there, my friend! I fancy I see you running, or rather limping, after all those pretty girls and women! I neither danced nor flirted with any of them, the former because I was too tired, and the latter owing to my natural bashfulness. I looked on, however, with the greatest pleasure while all these people flew about in sheer delight to the music of my 'Figaro', arranged for contradanses and German Dances.[11] For here they talk about nothing but 'Figaro'. No opera is drawing like 'Figaro'. Nothing, nothing but 'Figaro'.

> (Letter from WAM to Baron Gottfried von Jacquin in Vienna, 15 January 1787, in Anderson, 1985, p.903)

Not surprisingly, the success of *Figaro* in Prague encouraged Bondini to invite Mozart to compose a new opera for Prague, in the same *opera buffa* style, in readiness for the following season which would begin in the autumn of 1787. Once back in Vienna, Mozart no doubt contacted Da Ponte about the prospective opera, but he had other things to think about during the spring and summer. Public performance hardly featured in Mozart's schedule at that time, but he composed a series of works, apparently mainly for publication: string quintets, his last sonata for violin, the musically satirical *Ein Musikalischer Spass* (*A Musical Joke*) and the now-famous *Eine Kleine Nachtmusik*. He had various personal and domestic interruptions: he moved house in Vienna (probably to a cheaper apartment), he was ill for a period, and his father died in Salzburg. He also undertook some teaching; one of his short-term students may have been Beethoven, then on his first visit to Vienna. His father had commented on Mozart's tendency to leave composition until the last moment, but he probably had composed most of the score for *Don Giovanni* before he left for Prague with his wife on 1 October. It was expected that the first performance of the new opera would take place on 14 October, and would coincide with the honeymoon visit to Prague of Joseph II's niece, following her marriage to Prince Anton Clemens of Saxony. In Prague Mozart spent part of the time living at an inn in the city and part of the time at the Villa Bertramka, the home of Josepha Duschek, a singer friend from Salzburg days. Da Ponte arrived in Prague on 8 October to liaise with Mozart over the final arrangements for the libretto and the music; he stayed at a neighbouring inn so that the two could converse through the windows without either having to leave

---

[11] You will hear musical examples of these dance forms in Unit 3, in connection with the Act One finale of *Don Giovanni*.

his room. It seems very likely that, throughout the development of the composition of the opera, Da Ponte and Mozart were quite close collaborators, and it is even possible that Mozart contributed ideas to the opera's plot. What is certain is that the libretto (and thus the music) was under development right up to the time of the performances. An early version of the libretto was printed in Vienna and dated 1787 (see Figure 2.8); this may well have been a draft text that had been submitted for the Austrian censor's approval. Da Ponte would have supervised the printed libretto for the Prague production, and he also supervised some rehearsals there, but (like the royal couple) he had to leave Prague again before the first performance: he had urgent business in Vienna, including a commission for an opera to be composed by Salieri for the forthcoming wedding of Archduke Franz.[12]

The first performance of *Don Giovanni* in Prague was in any case delayed from its intended date. We can follow the events from a letter that Mozart wrote and added to in the course of ten days:

> *[October 15th.]* You probably think that my opera is over by now. If so, you are a little mistaken. In the first place, the stage personnel[13] here are not as smart as those in Vienna, when it comes to mastering an opera of this kind in a very short time. Secondly, I found on my arrival that so few preparations and arrangements had been made that it would have been absolutely impossible to produce it on the 14th, that is, yesterday. So yesterday my 'Figaro' was performed in a fully lighted theatre [i.e. without stage lighting effects] and I myself conducted ... 'Don Giovanni' has now been fixed for the 24th.

> *October 21st.* It was fixed for the 24th, but a further postponement has been caused by the illness of one of the singers. As the company is so small, the impresario is in a perpetual state of anxiety and has to spare his people as much as possible, lest some unexpected indisposition should plunge him in the most awkward of all situations, that of not being able to produce any show whatever!

> *[October 25th.]* My opera is to be performed for the first time next Monday, October 29th.

> (WAM to von Jacquin in Vienna, in Anderson, 1985, pp.911–12)

[12] Franz was the son of Joseph II's brother, who succeeded as Leopold II on Joseph's death in 1790. (It was for Leopold's succession that Mozart composed *La clemenza di Tito.*) Leopold himself died in 1792, to be succeeded as emperor by Franz.

[13] By this Mozart probably meant the singers and orchestra as well as the manager and theatre staff.

Figure 2.8   Title page from printed libretto of Don Giovanni, *Vienna, 1787, Gesellschaft der Musikfreunde, Vienna.*

On 4 November Mozart was able to write a further letter, reporting:

> My opera 'Don Giovanni' had its first performance on October 29th and was received with the greatest applause. It was performed yesterday for the fourth time, for my benefit.[14]
>
> (WAM to von Jacquin in Vienna, in Anderson, 1985, p.912)

---

[14] In theatrical practice, on a benefit night (usually the third or fourth performance) the author or composer was entitled to the profits of the house after expenses had been paid.

And on 19 December, back in Vienna (to which he returned soon after his benefit night), Mozart wrote to his sister:

> Of my writing 'Don Giovanni' for Prague and of the opera's triumphant success you may have heard already, but that his Majesty the Emperor has now taken me into his service will probably be news to you.

(WAM to Nannerl, in Anderson, 1985, p.914)

Mozart's court appointment (on 9 December) was not the result of the success of *Don Giovanni* but a consequence of the recent death of Gluck. His new office as *Kammerkomponist* ('chamber composer') to the emperor was not the major post for a court musician, which was *Hofkapellmeister* ('master of the court chapel'),[15] the post formerly held by Gluck and to which Salieri was appointed in February 1788. Mozart's post carried a salary of 800 florins (gulden) a year; Gluck had received 2,000. For *Don Giovanni* in Prague he had received a fee of 100 ducats (450 florins), and Da Ponte's fee had been about half of that amount. (It is quite difficult to convert these sums into modern equivalents, but the relative proportions in the payments are significant.)

Clearly, we can tell from Mozart's October letter that the opera company in Prague was not as luxurious in its arrangements as that in Vienna, but we need not doubt that *Don Giovanni* received a very successful production. There were seven solo singers: the impresario's wife played the role of Zerlina and one bass-baritone singer played both the roles of Masetto and the Commendatore (and thus the statue). The offstage chorus before Giovanni's descent may have comprised only the singers for Don Ottavio and the Commendatore, and the non-singing roles of lawyers in the final scene may have been played by stage hands. Mozart would have directed the performance from the keyboard, probably a harpsichord. The orchestra may have numbered about 30 to 35 players: not large in terms of later operatic practice but adequate enough for the building. The physical characteristics of the theatre, and the theatrical practice of the time, are essential elements to understanding the opera as Mozart and Da Ponte wrote and produced it (see Figures 2.9 and 2.10 on pp.108–9 and also Plate 2.1 in the Illustrations Book). The theatre was of wooden construction, very resonant and with good communication between the singers and the audience; the orchestra pit was shallow, also making for good communication but without obscuring the audience's view of the stage. The scenery was constructed mainly from painted canvas on wooden frames, which did not deaden the sound in the same way as curtains: in the theatre the climax of the second-act finale would probably have been pretty overpowering, through the combination of loud music and spectacular stage effects in a relatively small, enclosed

---

[15] This is a literal translation: in practice '*kapelle*' referred to the complete establishment of the musicians employed by the court, and not merely those employed for church services.

building. Once the curtain had risen for the beginning of an act, it did not fall again until the end; intermediate scene changes took place as transformation effects in full view of the audience. The deep stage provided a scenic spectacle, though the singers performed in the downstage area near the audience.

EXERCISE   A theatre in the same style as those in Prague and Vienna that saw the first performances of *Don Giovanni* survives today, with its original scenes and stage machinery, in the Czech Republic at Český Krumlov. A short sequence, illustrating the theatre and its scenic effects, is included on Video 1, band 2: *Staging Don Giovanni*. Watch this now and compare what you see of the theatre with the plan and section of the Prague theatre (Figures 2.9 and 2.10).

The 'original history' of *Don Giovanni* does not end with the Prague performance in 1787. The next year the opera was presented at the Burgtheater in Vienna under Mozart's direction, opening on 7 May (see Figure 2.11). A member of the audience, Count Karl Zinzendorf, recorded in his diary that he found the music '*agréable et très variée*'.[16] For this production Mozart, with Da Ponte's collaboration, made some important revisions to the score. These included a shortening of the opera's final scene, the insertion of a new aria for Don Ottavio ('Dalla sua pace') to replace 'Il mio tesoro' in Act One, and a substantial new scene-sequence in the middle of Act Two, including a major aria for Donna Elvira ('Mi tradi quell'alma ingrata'). Thus there are two authentic versions of the opera score, both carrying the authority of the composer and the librettist, one as performed in Prague and one as performed in Vienna. Although a large body of the opera remained unchanged, the alterations do affect some matters of pace and balance in the presentation of the story. Opinions vary as to whether the Vienna revisions were an improvement. On the one hand, the new material slows down some of the tighter, faster-moving section of the original Prague version, and the musical carpentry involved with the shortening of the final scene is not perfectly successful. On the other hand, the Vienna version includes some attractive new music, especially the arias for Ottavio and Elvira, and some people see the shortening of the final scene as an improvement. Most modern productions usually mix the Prague and the Vienna versions, inserting at least some of the Vienna music in an effort to gain the best of both worlds. But you could also regard this as the worst of both worlds, since it means that the opera is performed in a musical time-structure that reflects neither of those that Mozart or Da Ponte intended. The material on your CD follows the

---

[16] Pleasant and very diverse (quoted in Link, 1998, p.315).

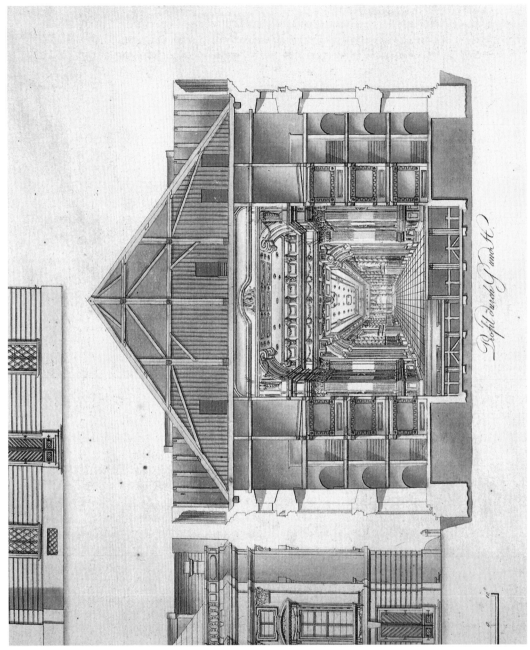

Figure 2.9   P. Heger, F. Heger and J. Berka, section through the Nostitz Theatre, Prague, showing the stage and proscenium arch, City of Prague Museum.

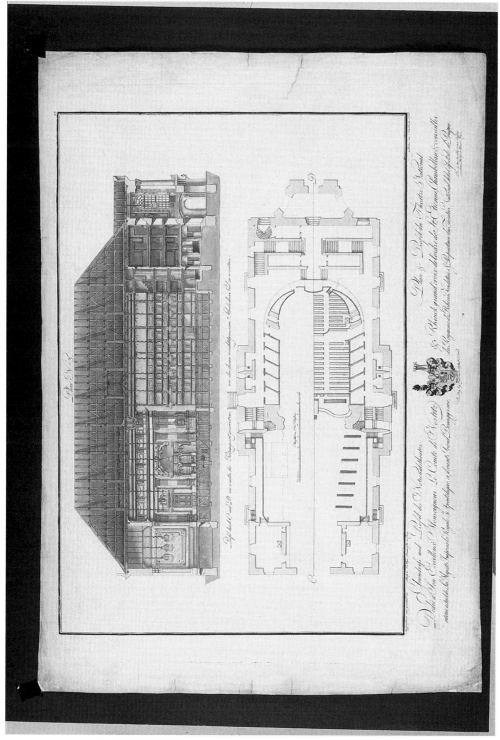

Figure 2.10   P. Heger, F. Heger and J. Berka, plan and section of the Nostitz Theatre, City of Prague Museum.

Prague version; most video and theatre performances incorporate the
new arias for Ottavio and Elvira from the Vienna version.

In 1788 *Don Giovanni* was performed 15 times at the Burgtheater in
Vienna. The last of these, on 15 December, was the last performance of
the opera that Mozart directed, and he had no further practical
connection with *Don Giovanni*. Nevertheless, there were productions in
at least 16 German cities before the time of Mozart's death in December
1791. In these, however, the opera was given in a very different form as
a *Singspiel*; Mozart's arias and ensembles were preserved (though not
necessarily completely), but the recitative was replaced by new spoken
dialogue to texts that bore little or no relation to Da Ponte's. The work
developed a divergence between coarse comedy (in the dialogue) and
serious aspects (in the musical movements), and in doing so destroyed
the delicate balance that is one of the fascinating features of the original.
Don Giovanni, or at least performances with that title and including
Mozart's music, reached Amsterdam in 1793, St Petersburg in 1797,
France in 1805, Italy in 1811, and London in 1817.

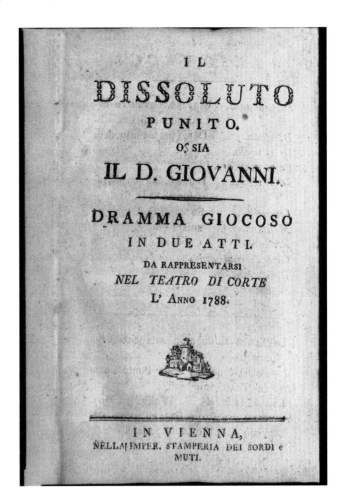

*Figure 2.11   Title page from printed
libretto of* Don Giovanni, *Vienna,
1788, British Library, London. Photo:
by permission of the British Library
(Hirsch iv.1378).*

7 Conclusion

In Unit 3 you will study selected scenes and musical movements from
Don Giovanni in detail, working in the order that they occur in the
opera, and then consider a number of issues relating to the work as a
whole. From Unit 2 you should take forward two things: a knowledge of
the opera's creative context and some basic experience in critical
listening. For the former, I suggest that you use items 1–5 on p.76 as a
checklist: the individual topics can also be located through the section
headings of the unit. In terms of approaching the musical aspects of the
opera, you may like to refer back to the listening exercises in section 4
(dealing with pitch, rhythm and the contribution of the orchestra) and
section 5 (dealing with harmony and keys). The use of particular voices
for the characters in the opera relates to both topics: Mozart used
'generic' voice types (e.g. the baritone for the servant Leporello and the
'serious' high soprano for Donna Anna) but also characterized them
individually in the particular music that he wrote for them.

In addition to these topics and techniques, Unit 2 has introduced you to
the experience of the opera itself. If you have time, you may find it
useful to watch the *Don Giovanni* video once more, as a complete
performance, but this is entirely optional.

Unit 3
Mozart's *Don Giovanni*: the opera

Prepared for the course team by Donald Burrows

Contents

1   Introduction

In this unit you will look in greater detail at some sections of *Don Giovanni*, in the sequence that they come in the opera, and then conclude this topic with a consideration of the opera's treatment of social and political issues in relation to the period of its composition. For the musical examples, the regular procedure will be for you to read my description and comments first, referring as necessary to the synopsis in the Anthology, and then to listen attentively and critically to the audio extract, using the texts in the AV Notes. In most cases, therefore, the exercises will involve recognizing features from my descriptions, rather than having to identify particular musical techniques unaided. Follow this type of activity in the way that makes most sense for you: it may be best initially to take the longer extracts in sections (individual audio track numbers are given in the AV Notes), and then go back to play the whole extract in order to appreciate the dramatic and musical continuity. Sometimes you may also find it helpful afterwards to watch the relevant section on the video as well, though this is not essential; the main thing is for you to remain open to the possibilities suggested by the musical extracts, with an imaginative perception of how they would have been treated on stage. It is important that you keep both the synopsis and the AV Notes to hand as you work through the unit.

2   The opening scene of Act One

The extract beginning with Audio 1, track 1 and ending at (i.e. just before the start of) track 15 takes you as far as the end of the duet for Anna and Ottavio. I now give a description and commentary for the scene.[17] You may prefer to read all of this and then listen to the complete score, or to take each section in turn at first, listening to it before proceeding to the next. Whichever you do, make full use of the track numbers which are provided for guidance in the AV Notes. In my commentary, track numbers are given both for the beginnings of the principal sections and for particular moments that you may wish to identify precisely as the music progresses. The principal sections begin at track numbers 1, 5, 6, 7, 11 and 12.

---

[17] As explained in the synopsis, I use 'scene' for a section of continuous action within a single stage setting. The musical score is arranged in 'Scenas' (as shown in the AV Notes), which are defined by the entrances and exits of the characters; thus there are three 'Scenas' within the first 'scene'.

Overture

According to a later anecdote attributed to Mozart's wife, the overture was composed the night before the first performance, and the orchestra played from the music before the ink was dry! This would indeed have been a remarkable achievement, for both composer and orchestra, as the overture is an extensive and cleverly written orchestral introduction to the opera. You may recognize for yourself that the opening is based on the music for the entrance of the statue at the climax of Act Two (which you listened to in Unit 2) but with one important difference: the orchestra at the statue's entrance is enhanced by the spectacular sound of trombones, which are not heard in the overture. Nevertheless, the forward reference to music heard later in the opera was relatively unusual in the 1780s, when the function of the overture was mainly to gain the audience's attention before the curtain went up. (In some later operatic genres the overture became a potpourri of songs from the show.) The 'statue' music leads into a faster section (track 2) which in a general way indicates the bustle of the opera to follow, and even possibly the energetic character of Giovanni himself, though there is no specific musical representation of him. The fast section is cast in a musical formal structure (later known as '**sonata form**') that was typical for orchestral music at this period; it is based on two themes with a clear return to the first theme (and key) at track 4. Although the music is generally cheerful (in the major key in contrast to the minor-key opening), it is not superficial and it has some 'serious' elements, including some adventurous key changes. The second theme, beginning at track 3 with the rhythm:

is also remarkable because it is almost immediately treated in a rather complicated way, in 'imitation', so that you hear one instrument after another entering with the theme in quick succession, creating a busy (and quite dissonant) effect. (Example 3.1 overleaf shows you this in musical notation.)

Most remarkable of all is the way that the overture does not close as expected, but changes key to introduce the first aria. (The shift at the end from the key of the overture, D major, to that of the aria, F major, is quite an abrupt one, as you will probably be able to hear.) Thus, the first dramatic episodes of the opera run together without a break.

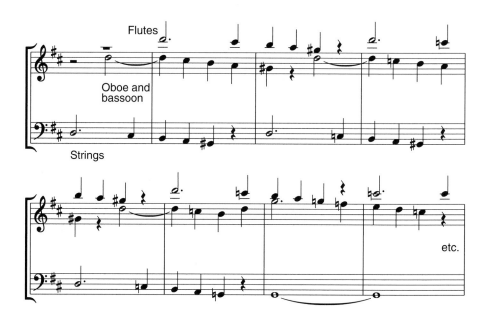

Example 3.1   This represents the orchestral scoring in a simplified way.

The first scene

Leporello (track 5)

Act One opens with an aria for Leporello: 'Notte e giorno faticar' (track 5). Superficially it is a representation of a typical 'comic servant' situation. Leporello, left to keep watch by Giovanni, complains about the contrast between the drudgery of his life and the freedom that his master enjoys in consequence; the contrast is there even in his opening phrases, as the simple repeated-note tune broadens out, almost with a swagger, on 'Voglio far il gentiluomo' ('I'd rather be a gentleman of fortune'). In the perspective of the opera as a whole, however, this aria takes on a greater significance, for Giovanni's behaviour undermines the social basis of the master–servant system. Later on in the act, Ottavio is reluctant to believe what he is told about Giovanni, because a 'cavalier' just doesn't behave like that.

Aria movements often had a short introduction for the orchestra before the singer began, and a similar postlude when the singer finished. (These orchestral sections of vocal movements were often called 'ritornellos'.[18]) Leporello's aria has a short introduction, but the orchestral link at the end is a transition rather than a conclusion – a musical representation of a moment of action on the stage, which leads

---

[18] In Britain the word 'symphony' was used for a ritornello, rather confusingly in view of the (related) use of the word for a genre of orchestral music.

straight into another musical movement (changing key at that point though the tempo remains the same) (track 6).

Anna, Giovanni and Leporello (track 6)

This begins with a phrase from Anna, who is trying to identify her intruder, answered by Giovanni's determined evasion, and it quickly develops into a trio for Anna, Giovanni and Leporello. This trio is the sort of ensemble that was characteristic of *opera buffa* (as distinct from *opera seria*, which almost entirely proceeded by solo arias).

Here we need to pause for a moment to consider the nature of 'realism' in opera. Obviously, at one level opera is an entirely unrealistic way of presenting drama: mostly, people in real life do not conduct all of their business in song. Where, as in *Don Giovanni*, the medium is of that of an all-sung opera (as distinct from, for example, a *Singspiel*, which has spoken dialogue), the musical mode of communication becomes the norm; it would be 'unreal' if someone spoke. Furthermore, in the more lyrical styles of music (including the style in which Mozart wrote), the mood or emotion of a particular moment is emphasized by being set within a form or structure that makes musical sense. As a result, words are often repeated or stretched into long musical phrases. This seems to go against reasonable experience in terms of normal conversational encounters, but in another sense it provides 'elastic time', which does bear some relationship to our *experience* of time. At moments of great emotion, events and the accompanying timescale become magnified in our perception: even at a more basic level, five minutes by the clock can seem a long time on some occasions and a short time on other occasions. The music therefore 'holds' dramatic moments suspended in time and allows us to come to grips more fully with the situation; in so doing it also gives us a measure of the significance that particular events have for the participants.

For the solo singer, the operatic medium overcomes the 'soliloquy problem'. Given the nature of operatic 'reality', there is nothing especially surprising about a character expressing his or her thoughts and feelings directly to the audience. Through the medium of a musical ensemble, it is possible for several people to express their different thoughts and feelings independently but united in one musical and dramatic event. The result becomes aurally complicated because of the number of things that are going on at the same time. In the case of this trio, two distinctly different things are taking place: the altercation between Giovanni and Anna, who are communicating (or avoiding communication) with each other, and the glum, almost fatalistic, exasperation that Leporello shares with the audience – effectively, 'Here's another fine mess he's got me into.' (Example 3.2, pp.118–19, shows the music for the transition into this section.)

Example 3.2   *The beginning of the trio. This is a 'vocal score', in which the orchestral accompaniment has been arranged for piano. Photo:* Don Giovanni, *Boosey & Hawkes, London, pp.10–11; the translation is not the same as that in the AV Notes.*

Example 3.2 (continued).

On the stage the situation is easier to see, and the music is easier to comprehend, than on a recording; video performances usually do not show you the whole picture of the stage groupings simultaneously, and audio recordings, although they may separate the sounds to left and right, do not have the physical presence of the singers to aid your comprehension. As you listen to the trio, try to pick out the individual voices, but don't be surprised if it's difficult!

Like Leporello's aria, the trio is an 'enclosed' musical movement in that it begins and ends in the same key. Also like Leporello's aria, however, it does not finish in a conventional way, because the orchestral postlude turns into another link, as Anna escapes and the Commendatore enters (track 7).

The Commendatore, Giovanni and Leporello (track 7)

The regular background tempo of the music is maintained, but the exchanges between Giovanni and the Commendatore are much more broken up, less tune-like, than the singers' phrases in the previous sections. Once again a trio of voices is involved, as Leporello continues his own comments underneath, even using the same musical phrases as Giovanni: the servant is reduced simply to echoing his master. The banter is silenced, however, when Giovanni accepts the Commendatore's challenge ('Misero, attendi', track 8). At this moment Mozart uses the same key, and the same type of music, as the Statue will use to address Giovanni at the climax of the opera (and to which reference was made at the opening of the overture). It's doubtful that Mozart expected his audience to recognize the key relationship consciously, but no one could have been in any doubt of the earnestness of this moment. The sword-fight follows, and there's also no doubt at all about the moment of the fatal thrust, when the music is arrested by a special chord known technically as a 'diminished seventh' (track 9). This chord introduces a particular type of momentary tension into the harmony, and forms the climax to the agitated music for the sword-fight; although there is a pause on this chord, by its nature it is a musical hinge rather than a conclusion.

Immediately the mood changes: a new tempo, and a new type of music, though the trio ensemble continues, the Commendatore gasps out the rest of his life, Leporello's apprehension increases, and even Giovanni seems aghast at what has happened. The last is made amply clear by Mozart's musical treatment of the text, and it is quite important for establishing his character. Giovanni is a seducer but not, by intent, a murderer: the death of the Commendatore was an inevitable consequence of the duel challenge. His two seductions which are directly portrayed in the opera are both unsuccessful (in spite of his multiple success rate elsewhere, which is later enumerated by Leporello in the 'catalogue aria'), and in each case Giovanni turns his energies to dealing with the social *contretemps* that follow, rather than taking out his resentment on the lady concerned. Win or lose, Giovanni seduces his women and then passes on. This does not mean that the effect on the women themselves is trivial: of all the treatments of the Don Giovanni story, that of Mozart and Da Ponte is most powerful in leaving us wondering about the nature of sexual relationships and the psychology of the compulsive womanizer, as well as wondering about divine retribution. One of the reasons for this is that, as their characters are developed in the course of the opera, the women themselves are portrayed as strong individuals, on equal terms dramatically with the men. Indeed, it is one of the remarkable aspects of Mozart's great Viennese operas that the theatrical, musical and social circumstances of the time gave the opportunity for roles (and careers) in which women had an unusual level of professional comparability with men.[19]

Giovanni and Leporello (track 11)

At the end of the second trio the orchestral postlude accompanies the Commendatore's dying moments (track 10), and leads into the first passage of **simple recitative** (track 11). Simple recitative consists of conversational exchanges which are accompanied by a keyboard instrument rather than the orchestra. (At this moment, the dramatic necessity for the conversation to take place in whispers usually means that the accompanying instrument is hardly audible, but you will hear clearer examples later.) This form of recitative is sometimes called *secco* ('dry') recitative, on account of the sparseness of the accompaniment, but a better term is *semplice* ('simple') recitative – Mozart would probably not have liked to hear his music described as 'dry'! Although the written music is notated with rhythmic regularity (that is, with the same number of beats – usually four – in each bar), recitative was intended to be taken rather freely, following the differences in pace and strength of delivery that are typical in normal conversation.

Anna and Ottavio (track 12)

As regards techniques of musical presentation, somewhere between *semplice* recitative and the more measured expression of solo arias and ensembles comes another form: ***accompagnato*** **('accompanied') recitative**, in which the orchestra introduces, accompanies or punctuates the 'conversational' delivery of the singers. An example of this follows (track 12), when Anna returns with Ottavio and discovers the body of her father: a situation of powerful and unsettling – often fast-changing – emotions for which accompanied recitative is the best musical medium.[20]

---

[19] This was true of Italian opera in many centres throughout the eighteenth century; it was combined with a general social denigration of those who followed stage careers, complemented by a fascination with star performances.

[20] The headings in the libretto extracts (AV Notes) follow Mozart's own conventions: *recitativo* indicates *semplice* recitative, as distinct from *recitativo accompagnato*.

The scene begins in simple recitative, but quickly converts to the more expressive form when Anna sees her father's body. Here the music is led by the text as it unfolds, with few repetitions of words except for immediate emphasis. As the initial shock subsides, the music moves into a more measured and lyrical phase with the duet 'Fuggi, crudele' (track 13), but the progress of the duet is interrupted by *accompagnato* recitative once more as Anna demands that Ottavio take an oath of vengeance ('Ah! vendicar', track 14). The duet then proceeds with the two voices singing together (for the first time): the repeat of the oath later is a confirmation which requires less forceful treatment than before. In the tonal style of music that is represented by *Don Giovanni*, ends of movements were marked by clear formulas of chords known as **cadences**, which bring the music clearly to rest in the 'home' key. The orchestral ritornello at the end of the duet is the first one in the opera to end with a clear final cadence; all the action up to this point had been composed by Mozart into one continuous musical 'scene', carrying forward the twists and turns of the various situations.

EXERCISE   Listen to the complete 'scene' now (tracks 1–14), even if you have already listened to it as individual sections. Then, making use of my descriptions, list the means that Mozart uses to delineate the characters and the stage action, with examples of their use. Your list should include, for example, examples of the use of individual chords, key changes, different types of melodies, ensembles, and the orchestra.

DISCUSSION   As a prompt, I'll give you just one example from each of the categories that I mentioned. You should be able to find more examples than this from my previous descriptions, and in any case as you become more experienced in listening you may well find extra examples for yourself.

Chords: the 'diminished seventh' chord that marks Giovanni's fatal sword-thrust to the Commendatore.

Key changes: the key change at Anna's first entry, pursuing Giovanni.

Different types of melody: the 'broken-up' phrases of Giovanni, the Commendatore and Leporello in their trio, in contrast to the more 'tune-like' initial aria for Leporello.

Ensembles: the trio for Anna, Giovanni and Leporello, following on from Leporello's first aria.

The orchestra: orchestral accompaniment for *accompagnato* recitative when Anna discovers the Commendatore's body; *accompagnato* is often used instead of *semplice* recitative at moments of solemnity or heightened emotion.

EXERCISE   Before proceeding further, listen to one other example of *accompagnato* recitative, again involving Anna and Ottavio. In this, Anna describes what happened in the moments before the action of the first scene began (track 23 – use the track number also to find the text in the AV Notes). Once again, a powerful emotional situation is involved, and Mozart's music is the perfect vehicle for Anna's distracted recollections. Also you will hear how, as both a climax and a release, the recitative flows into an aria (track 24) – in this case one that you already listened to in the previous unit.

3   Giovanni and two other women

You may remember from Unit 2 that when Mozart arrived in Prague in January 1787 he found people singing or whistling tunes from *Figaro*. One of the essentials for a successful Italian opera, along with a good '*dramma*' (to use the Italian spelling of the period), was the incorporation of some memorable tunes. Although the extracts you have listened to so far have included some quite lyrical and tuneful movements, they were essentially musical carriers for the dramatic action. But *Don Giovanni* did have its 'hit tunes', and foremost among them was the duet 'Là ci darem la mano'. One of the early successes in the career of the pianist-composer Frédéric Chopin was a set of variations on this tune, which he performed to great acclaim in Vienna in 1830 and at Paris and London in 1833; the audiences were no doubt dazzled by Chopin's piano playing, but they also knew the tune. In the context of the opera, the very attractiveness and character of the music fulfils a dramatic function: this is the moment when Giovanni succeeds in winning the attentions of the young bride Zerlina.

EXERCISE   Read the text of the duet and its preceding recitative ('Alfin siam liberati – Là ci darem la mano') in the AV Notes (tracks 15–18). The context is that Giovanni has just sent Zerlina's husband away with Leporello, though under protest. Masetto is under no illusions about Giovanni's intentions towards Zerlina, and in his preceding aria ('Ho capito, signor, sì', which is not in your extracts) he had expressed his frustration that a 'gentleman' like Giovanni apparently had the right to do whatever he pleased. In the recitative Giovanni proceeds briskly with his seduction of Zerlina; the duet comes at the moment when he persuades her to hold his hand, having invited her to come with him to his nearby villa.[21] The 'hand' idea obviously has wider reference in the opera; later on, it will

---

[21] Or cottage: the word that Giovanni uses is a double diminutive from '*casa*' (house or home) → *casino* → *casinetto*. This is clearly a different building from the mansion in which the Act One finale is set.

be the handshake (and the accompanying invitation) between Giovanni and the Statue that changes his fortunes.

Then listen to the recitative and the duet (tracks 15–18), followed by one or two playings of the duet by itself (tracks 16–18). Stop at the music which follows, track 19. As you listen to the duet, try to answer the following questions:

1   What is remarkable about the opening of the duet, and what are the implications of this for what happens on stage?

2   In Unit 2 you listened, for comparison, to an aria for Anna and one for Zerlina, as representing the musical styles for *seria* and *buffa* characters in the opera. Which of these is closer to the musical style that Mozart uses in the duet, and how does this relate to the situation in the opera?

3   The opening theme of the duet comes back at track 17, in the original key, but with a difference in the participation of the singers. What is this difference, and what is its dramatic implication?

4   Eventually Zerlina agrees to Giovanni's proposal. What happens to the music at that moment (track 18)?

DISCUSSION   This exercise requires careful listening, the application of some ideas that you met in Unit 2, and also some imagination as to how Mozart's music relates to what happens on stage. I hope you have been led to at least some of the 'answers' that I give below. Compare them with yours, and in any case listen to the duet once more when you have read them.

1   The duet begins without any orchestral introduction or ritornello. Giovanni's seduction relies for its success on keeping up the pressure: he goes straight from the invitation at the end of the recitative to the physical contact of holding hands.

2   The style of the duet is closer to that of 'Batti, batti' (Zerlina's aria) than to that of Anna's aria (the opening of which you were reminded of in the previous section of this unit). The simple, apparently regular, phrases of the melody and the mainly step-wise movement of the pitches in the tune are characteristics of the 'lower-class' characters (as in 'Batti, batti'), and yet the duet is initiated by the 'cavalier' Giovanni. The explanation is that, for his present purpose, Giovanni is bringing himself down socially to Zerlina's level, while including a flattering implication that Zerlina is a lady who deserves better than the peasant Masetto for a husband. So the music reflects a levelling-off process; the language is basically that of a *buffa* character, but the melodies are elegant enough for a gentleman.

3   At the opening Giovanni and Zerlina sing their complete statements (four lines of verse each) in turn. When the music comes back, however, Zerlina's phrases immediately answer each of Giovanni's,

and then Zerlina's melody gradually becomes more elaborate as she gains more confidence (or is more persuaded). Musically, the alternation of the phrases indicates Giovanni and Zerlina coming together in agreement (and probably physically closer together as well on the stage).

4   When Zerlina finally says 'Yes', the rhythm of the music changes to a more joyous character as the pair prepare to go off together. In technical terms, this is a change from the simple-time rhythm (see Example 3.3) to compound time (see Example 3.4).

Example 3.3

Example 3.4

This change repeats the same process from simple to compound time that you heard in Zerlina's aria 'Batti, batti' in Unit 2, section 4. (If you have forgotten about this, listen once again to the audio demonstration on Audio 2, track 19 and see pp.94–5 above.[22]) You may have noticed, however, that although there is a new rhythm and a new melody when the duet changes to compound time, the tune once again moves mainly in simple pitch-steps. The melodies are shown in Examples 3.5 and 3.6.

Example 3.5

Example 3.6

---

[22] Compound-time rhythms are characteristic of many folk dances, and indeed a similar rhythm introduces the villagers at their first appearance in the opera, at No. 5 (Act One, Scene 7 – see the synopsis in Anthology I).

At the end of the duet, the progress of Giovanni and Zerlina towards his villa is interrupted by the arrival of Elvira, who upbraids Giovanni for his latest 'amusement' and warns Zerlina not to believe anything that he says; Giovanni, for his part, tells Zerlina that he had pretended to love Elvira out of the kindness of his heart. Elvira's aria, in which she warns Zerlina, is a startling musical contrast to the preceding duet. It is unmistakably a *seria* piece, with angular, impassioned melodic lines for the singer, and an orchestral accompaniment that adds tension to the music. (In the duet the orchestra had, by contrast, provided soothing, confirming interludes and commentary.) The jerky, dotted-rhythm musical rhetoric of Elvira's aria (sustained almost continuously in the orchestral part) is in the old-fashioned tradition of *opera seria* from the high Baroque era earlier in the century, though the harmony and the structure of the movement are typical of Mozart's Classical musical style.

EXERCISE   Listen now again to the duet (track 16), proceeding into the following recitative and then the aria (track 20). (This section of the performance, incidentally, gives you a clear example of *semplice* recitative at track 19.) Listen for the contrast in the musical language between the duet and the aria; once again, the music reinforces contrasts both of character and of situation. Read the libretto in the AV Notes first.

Then listen separately to Elvira's aria a couple of times. The aria, although short, is in a recognizable musical 'form' which relies on a sense of tonality – establishing a key at the beginning, moving away from it and then returning to it later. There are three distinct sections: an opening section, a middle section and then a recapitulation which returns to the opening music and key. With the help of the libretto in the AV Notes (at tracks 20–2), see if you can identify the sections. As an extra hint, I'll mention that the musical structure follows that of the words.

DISCUSSION   The most important 'landmark' in the musical structure comes at the return of the words 'non lo lasciar più dir' (track 22). The music here reinforces Elvira's principal message that Zerlina should not place any faith in Giovanni's words, and returns to the tonic key. The sections are:

Opening section: up to the words 'fallace il ciglio', followed by a short orchestral link. At this point the music has moved away from the tonic key to the 'dominant' key. (The latter is based on a 'home' note that is closely related to the tonic, so it's not a matter of an abrupt, arresting gesture, but rather the key change has the effect of 'lifting' the music and moving it on.)

Middle section: beginning with the words 'Da miei tormenti impara' (track 21), and passing through several keys.

Recapitulation: the return to the tonic key (track 22), as just described. Although the 'home' key returns, and there is a brief reference back to the opening music, Mozart does not repeat the opening section exactly, but extends the melody in a new way, leaving us with the memory of the singer's flourish on the word 'fallace' (false). Because of the subtlety of Mozart's return to the tonic in the midst of the repeat of the first verse of the text, I would not have expected you to hear the return to the tonic key for yourself. With the help of the track number you may nevertheless be able to hear the passing reference to the opening melody.

If you managed to spot the structure for yourself, well done! Whether you did or not, listen to the aria a couple of times more, concentrating on the structural pattern. The changes in the track numbers will identify the 'landmark moments' for you.

Elvira's music there was clearly that of a serious, high-status character, and this is true of her music throughout the opera. One of Mozart's remarkable achievements was to delineate and distinguish the individual characters of Anna and Elvira in their music, while at the same time dealing with voices that were fundamentally similar in expressive style and vocal range. The same is true of the men: Leporello, Masetto, the Commendatore and Don Giovanni are all roles for singers with voices in the baritone range, but Mozart's music leaves you in no doubt as to which of them is singing at any moment.

As already noted, there is a remarkable equality of dramatic and musical status between the men and the women in Mozart's operas; Giovanni, Leporello and Masetto are matched by equally powerful roles for Anna, Elvira and Zerlina. Although Anna and Elvira are both high-status roles, there does seem to be a fundamental generic difference between their musical portrayal; Mozart may well have regarded Elvira as a 'medium' character role. The 'mediumness' is not a matter of social position, however: Elvira is clearly a 'Donna' like Anna (but not like Zerlina). In terms of social status there are no 'middle-class' roles in *Don Giovanni*. The difference seems to be that Elvira comes from 'outside'; she is 'a lady from Burgos, abandoned by Don Giovanni' and apparently anxious to resume their relationship. Anna, Ottavio, Masetto and Zerlina are all part of one community, and relate to each other as such. Elvira has come from somewhere else in pursuit of Don Giovanni and is unwilling to be abandoned; she is seeking Giovanni in order to keep him to his promises. As an outsider, she is the obvious counterpart to Giovanni himself, who may have a villa at the scene of the opera, but whose conquests (and therefore connections) cover Germany, France and Turkey as well as Spain. (The action of the opera takes place in 'a city in Spain'.)

4   The Act One finale

The ensemble act finale was one of the distinguishing features of the *opera buffa* genre, and one that developed from a simple brawl between three or four of the characters in the early examples of the *buffa* genre into more elaborate, extended and dramatically relevant musical structures. As in the first scene of Act One that you studied earlier, the act finales of the Mozart/Da Ponte arias are essentially chains of events and situations, and therefore chains of musical movements with linking passages. The remarkable qualities of Mozart's operatic finales, which were probably never surpassed by any other *opera buffa* composer, concern the pacing of the incidents and the overall sense of dramatic direction and coherence. Although the text was supplied by a librettist, it was the composer who controlled the pace of the drama: how long was spent on each incident and the placing of the main events within the overall time-frame. This is, in fact, one of the attractions of opera in the hands of the best composers: the clockwork runs to time.

The dramatic content of the first act finale of *Don Giovanni* was largely an invention of Da Ponte's, owing little to Bertati or to other preceding treatments of the story. (It does not even appear in Da Ponte's Viennese printed draft libretto dated 1787, which ends with Scena 12 as found in the Prague version.) The principal dramatic incident of the finale is Giovanni's further attempt to complete his seduction of Zerlina; the dramatic conclusion of the finale is the unification of the various forces opposed to Giovanni – Anna, Ottavio, Elvira and Masetto, all variously persuaded of his guilt as a seducer and as the murderer of the Commendatore. The finale also incorporates a spectacular effect, both visual and musical: the presentation of a ball scene in which a number of dances are taking place simultaneously, thus separating a number of social groupings and multiplying the centres of activity in a manner that is sufficiently complex and distracting to allow Giovanni to sneak away with Zerlina. At the height of the physical complexity/confusion, three simultaneous dances are going on, in different styles, metres and speeds. The stage direction for the scene is simply 'Hall in Don Giovanni's house, lit up and decorated for a festive ball', but the stage must have been divided into three clearly distinct spaces, indeed possibly even three physically separate 'rooms'. The previous scene had taken place outside Giovanni's house; when Anna, Ottavio and Elvira arrive, they already hear the dancing in progress as Leporello opens a window to welcome them. These three guests follow an upper-class social tradition of the period by treating the ball as a masquerade. They are 'masked' and thus formally concealing their identities, which allows them to take part in an event with the villagers. The scene opens as the guests at the ball (which initially consist only of the country folk celebrating the wedding of Masetto and Zerlina) take their seats again, following the dance that the maskers overheard; the maskers themselves have not yet reached the ballroom.

EXERCISE   Read the synopsis for the Act One finale (Anthology I, pp.11–12) and the text of the extract in the AV Notes; then listen to the extract, which begins at track 26. After that, read my description below, which describes the individual musical movements of the finale, before listening again. (As with the opera's opening scene, you may find it helpful also to read the commentary for each section in turn and then listen to that section before proceeding to the next.) When reading the synopsis and text, don't forget that, here especially, the stage directions are as important as the words that are sung! As you proceed, make a note for yourself of further examples of the features that I listed in the exercise at the end of section 2, and any others (for example, concerning rhythm) that you notice.

The finale has the following sections:

1   (Track 26) Refreshments are served in the break between the dances, and after a time Giovanni approaches Zerlina (*Fa carezze a Zerlina*), while Masetto is beside himself with apprehension and jealousy. The conversations take place over a complete and unbroken orchestral movement in the compound-time rhythms which characterize the country folk.

2   (Track 27) The music changes with a fanfare to something more formal as the maskers enter and are welcomed by Giovanni and Leporello. They all take up Giovanni's toast 'Viva la libertà!' with surprising emphasis. The sentiment is perhaps ambiguous. Superficially it refers to the temporary suspension of formal social restrictions during the ball, but no doubt Giovanni and Leporello also have their own ideas of 'libertà', while for the maskers the freedom they seek is perhaps freedom from Giovanni. The text of this passage is not included in the 1787 Viennese draft libretto; 'libertà' was toasted at Prague, but when it came to the Vienna performances in 1788 the word had been changed, perhaps at the censor's insistence, to 'società'.

There then follows an accumulating succession of dances which, following eighteenth-century ball practice (in England as well as in Vienna), occur in a conventional generic order – beginning with the most formal and aristocratic, and then proceeding to less elegant (and more energetic) forms.

3   (Track 28) The dances begin with a stately minuet (a moderately paced triple-time dance) for Anna and Ottavio; while dancing, Anna's attention is drawn by Elvira to the presence of Zerlina. During the dance Giovanni instructs Leporello to distract Masetto by leading him

away to another dance area, and then he takes Zerlina in the opposite direction to a different dance.

4   While the minuet is still going on (with its own orchestra of oboes, horns and strings on the stage), a second orchestra of violins and bass instruments gathers (Mozart writes in a 'tuning-up' sequence for them) and then begins a *contradanza* (a 'country dance', with two beats in a bar) (track 29). Giovanni dances this with Zerlina. Soon afterwards a third orchestra (similarly of violins and basses) starts up with a '*Teitsch*' (a 'Deutsch' or 'German dance' in fast triple time[23]) (track 30). Example 3.7 shows you a page of the music with all three dances going at once. Leporello leads Masetto, under protest, to the 'Teitsch', and as soon as that dance is under way Giovanni pulls Zerlina out of the ballroom. The exchange between Giovanni and Zerlina adds yet another metre to the music.

In the theatre, where you have a view of all three dances at the same time and they have been built up one after another, the situation is more comprehensible than on an audio or video recording, though even so the complexity is such that (if you don't know the details beforehand) it is quite difficult to decide where to focus your concentration at any given moment. You may have found it difficult to pick out the three dances on the audio extract and to hear how they fit together. On Audio 2, track 21 there is a demonstration of the music of each dance separately, showing their individual character in melodies and rhythms.

EXERCISE   Listen to this now before proceeding.

5   Both Masetto and the minuet dancers have noticed Giovanni's manoeuvre; Masetto breaks free of Leporello and goes to follow Zerlina, and Leporello also leaves, presumably to prevent Masetto from harming his master. Behind the scenes on the right Zerlina screams and a struggle is heard (track 31). The stage bands depart in confusion (as also do the villagers), Masetto is heard off-stage crying 'Ah Zerlina', and a further struggle is heard on the other side, with Zerlina crying out 'Scellerato' ('scoundrel'). The maskers break down the door but Zerlina enters from another direction, and Ottavio, Anna, Elvira and Masetto rush to her aid. All this only takes just over half a minute: Mozart's music for both singers and orchestra conveys the bustle and confusion of the situation. Even if you have not much experience of listening to music, I'm sure that you'll be able to hear

[23] Although this is not made explicit in the libretto, it is probable that some of the country folk also participated in the second and third dances.

*) la Teitsch = Danza „alla tedesca" („Deutscher").

Example 3.7   The three dances: a page from the full score of Don Giovanni, Bärenreiter, *Kassel, 1968, p.224.*

the startling key change that is precipitated by Zerlina's initial scream, abruptly breaking off the key in which the dances had taken place.

6   (Track 32) With another change of key and tempo, back to a more *seria* style, Giovanni enters, sword in hand, leading Leporello by the arm: he makes as if to stab Leporello, but the sword does not leave its scabbard. Giovanni claims to have caught Leporello in the act of attacking Zerlina. Don Ottavio, pistol in hand, challenges the truth of this story; he, Anna and Elvira remove their masks, and with Zerlina and Masetto they round on Giovanni, saying that they are now convinced of his infamy and that the thunderbolt of vengeance will pursue Giovanni that very day.

7   (Track 33) In response to their threats, Giovanni is at first disconcerted, but then regains his courage ('Ma non manca in me coraggio', track 34) and defies them. The act ends with an unresolved confrontation between Giovanni (supported by Leporello) and the others. This is a typical *opera buffa* conclusion, with lots of energetic music to support the confrontation, and a prolongation of the situation in order to make a rousing musical finale. The long section from the unmasking (beginning at the words 'Tutto tutto già si sa') has been firmly grounded in one key, and mainly sticks to simple key-affirming music. The exception, the chromatic phrase (using notes from outside the key) when the pursuers scream 'la tua fiera crudeltà' at Giovanni, thus becomes all the more powerful.

Both in its detailed musical choreography of particular incidents and in its overall drive, this finale is one of the most remarkable extended scenes in all opera. In the theatre some things are much easier to grasp than on a recording: not only the separation of the stage bands but also the groupings of singers. You may nevertheless have noticed the great variety of character combinations that Da Ponte gave to Mozart – single voices in conversation while other things are going on behind them, two or three singers united together, or one group of singers versus another group. Mozart also makes full use of other means to support and push along the drama: varied rhythms, sudden changes of key, and orchestral accompaniments that by turns set up new situations (such as the entrance of the maskers) and enhance the activity on the stage, sustaining the background to the longer scenes and heightening the activity at moments of confusion.

EXERCISE   I suggest that you listen to the finale once more, from track 26, and then watch the video of the complete Act One before proceeding.

---

5   The first scenes of Act Two

Some commentators have seen the first half of Act Two as the weakest area in *Don Giovanni*. Here Da Ponte stretches out the story in an episodic manner, without advancing the main plot substantially or strongly following up the confrontation with which Act One ended. Certainly Da Ponte had to create some diversions at this point in order to turn Bertati's single-act scenario into a full-length opera, and he took the opportunity to entertain the audience with some comic business involving disguise and mistaken identities. However, he also used the opportunity to develop some aspects of the characters – in particular the role of Leporello – for which the plot would not otherwise have given space. Furthermore, it would have been too simplistic to run straight from the threat of vengeance (at the end of Act One) to its enactment. Although the opera's plot can be seen as linear, moving from the Commendatore's murder to Giovanni's downfall, it is also circular (or perhaps spiral). Giovanni's opponents make successive attempts to catch him and bring him to judgement, but fail each time for different reasons: because the identity of the murderer is initially uncertain, because Giovanni brazens out the social consequences of his misbehaviour, or because he is clever enough to escape. There are in fact two complementary and competing motivations for Giovanni himself: his irresistible attraction towards women (before Elvira appears in Act One Giovanni tells Leporello that he can 'smell a woman', and at the beginning of Act Two his response to Leporello's appeal to abandon his profligate lifestyle is that he needs women more than bread or air) and his constant desire to outwit his opponents. When the two are in combination, he clearly enjoys the challenge of getting out of the mess that his escapades bring upon him. The first half of Act Two presents one elaborate spiral; Giovanni creates a confusion of identities that gives him the cover to pursue a new woman, and also enables him to escape from his pursuers. By exchanging clothes with Leporello he is able both to dispose of the unwelcome attentions of Elvira and to attempt the seduction of her maidservant.

EXERCISE   Listen now to the *canzonetta* with which Giovanni (dressed as Leporello) serenades Elvira's maid in an effort to bring her to the window of her room (track 35). There's a novelty in the instrumentation: Giovanni accompanies his song on the mandolin, which is incorporated into the orchestral texture (see Figure 3.1). How does the style of the music suit the action at this point?

DISCUSSION   Since Giovanni is taking on the role of his servant for the purpose, it's not surprising that, as with 'Là ci darem la mano', he adopts a simple style, this time in swinging compound-time rhythm, with a graceful melody (moving mainly in repeated notes and pitch-steps) and straightforward harmony. (The term '*canzonetta*' in fact refers to a song in fairly simple style.) The song has two verses, with virtually identical music for each verse; as in his duet with Zerlina, Giovanni is adopting a simpler musical style appropriate to the social level of the woman he is hoping to attract.

Giovanni's attempt at seduction does not get very far, because at the end of the song he is interrupted by the arrival of Masetto and a group of his friends seeking to avenge the attack on Zerlina; they are inevitably sent on their way by 'Leporello'. Meanwhile, the real Leporello develops troubles of his own in his fictional role as Giovanni. The climax of this sequence is a sextet (an ensemble involving six voices) when the various pursuers come together, which is nearly as extended as an act finale and equally brilliant in its musical-dramatic execution by Mozart.

Figure 3.1 Medardus Thoenert, Luigi Bassi as Don Giovanni, *1787, engraving, 9.1 x 5.8 cm, Theatre Collection, University of Cologne. Photo: reproduced by courtesy of Theaterwissenschaftliche Sammlung, Universität zu Köln.*

The scene shows the original singer for the role of Don Giovanni during the canzonetta.

In the space of two units it is obviously not possible to explore every facet of *Don Giovanni*, nor to look in detail at all of the events and all of the characters. You may have noticed that I have not paid much attention to Ottavio, and indeed he is perhaps the least developed character in the opera. His role is mainly as a supporter (and to some extent a sounding-board) for Anna, to whom he is devoted in spite of her repeated insistence on delaying their union. Nevertheless, his role is musically significant, for he receives some splendid arias. (The only character who never receives a complete solo aria is Giovanni himself.) Ottavio is also clearly distinguishable from the other male characters because he is the only one with a voice in the higher (tenor) register: a high voice for high social status, perhaps.[24]

EXERCISE   Listen now to Ottavio's Act Two aria, 'Il mio tesoro intanto' (beginning at track 36), having first read the text in the AV Notes. This aria comes at the moment in the opera when Ottavio has become finally convinced that, in spite of his 'cavalier' status, Giovanni is the murderer of the Commendatore, and he promises to fulfil the vow that he made in the opening scene of Act One. He asks that his resolution be conveyed to Anna. The accompaniment (and introduction) to the aria includes a prominent role for the clarinets as a colourful part of the orchestral texture.

How does the music reflect the status of Don Ottavio?

Referring to the text while listening to the music, try to identify the musical structure of the aria, listening for musical 'landmarks'.

DISCUSSION   Initially, the theme of the aria has the step-wise melody that we have associated with the less socially exalted characters in the drama, but the melody soon develops elaborate, extended phrases (also including long-sustained notes and running passages in shorter notes) and a wider pitch-range which leave no doubt that this is the music of a *seria* character.

You will, I hope, have spotted the return of the opening theme at the half-way point. The two halves of the aria each comprise two sections. The first section begins and ends in the same key, and is followed by a more varied section, moving away from the original key, beginning at the words 'Ditele che i suoi torti' (track 37); the opening section then returns complete in the original key, and is followed by a closing section to the second text, this time re-composed to stay in the tonic key.

[24] In *opera seria*, as noted in Act One, the leading male roles were played by *castrati* singing in the soprano or alto register. (When a *castrato* was not available, these male roles were often sung by women.) In other genres of opera, including *Singspiel*, it was not unusual for the leading male role to be for the tenor voice, and this trend developed further in nineteenth-century opera.

I hope that you recognized the main points of the structure. The identifications of keys were beyond the scope of what I was asking, but I suggest that you listen to the aria at least once more. Now that it has been pointed out, you may well be able to recognize that the original key as well as the theme return at the half-way point.

6   The graveyard scene

In the original (Prague) version of the opera, the graveyard scene followed directly after the aria that you have just heard, and there could not be a greater contrast than that between Ottavio's earnest seriousness and the levity that opens the following scene. Giovanni has named a graveyard, of all places, as his meeting-point with Leporello to report on their various adventures (amorous, as usual, in the case of Giovanni) and to plan the next step. Here *semplice* recitative comes into its own as the conversation proceeds, only to be interrupted dramatically (in every sense) by the solemn pronouncements of the monumental statue of the Commendatore. This is followed by a trio[25] (track 40) in which Mozart brilliantly conveys the successive actions and emotions of Leporello and Giovanni within a single overall tempo. Leporello advances and retreats between his master's insistence that he invite the statue for a meal and his own dread as he approaches too close to the statue. The situation has simultaneously a deadly serious and a ridiculous aspect, at least until the Statue actually signifies its assent, first by nodding and then by replying (once only) 'Sì' to Giovanni's personal invitation. Thereafter Giovanni is entertained by the novelty of the situation, while Leporello is simply terrified (Figure 3.2).

EXERCISE   Read the text of the scene through (AV Notes, Scena 11) and then listen to the complete scene (tracks 38–40). In this case, try to follow the text carefully while the scene is played, because every phrase of the text, particularly from the moment of the Statue's participation, contributes to the drama and is brilliantly conveyed through the music. You may need two or three playings to get a full grasp of the details of the music and the action.

---

[25] The movement is described as a *duetto*, but obviously the Statue is also part of the dramatic action, even though his musical contribution is limited to 'Sì'.

Figure 3.2   François Boucher, Don Juan and his Servant at the Tomb, *from* Oeuvres de Molière, *Paris, 1749. Photo: by permission of the British Library (640.a.1-8).*

The music for the Statue (beginning at track 39) obviously presents the greatest contrast to the surrounding recitative, as the fast patter of the previous conversation between Giovanni and Leporello is interrupted by slow, measured minor-key harmonies. (These harmonies, incidentally, include the use of the diminished seventh chord which signified the fatal sword-thrust at the beginning of the opera, and now point up the word 'finirai'; the chords that accompany the surrounding recitative are much simpler and are mostly in major keys.) The orchestral scoring to accompany the Statue in its interruptions to the recitative is also aurally spectacular: this is the first entry of the trombones in the opera, and they form part of a wind ensemble with oboes, clarinets and bassoons. (Of the string instruments, only the cellos and double basses participate at that moment.) In the eighteenth century trombones were not regularly used in the orchestra. There were probably only a limited number of the instruments (and their players) in Europe, but they were conventionally used in Vienna and Salzburg to accompany the voices in church music.

So, quite apart from the surprising and rather eerie effect of their use in the theatre, the trombones brought with them their association with the solemnities of religious ritual.

7   The supper scene

The supper scene is the logical consequence of the invitation in the graveyard, but of course it does not follow directly in the opera; there is an intermediate scene for Anna and Ottavio, while Giovanni returns home. You listened to a substantial portion of the supper scene at the beginning of Unit 2: that extract is preceded, at the beginning of the finale, by the table preparations for the meal and by the background musical entertainment to Giovanni's feasting which is provided by a 'harmonie' ensemble: an on-stage band, principally of wind instruments. Giovanni is played tunes from recent operas (on which he comments while he eats): *Una cosa rara* (by Martín y Soler, to a libretto by Da Ponte), *I due litiganti* (by Guiseppe Sarti, to a libretto based on Goldoni), and Mozart's own *Le nozze di Figaro*.[26] The audio extract begins with the third tune.

EXERCISE   Replay this scene (Audio 2, track 1), referring beforehand to the synopsis in the Anthology I (pp.15–16) and the text in the AV Notes. I suggest that you play the complete extract twice (as far as the beginning of track 16), the first time following the text.

With the experience that you have gained from listening to and following other sections of the opera, this extract should make much more sense to you now than it did when you listened in Unit 2; you know much more about the plot background to the scene, and are more familiar with Mozart's music (and the sound of sung Italian). I list below some individual points for you to listen for; replay sections of the extract as you need to in order to check them for yourself. Treat this as an extended listening exercise and, as usual, note for yourself the musical features that contribute to the effectiveness of the stage action.

---

1   (Audio 2, track 1) This is an enclosed musical 'movement', beginning and ending in the same key – not surprising in view of the fact that it is based on pre-existing music from *Figaro* over which new words are added (sometimes to the original tune!). The section obviously carries the stage business of Leporello helping himself to the food.

---

[26] These were all recent Viennese productions, and Da Ponte could not resist putting some critical comments into Giovanni's mouth, notwithstanding the supposed location of the opera in Spain.

2   Elvira's entry (track 2) does not involve a change of key but instead changes of speed and metre (fast three-in-a-bar in place of a moderate-speed four-in-a-bar). The following section also forms a complete 'movement' in itself, beginning and ending in the same key. Mozart's use of key is carefully paced to the action. There is a brief movement towards another (closely related) key up to the moment when Elvira begins 'Ah! non deridere' (track 3). The following passage relies on the fact the music prepares for a return to the tonic, but the expected resolution is delayed until Giovanni says 'Lascia ch'io mangi' (track 4), from which point onwards the music uses formulae (in melodies and harmony) which re-emphasize the tonic key in a rather repetitive way until the end of the movement. Thus Mozart's music, by remaining rather obstinately in one key, supports the situation in which nothing is happening. Elvira's desperate appeal to Giovanni falls on indifferent ears, ultimately rejected at 'Lascia ch'io mangi' (with the sense, 'Let me get on with my food'), and is succeeded by a non-conversation between Elvira and Giovanni, under which Leporello as usual makes his own comments. The music conveys the passing of time in which plenty of statements are made but there is no progress in the relationship. The musical technique that Mozart uses, which relies on an expectation of a return to the tonic key, is quite subtle, but I hope that you will be able to sense the stalemate effect that is produced until Giovanni cuts off the conversation. As you listen again to this section, see if you can sense the musical game with keys which mirror the personal 'game' that is taking place on stage.

3   The tonic-key closure of the preceding movement is disturbed by the interruption when Elvira sees the Statue and screams over another diminished-seventh chord (track 5). In the link that follows, a point to listen out for is the bass line of the harmony (played by the lower-pitch instruments in the orchestra – cellos, double basses and bassoons). The rising bass pushes forward a tension in the harmony towards the key of D minor (associated with the Statue in the graveyard scene), but there is a sudden diversion (to F major) as Leporello breathlessly reports what he has seen in a new speed and metre (a faster four-in-a-bar) (track 6). This leads on, in the same tempo, to the knocks on the door (track 7), which are irregularly spaced to carry the Statue's urgent insistence; there are three double knocks (the second and third closer in time than the first and second) and then two separate ones. In spite of the tension and disruption in the situation (carried by accordingly lively music), the key of the music remains solidly in Leporello's key of F major.

4   (Track 8) However, the Statue enters,[27] with full majestic orchestral accompaniment, interrupting the harmony in the same diminished-

[27] The Statue enters musically but perhaps not physically; he is revealed when Giovanni opens the door, and may have remained in the doorway thereafter.

seventh chord with which he was killed in Act One, and turning the music to the key of D minor which had been set up earlier. In fact, this final section of the scene replays the keys that were heard in the opening scenes of the opera: the first part of Act One that you listened to at the start of this unit began and ended in D minor, but Leporello's first aria ('Notte e giorno faticar') was in F major. You may think that this is very technical and would only have been understood with reference to the written music, but in fact many people seem to be instinctively aware of this kind of long-term reminiscence, especially when the incidents (dramatic and musical) are themselves memorable. Certainly, we must suppose that the overall key scheme was the result of deliberate planning on Mozart's part.

I mentioned earlier Mozart's use of some elements from this scene in the overture: these include the basic rhythm and the cross-rhythms ('syncopations') in the orchestra (marked 'a' and 'b' on Example 3.8), which pervade the accompaniment following track 8, and then the scales from the violins beginning at 'Altre cure più gravi di queste' (track 10), which perhaps represent smoke curling round the Statue. Otherwise there is little that I want to add in the way of commentary to this section of the finale. The dramatic sequence is clear, and is brilliantly carried by the shifting harmonies and the interplay of the characters in Mozart's score. Listen, nevertheless, for the rising bass to the harmony which marks the menace that the Statue brings to Giovanni; there are particularly clear examples under the Statue's phrase beginning 'Tu m'invitasti a cena' (track 12), and following the entry of understage chorus (track 15). The final screams of Don Giovanni and Leporello match Elvira's earlier in the scene, but also those of Zerlina in the Act One finale. The threat posed to the women has been exorcised by the punishment of Giovanni.

One other aspect of the scene, however, requires special comment. Obviously, this is the climax of the opera, and the business conducted between Giovanni and the Statue is deadly serious. But the scene also has its *buffo* aspect, as Leporello hides under the dining table, much more frightened than his master, yet continuing the mode of complaint about his situation as Giovanni's servant that has been one of the threads throughout the opera. It is scarcely possible to imagine the continued participation of Leporello in this manner in a spoken drama: it would have undermined the principal thrust of the scene. Yet the musical medium of opera allows both the 'serious' and 'comic' elements to be presented simultaneously (track 11), and indeed Leporello's reactions heighten rather than diminish the force of the remarkable things that are being enacted before his eyes.

Example 3.8   The entry of the Statue in the vocal score. Photo: Don Giovanni, *Boosey & Hawkes, London, p.276.*

Figure 3.3   A page from Mozart's autograph score of Don Giovanni, *the moment when the Statue demands Giovanni's repentance, Bibliothèque Nationale de France, Paris.*

8   The 'Scena ultima'

With Giovanni vanished below the stage into the fire, the business of the opera would appear to be finished: the dissolute one has met his punishment. But it is not the end of the opera. In the final scene the other characters return, discover from Leporello what has happened, make their plans for the future, and comment on the 'moral' of the story.

EXERCISE   Read the 'Scena ultima' in the AV Notes and then listen to this final scene. Go into it by picking up the end of the previous scene (i.e. track 15, followed by track 16).

What is the function of the final scene, and what is its effect?

DISCUSSION   The function of the scene is to tie up the other ends of the plot. Anna and Ottavio are to be united (after a delay) (track 17), Elvira will enter a convent, Masetto and Zerlina will go home to celebrate, and Leporello will have to find a new master. The effect is to return from the supernatural, melodramatic world to the more prosaic one of ordinary life, which now goes on without the threat from Giovanni but also without the energy and zest that he represented. The scene therefore takes out the tension, and provides a buffer for the opera audience between the high emotions of Giovanni's destruction and the world to which they will return outside the theatre. The effect is comparable to that of a cinema shot which moves from a close-up to draw back and show you the whole scene. The 'moral' in the closing lively *buffo* sextet (track 18) completes the transition by depersonalizing the singers: they are no longer individual characters but address the audience together. (There are obvious parallels here with the function of the 'chorus' in classical Greek drama.)

It did not take long for this final scene to be perceived as a 'problem'. In the nineteenth century it became virtually standard for the opera to end with Giovanni's destruction, which was regarded as the conclusion of the story. What we are dealing with here may be characterized as the difference between 'Enlightenment' and 'Romantic' expectations of opera (and drama). To end *Don Giovanni* with the melodrama rather than with Mozart's final scene brought it into line with later fashions in Italian (and German) opera: Donizetti's *Maria Stuarda* (1835) ends with Mary Stuart going to her execution and, to take two famous but much later examples from the Romantic tradition, Wagner's *Ring* cycle (premiere 1876) ends with the destruction of Valhalla, while Puccini's *Tosca* (1900) ends with Tosca's suicide leap. The 'Romantic' rationale for the omission of the original final scene has been well described by Isaiah Berlin:

> In the nineteenth century this perfectly harmless sextet, which is one of the most charming of Mozart's pieces, was regarded by the public as blasphemous, and was therefore never performed
> ...
>
> The reason is this. Here is this vast, dominating, sinister symbolic figure, Don Giovanni, who stands we know not for what, but certainly for something inexpressible. He stands, perhaps, for art as against life, for some principle of inexhaustible evil against some kind of philistine good; he stands for power, for magic, for some sort of infernal forces of a superhuman kind. The opera ends with an enormous climax, in which one infernal force is swallowed by another, and the vast melodrama rises to a volcanic culmination, which was meant to cow the audience, and to show them amidst what an unstable and terrifying world they lived; and then suddenly this philistine little sextet follows, in which the characters simply sing peacefully about the fact that a rake has been punished, and good men will continue their ordinary, perfectly peaceful lives thereafter. This was regarded as inartistic, shallow, bathetic and disgusting, and therefore eliminated.

This elevation of *Don Giovanni* into a vast myth, which dominates over us and which must be interpreted so as to convey the profoundest and most inexpressible aspects of the terrifying nature of reality, was certainly very far from the thoughts of the librettist, probably very far from the thoughts of Mozart.

(Berlin, 1999, p.123)

The end to *Don Giovanni* as conceived by Da Ponte and Mozart is much more cool and rational. It is not unreasonable to see the difference between the original opera and its later presentations in terms of the transition from 'Enlightenment' to 'Romanticism', and indeed eighteenth-century opera is often described with reference to concepts that bear the 'Enlightenment' label.

EXERCISE   Read now the following extract describing trends in eighteenth-century opera from the leading English-language dictionary of music. Note particularly its references to 'Enlightenment'.

In the narratives of cultural history, the 18th century seems to cross a major division or watershed, from whatever standpoint it is viewed: it bridged *ancien régime* and Revolution, Baroque and Classicism, absolutism and Enlightenment, and so forth ...

Given, however, the strength of opera – Italian and other – in its appeal to fantasy, popularity or spontaneity, it is no wonder that so many artistic, intellectual and political trends in 18th-century Europe seized upon the genre to promote themselves. One of these trends was surely the emancipation of dramatic music, another the emancipation of the thinking individual (the Enlightenment).

(Reinhard Strohm with Michael Noray, 'The 18th century', in Sadie, 2001, vol.18, p.427)

The idea of the Enlightenment as 'the emancipation of the thinking individual' is one that you might like to consider further as you study the course. Concern with 'the individual' is, however, also a feature of 'Romantic' attitudes. This raises a broader issue. The passage just quoted came from a modern musical dictionary, and assumed terms of periodization which are specific to the usages of musical history in which 'Baroque' applies to the style of music composed between about 1600 and 1750, 'Classical' to music composed between about 1750 and 1820, and 'Romantic' to music composed from about 1820 onwards. The chronology, and the style concepts involved, may not coincide at all with the usage of these terms by, for example, art historians. Nor are usages even watertight within music. Some musical historians see 'Classical' and 'Romantic' as simultaneous and complementary forces in music composed from about 1780 onwards; the model for 'Classical' is normally taken to be the music by Viennese composers (including Mozart) from the period between 1780 and 1820, but there is a different application of the word within French music. 'Classical' and 'Romantic' when applied to music may therefore refer either to specific historical style periods or to ways of approach to musical composition that could overlap or even be concurrent. You will find that there is a similar problem with the use of 'Enlightenment' and 'Romantic': some writers regard these as describing characteristic ways of thinking, while others see them as describing the dominant intellectual ideas of particular chronological periods. The relationship of *Don Giovanni* to the Enlightenment is considered further in the next section, and it is relevant to remember that the opera was written at a time of great social and political change. You might like to try to decide for yourself at the end whether *Don Giovanni* was in any way an opera that 'promoted' any artistic, intellectual or political trend.

I suggest that you now watch the complete Act Two of the opera from the video before proceeding.

9   Giovanni and society

These units have concentrated on *Don Giovanni* in terms of its original conception, with various reminders that in order to come to an imaginative understanding of that conception it may be necessary to see through (and indeed set aside) various subsequent Romantic traditions of interpretation in the performance of *Don Giovanni*. We now need also to consider how the artistic conception related to the intellectual and social context of its period. The Giovanni of Da Ponte and Mozart is clearly in opposition to the forces of his society as depicted in the opera, but is he an enlightened 'thinking individual'? One of his characteristics seems to be that he rarely 'thinks' at all but rather operates by instinct, improvising his way through the consequences. The moralistic view of Giovanni as simply a bad man who gets his just deserts, which was certainly present in the origins of the story and resurfaced again in Romantic interpretations of the opera, seems too specific and too simplistic for the character as presented by Mozart and Da Ponte in 1787, for many aspects of the story and of the characters are left ambiguous. We watch the story in sympathy with the characters, but not understanding everything about them.

No aspect of the opera is more enigmatic than the character of Giovanni himself, and how this is intended to be perceived by the audience. While he is the 'dissolute one' who is punished, he is also (in his personal courage and independence) presented as something of a hero; it is unclear whether we should sympathize with him and enjoy his antics or

condemn him – or both at once. There is an underlying moral problem
here, for Giovanni appears to promote the sensual in an age that was
committed outwardly to intellectual enlightenment. There was, however,
a strand of thinking at the time (represented, for example, by the article
on 'Enjoyment' in Diderot's *Encyclopédie*) that regarded the liberating
pleasures of sensuality as an entirely rational objective. In this aspect the
opera raises a general problem about the presentation of 'heroism' in the
individual. Giovanni's unrepentant death effectively represents a
martyrdom on behalf of his own belief system: he rejects the sanctions
conventionally associated with punishment in the afterlife, and indeed he
seems to recognize no sanctions at all.[28] There is thus a lack of a clear
moral resolution: the individual's flaunting of liberty runs counter to the
Enlightenment quest for universal solutions, and the opera draws
attention to the problem of trying to resolve an individual's personal
imperatives (some of which may be a logical consequence of
Enlightenment ideals) with the needs of society as a whole.

Within the opera, this theme is obviously played out in terms of gender
politics: Giovanni's 'dissoluteness' lies in his irresponsible multiple
seductions, successful or attempted. Modern psychologically-based
studies have suggested various interpretations of Giovanni's motivation,
ranging from underlying homosexuality to various forms of emotional
inadequacy, though it has to be said that the character as portrayed in
the opera seems to be almost worryingly self-aware and well balanced;
he seduces women because he enjoys the experience of the simple
animal attraction. The nature of his activities has also been the subject of
much speculation: was Giovanni not merely a seducer but a rapist? The
libretto is inconclusive on this point. As far as we can tell, his physical
relationships with Anna and Zerlina did not get very far, and in the
'catalogue aria' Leporello refers to Giovanni's long list of women not in
terms of conquests but simply as girlfriends ('belle'). It is probably true
that the conventions of theatrical decorum in Prague in 1787 (as enforced
by the Viennese censor) would not have admitted the representation of
explicit physical/sexual relationships, but perhaps the audiences
interpreted the hints in those terms. On the other hand, it is arguable that
this was unnecessary, or even irrelevant, to the drama. The essential
factor is the emotional hold that Giovanni achieves over women, which
manifestly damages Anna's relationship with Ottavio, Zerlina's with
Masetto, and Elvira's with men in general.

Because Da Ponte and Mozart characterized the individual women so
powerfully – indeed, more so than the male protagonists – the
interactions are more subtle than a simple war between the genders.
Thus, although *Don Giovanni* deals with a subject that was
acknowledged as a vehicle for exploring the nature of gender

---

[28] It is arguable, of course, that Giovanni does in fact recognize 'judgement' (and
punishment) when it comes to him, but up to that moment refuses to believe that it
can happen to him.

relationships, it also opens up wider issues. It is impossible to know how far the dramatization of the story may have been affected by the personal experiences of Da Ponte (and Casanova), but the activities of the seducer seem to be less important than their effects. Perhaps, indeed, Da Ponte was using the sexual relationships as a way of dramatizing broader issues about society. In particular, this could relate to the functioning of a property-based society in which personal relationships are based on the principle that one person would become the property – and under the control – of another, a materialistic practice usually promoted under cover of concepts such as 'commitment'. Giovanni's offence – and assertion of independence – is that he refuses to be 'owned'; this is the significance of the list of his 'belle', in demonstrating to Elvira that her plans to bring Giovanni under her power are futile. There is an unresolved conflict, therefore, between the needs of the individual and the operation of economic and political systems that are property based. Since most societies are in fact so based (the principal issue concerning which group holds the property), this conflict may be not only unresolved but unresolvable. The 'state of nature' that Rousseau saw as representing an ideal of human happiness thus clashes with human institutions, and one person's liberty may be damaging to the well being of another person or group: a distinctly disturbing problem for the orderly social world to which the Enlightenment strove. Giovanni consistently breaks (or perhaps refuses to make) promises, thus threatening the entire contract-based system.

Don Giovanni was a theatrical entertainment, not a social or political tract masquerading in dramatic clothing, but the opera does raise questions in its treatment of the story about issues that are in the broadest sense political, concerning the rights and freedoms of individuals within society. It is in fact virtually impossible to avoid considering this aspect in view of simple historical chronology. *Don Giovanni* was written and composed for performance at the centres of power for the Austro-Hungarian empire, and implicitly under court approval if not its direct patronage. Joseph II's reign, at least until its latest years, was a model example of the rule of the 'enlightened despot': Joseph reformed old institutions and freed up the old formal court etiquettes, but the social structures remained fundamentally those of the *ancien régime*. *Don Giovanni* was first performed in Prague in 1787 and in Vienna in 1788; 1789 was the year of the French Revolution. We may well wonder what was in Da Ponte's mind when he made *libertà* the toast in the Act One finale, and what was in Mozart's mind when he chose to set this with such repeated emphasis. In one aspect the opera is certainly about 'liberty', as Giovanni adopts his own standards of freedom which cross both accepted social conventions and the class structures of his society. One aspect of the libretto which is clear enough is that Giovanni's activities rely on the privileges deriving from his social status. His seduction of Zerlina is clearly promoted on this basis, and he at first avoids suspicion as a hit-and-run murderer because he is a 'cavalier'. Although dramatized in terms of sexual activity, the opera raises wider questions about the proper extent of personal liberty: how much restriction should society place on individuals, how far should an individual accept that restriction unquestioningly and, above all, how should such restriction be applied? Through the cyclic pattern of the plot, there are repeated attempts to bring Giovanni to justice (or retribution), and the outstanding thing is that all of them fail. The punishment of Giovanni is ultimately effected only by a supernatural force; it is almost as if hell has to be provided (in reality or in human imagination) to deal with those who are too clever, and too independent, to be caught.

The subject matter of *Don Giovanni* thus carried some political overtones which meant that Da Ponte probably had to take some care not to be too explicit in matters that might give offence to the court; to do so might have prevented the opera from reaching the stage. We have no evidence that the librettist or the composer were put under any official pressure when creating *Don Giovanni*, and in any case it seems very likely that they would have regarded a specific 'political' message as being too limiting; essentially, the opera deals with humans in particular situations. Nevertheless, it is legitimate for us to look at *Don Giovanni* as a work that was written at a particularly interesting time from the social and political point of view, while recognizing that it deals with its subject matter in a rich manner that has much wider relevance.

EXERCISE   To conclude your present study of *Don Giovanni*, read the following long extract, a modern essay about the opera from Anthony Arblaster's book entitled (appropriately enough) *Viva la Libertà!: Politics in Opera* (1992). It has references that go beyond the original period of the opera to the experiences and ideas of (for example) Rousseau, Mary Wollstonecraft and Freud. (It also refers to the Marquis de Sade, about whom you will find more in Unit 4.) The essay is one modern author's commentary on the political and social issues which are raised by *Don Giovanni*, but it also has a revision function for you, as a reminder of some of the things that you have seen and heard from the opera, and also a reminder of the strength of its subsequent influence.

After *Figaro* came *Don Giovanni*, premiered this time in Prague, a city whose more liberal atmosphere had ensured a greater success for *Figaro* there than it had enjoyed in Vienna. With *Figaro* it is always possible to prise open a gap between Beaumarchais on the one hand and Mozart and Da Ponte on the other, blaming the French playwright for the radical or subversive elements from which some commentators have always been anxious to dissociate 'the divine Mozart'. With *Don Giovanni* no such strategy is available. In this case there could be no question of simply adapting a single extant text. There had been seven operas based on the Don Juan theme in the previous ten years alone, and there were, of course, famous dramatic treatments by Molière and Goldoni. From all these, Da Ponte and Mozart had to fashion their version, and the emphases and balance of the work that emerged have to be taken as what they intended ...

Le nozze di Figaro was manifestly a social comedy, with a clear narrative and explicit themes. *Don Giovanni*, by the nature of its tale, could never be so straightforward. Some commentators have stressed its *buffo* character and the work is subtitled *dramma giocoso*, but a 'comedy' that begins with the murder of an old man who is trying to protect his daughter against seduction or rape, and ends with the same man's statue visiting the hero for supper and dragging him down into the flames of hell, is clearly something more than a bundle of uncomplicated laughs.

However we react to it, the figure of Don Juan is one of the key myths of post-Renaissance Europe. It is not simply the male-invented, self-congratulatory myth of the irresistibly attractive man, but the more ambiguous conception of a man who is fatally attractive to women, even though he is known to be a faithless, restless philanderer – so that even when his servant reads out to one infatuated or obsessed woman a list of his 'conquests', it fails to repel her. This is a very potent image, and not only for men. Juan/Giovanni is a dream figure, the person who indulges his or her sexual appetites entirely without restraint, inhibition or guilt ... Giovanni simply ignores the conventional restraints on desire or libido, the repression or self-discipline on which, according to Freud, all civilized life depends. The final outcome of following Giovanni's course of self-indulgence is to be found in the exactly contemporary lurid sexual fantasies of the Marquis de Sade, which Sade explicitly justifies in terms of following the dictates of nature and disregarding the restraints imposed by conventional society. That Sade's sexual tastes were less orthodox than Giovanni's is irrelevant. The same philosophy of the uninhibited pursuit of personal pleasure is basic to both fictions.

Following Rousseau, the idea of obedience to nature rather than convention was usually turned into a radical or even revolutionary political and social challenge to existing society. The idea of the 'natural rights' of men – and sometimes women too – provided a moral measure by which the actual rights conceded by actual governments could be tested, and usually found wanting. But Sade's idea of following nature and defying convention, which he certainly associated with the revolutionary project of 1789 and after, was ultimately not political at all, but destructive of any conceivable community or social structure. It is doubtful that it is even compatible with anarchism, since it explicitly rejects the principle of respect for the autonomy and rights of others. 'Others' are simply objects to be used for the individual's own (sexual) convenience. This is Giovanni's philosophy too. Courageous and true to his own self, as he shows when, on the brink of damnation, he defies the statue's exhortations to repent, he is nevertheless an egoist; and this is undoubtedly part of his fascination. A part of each of us perhaps longs secretly to be equally ruthless, and guilt-free, in pursuit of our own gratification. But unlike Sade, unlike Giovanni, we dare not.

Don Giovanni is also, however, a social comedy ... Giovanni's licentiousness is class-based ... he takes advantage of his aristocratic position to seduce women of the lower classes as well as of his own class. When it comes to sex, he is not a snob, but he knows how to exploit both his position and its economic and social attractions, as we can hear in his brazen wooing of Zerlina. You were not born to be a peasant, he tells her. To which she replies that it is only rarely that you gentlemen (*cavalieri*) are honest and sincere with women. That is a slander put about by the common people, he retorts. Zerlina is not a fool, but she finds it hard to resist Giovanni's social as well as sexual appeal. But when he thinks that his rank might prove a disadvantage in seduction, as with Elvira's maid, he employs his servant Leporello to do the wooing on his behalf.

Zerlina and Masetto represent the lower orders in this opera, and they make a striking pair. Neither of them really belongs to the gullible country booby type who often appears in opera. Although Masetto is outwitted twice, by Giovanni and Leporello, he is under no illusions about what is happening, and on the first occasion he submits only to *force majeure*. The whole of his brief aria 'Ho capito, signor, sì!' is an exercise in heavy sarcasm that makes it abundantly clear that he neither trusts nor respects this lecherous, bullying aristocrat. Throughout the Act One finale Masetto is in a state of rage at what is going on between his fiancée and Don Giovanni, uttering against the latter dire threats whose fierce resentment against aristocratic presumption might well be seen as pre-revolutionary. These are not altogether empty threats either, for when he reappears in Act Two, it is with a band of armed peasants, and with the decided intention of killing Giovanni. Zerlina rebukes him for his jealousy, but more than jealousy is involved. Under the normal circumstances of feudal society, peasants did not set out to murder aristocrats who seduced their fiancées: it was far too common an occurrence, and all the sanctions of class society and class-based law were stacked against such rashness. Masetto's impetuosity is an indication that traditional deference is crumbling.

Zerlina is a more ambivalent figure. She seems to be flattered by the Don's attentions, but not really deceived ... Theodor Adorno's characterization of her ... is shrewd: 'neither shepherdess nor citoyenne, she belongs to that historical moment between rococo and revolution' ...

The third representative of the lower orders is Don Giovanni's servant and accomplice, Leporello. Servant–master or servant–mistress relations are a recurring feature of opera as they are of spoken drama, but the relationship between Giovanni and Leporello is surely the most detailed and subtle of all such portraits. This is more than a cash connection. There is mutual dependence here, partly because Giovanni knows that no ordinary employee could be expected to perform some of the outrageous tasks that he demands of Leporello. Leporello knows this too, and it gives him a certain licence to criticize and cheek his master. But in this respect he plays the part of jester, all-licensed fool, at Giovanni's court. More than once he resolves to leave his dissolute master, but is easily dissuaded by money. He is particularly active in the constant baiting and tormenting of Elvira. In the last analysis he is the epitome of the abject servility that such perpetual personal availability to an employer has always required.

Of the remaining four characters, three – Donna Anna, her father the Commendatore and her lover Don Ottavio – represent the respectable upper classes; appropriately both Anna and Ottavio seem almost like refugees from *opera seria*: repetitive, fixed characters whose music usually has a formality very different from Elvira's more personal outbursts, or from the songs of Giovanni on the one hand and Zerlina on the other. When Donna Anna reveals her conviction that Giovanni was the man who tried, unsuccessfully by her own account, to rape her, Ottavio is shocked to think that a gentleman (*un cavaliero*) could behave so badly. Is it anachronistic to suggest that the formality of relations between this pair is meant to be contrasted unfavourably with the spontaneity, the relaxation and the real, if shallow, feelings that characterize Giovanni's relationships and brief liaisons with Elvira and Zerlina? And is not Anna more deeply disturbed by her encounter with Giovanni than she cares or dares to admit? Her account of what happened may not be truthful, and the excuse of her father's death as a reason to delay further her wedding to Ottavio seems thin. She can be seen as the epitome of that repression of powerful feelings by convention that is the exact antithesis of Giovanni himself; her music, powerful yet formalized, reflects this.

Elvira is a different matter. She is decidedly an independent and unconventional woman. For – whether she genuinely regards

Giovanni as her husband, or whether she is simply infatuated
with him and determined to hold him to his promises and avenge
her desertion – her action in pursuing him across Spain is not
that of an ordinarily respectable woman. Perhaps she belongs to
a different social stratum from Anna and Ottavio. At all events
she is spirited and resourceful enough to belong in spirit to the
age of Mary Wollstonecraft, who showed a similar independence
in her personal life, and whose *Vindication of the Rights of
Woman* appeared five years after this opera.

What *Don Giovanni* depicts is a traditional stratified society still
in full operation at the formal level, but substantially in serious
decay: subverted both by challenge from below (Masetto and his
armed peasants) and by the irresponsible abuse of wealth and
privilege by the aristocracy itself. We can see this class society
musically in operation at Don Giovanni's ball. In a virtuoso
display Mozart brings three separate instrumental ensembles on
stage, each playing simultaneously a different dance with
different social connotations: a minuet for the gentry, a
contradanza for the middling folk, and a Deutscher or fast waltz
for the peasantry (this is danced by Leporello and Masetto).

But this display is a symbol of disorder as well as order ...
Giovanni has in any case arranged the celebration simply as an
opportunity for licentiousness, and specifically to facilitate the
seduction of Zerlina. So the formality and grandeur of the
occasion barely conceal dissipation and indulgence. And when
the three masked avengers arrive as uninvited guests, Giovanni is
hospitality itself:

> E aperto a tutti quanti:
> Viva la libertà!

Or, in modern parlance, this is liberty hall. It is doubtful that he
means much by this except that he is keeping open house. But
Mozart makes much of these words: they become a grand climax
to this section of the finale, being sung no fewer than thirteen
times by the guests and their host, and it seems likely that the
composer was adding a political meaning to an ostensibly social
flourish. At all events that is how it must have been perceived by
the Austrian authorities, since the words were altered to 'Viva la
società' in the Viennese libretto. Giovanni's ball, in the responses
it evokes, becomes the focus of all the forces that are gnawing
away at the fabric of the old order: upper-class irresponsibility,
bourgeois militancy and the anger and resentment of the lower
orders.

A final word must be said about the opera's extraordinary
denouement. The opera's subtitle, *Il dissoluto punito*, sometimes
came to dominate advertising for the work, as if to reassure

potential audiences of its moral character. The trouble is that the dissolute man is only punished as a result of the unlikely intervention of a statue which invites itself to supper and then drags his host down to hell. As Bernard Shaw sensibly pointed out, 'Gentlemen who break through the ordinary categories of good and evil ... do not, as a matter of fact, get called on by statues, and taken straight down through the floor to eternal torments; and to pretend that they do is to shirk the social problem they present.' This penultimate scene is one of the most powerful in all opera. The Commendatore as the angel and messenger of death is a terrifying figure, and Don Giovanni's fearless defiance, contrasted with Leporello's comic terror, gives him at the last a nearly heroic stature.

But Shaw is right. Considered as a device for dealing with the challenge presented by Giovanni to the established social order and conventional morality, the statue's intervention is no more than an evasion. And this is in itself revealing ... When we come to Giovanni, the disruption caused by this entirely egoistic figure is so damaging, so disturbing, that no reconciliation, no truce with those he has wronged and abused, is possible. But nor, within pre-revolutionary society, is there any possibility that society will be able to check, contain or punish him. Aristocratic privilege was of the essence of that social order. Hence only supernatural intervention can override its abuse. The sheer unreality of that solution indicates the depths of the crisis posed by Giovanni's challenge. The Commendatore's arrival can be seen as a mythical picturesque parallel to the Revolution itself, which only two years later was to bring upon the aristocracy of France their long-expected, long-delayed retribution.

(Arblaster, 1992, pp.24–31)

10   Conclusion

The *Don Giovanni* of Mozart and Da Ponte is both a powerful theatrical experience and a fascinating treatment of issues relating to politics, society and gender relationships. The riddles that it raises about the resolution of individual liberty with social responsibility are probably relevant to all human societies, before or since. Nevertheless, there were reasons why the issues found special urgency in the Europe of the later 1780s. Don Giovanni presents a challenge to the tidy world of Enlightenment ideals, at a time when the forms of society in which the Enlightenment had flourished were crumbling at the edges. Hedonism and amoralism were one possible logical consequence of Enlightenment materialism: the Enlightenment itself fostered an emphasis on individual pain and pleasure and, by challenging a belief in the supernatural soul, left the way open to the pragmatic lifestyle pursued by Giovanni. On the other hand, Enlightenment attitudes would have strongly supported the clear identification of vice and the punishment of the wicked. The opera is thus suspended between the rational (but questioning) attitudes of the Enlightenment and the emphasis on the individual that would be taken up in Romantic thinking. Don Giovanni's defeat requires the intervention of the supernatural as the 'rational' means of achieving the resolution of competing values. This goes against the Enlightenment's general rejection of the supernatural, though the supernatural (not necessarily in a traditional Christian mode) would resurface strongly in Romantic thinking (and drama). Elsewhere the opera suggests challenges to existing political authority, for example in the attitudes and actions of Masetto, in the same way that Giovanni's secular, liberal attitudes (perhaps open to interpretation in terms of proto-revolutionary radicalism) challenge the residual patriarchal religious ideology.

EXERCISE   At the end of Unit 2 I referred you back to the list that had been given at the beginning of that unit (p.76). Return to this again, in the light of the greater experience and understanding of *Don Giovanni* that you now have. I suggest that, as a revision exercise, you not only check through the various aspects that are given in the list, but also prepare your own checklist under two broad headings:

1   The technical means that are used by Mozart to convey character and situation – examples are the use of (for example) rhythm, melody, harmony, keys and key changes, particular voice types, and the use of the orchestra. Include also features that may be attributable to Da Ponte, such as the arrangement of the plot and stage business. There are a number of important areas where the technical means may be their joint responsibility – such as the choice of passages to be set as *accompagnato* recitative.

2   Examples of the way in which the opera presents issues of gender and politics, particularly in relation to Enlightenment and Romantic attitudes.

Finally, you may find it useful to watch the complete opera again from the video, but this is entirely optional. You should, as a result of your studies, be in a much better position to understand (and enjoy) the experience than when you saw it first, and to appreciate that it is both a remarkable creative achievement (which well deserved its subsequent reputation, in spite of the elements of misrepresentation) and a significant 'text' for the time and place of its creation.

References (Units 2 and 3)

The score and the libretti

Mozart, W.A. (1968) *Il dissoluto punito ossia il Don Giovanni*, ed. Wolfgang Plath and Wolfgang Rehm, *Neue Ausgabe sämtlicher Werke*, Serie II (*Bühnenwerke*), Werkgruppe 5, Band 17, Kassel, Bärenreiter.

Warburton, E. (ed.) (1992) *The Librettos of Mozart's Operas*, 7 vols, New York, Garland.

Text references

Anderson, E. (ed.) (1985) *The Letters of Mozart and his Family*, 3rd edn, revised by Stanley Sadie and Fiona Smart, London, Macmillan.

Arblaster, A. (1992) *Viva la Libertà! Politics in Opera*, London, Verso.

Badura-Skoda, E. (1973–4) 'The influence of the Viennese popular comedy on Haydn and Mozart', *Proceedings of the Royal Musical Association*, vol.100.

Berlin, I. (1999) *The Roots of Romanticism*, London, Macmillan.

Johnson, S. (1961) *Lives of the English Poets*, intro. L. Archer Hind, 2 vols, London, Dent.

Link, D. (1998) *The National Court Theatre in Mozart's Vienna: Sources and Documents 1783–1792*, Oxford, Clarendon Press.

Rushton, J. (ed.) (1981) *W.A. Mozart: 'Don Giovanni'*, Cambridge, Cambridge University Press.

Sadie, S. (ed.) (2001) *The New Grove Dictionary of Music and Musicians*, 2nd edn, 29 vols, London, Macmillan.

Further reading (Units 2 and 3)

All suggestions for further reading in the blocks are intended to help you pursue topics of interest after the end of the course; you are not required to read beyond the course materials as preparation for assignments or the examination.

Clément, C. (1988) *Opera: or, the Undoing of Women*, trans. Betsy Wing, London, Tauris (first published 1979).

Donington, R. (1981) 'Don Giovanni goes to Hell', *The Musical Times*, July, pp.446–8.

Heartz, D. (1990) *Mozart's Operas*, Berkeley, University of California Press (includes four chapters about *Don Giovanni*).

Hunter, M. (1999) *The Culture of Opera Buffa in Mozart's Vienna: The Poetics of Entertainment*, Princeton, Princeton University Press.

Kerman, J. (1989) *Opera as Drama*, 2nd edn, London, Faber.

Link, D. (1998) *The National Court Theatre in Mozart's Vienna: Sources and Documents 1783–1792*, Oxford, Clarendon Press.

Miller, J. (ed.) (1990) *The Don Giovanni Book*, London, Faber.

Pirrotta, N. (1994) *Don Giovanni's Progress*, trans. Harris S. Saunders, Jr, New York, Marsilio.

Rice, J.A. (1998) *Antonio Salieri and Viennese Opera*, Chicago, University of Chicago Press.

Rushton, J. (ed.) (1981) *W.A. Mozart: 'Don Giovanni'*, Cambridge, Cambridge University Press (includes essays on 'Don Juan before Da Ponte' by Edward Forman and 'Don Giovanni as an idea' by Bernard Williams).

Sadie, S. (ed.) (1992) *The New Grove Dictionary of Opera*, 4 vols, London, Macmillan.

Sheppard, L.A. (trans. and ed.) (1929) *Memoirs of Lorenzo da Ponte*, London, G. Routledge & Sons.

Steptoe, A. (1988) *The Mozart–Da Ponte Operas*, Oxford, Clarendon Press.

Till, N. (1992) *Mozart and the Enlightenment*, London, Faber.

Webster, J. and Hunter, M. (eds) (1997) *Opera Buffa in Mozart's Vienna*, Cambridge, Cambridge University Press.

Unit 4
Faith and death in the late Enlightenment: David Hume

Prepared for the course team by Alex Barber

Contents

Study components (Units 4 and 5)

Weeks of study	Supplementary material	Audio-visual	Anthologies and set books
2	AV Notes Illustrations Book	Audio 2 Video 1	Anthology I

Units 4 and 5 are effectively continuous and have been split into two parts solely to facilitate workload planning. The readings in Unit 4 are shorter but slightly more challenging than those of Unit 5.

Objectives

Having read Units 4 and 5 you should gain:

1   Familiarity with debates in the late Enlightenment concerning suicide, immortality, the nature of evidence, the existence of God and related topics, plus some experience of participating in these debates.

2   Acquaintance with some characteristic shifts and continuities in the move from Enlightenment ideals towards Romantic ones, including the new respect for **sentiment**; the increased emphasis on individualism, privacy and personal response; new conceptions of nature, including human nature; the continuing fascination with non-European cultures.

3   Confidence that study can transform a centuries-old text into an enjoyable, informative, articulate and reasoned discussion of a familiar topic, even if at first that text seems obscure or arcane.

4   Direct experience of this transformative process, through careful examination of the set readings and appreciation of some necessary background information.

1   Prelude: Hume's death

In mid-August 1776 crowds formed outside the family home of David Hume. Hume was a pivotal figure in the Scottish Enlightenment, and his imminent death was widely anticipated. The crowds were anxious to know how he was facing up to his coming demise.

Hume is best known today as a historian (through his *History of England* of 1754–62) and a philosopher. His *Treatise of Human Nature* is regarded by many as one of the most significant philosophical works to have been written in English. But when it originally appeared in 1739 it had, in Hume's words, 'fallen dead-born from the press' (Hume, 1962, p.305). Hume attributed this lack of commercial success to an overly academic style, and set about publishing a more reader-friendly version in the form of two *Enquiries* in 1748 and 1751 (Hume, 1975). He dithered over whether or not to include some new material in the first of these, eventually choosing to do so in a chapter called 'On miracles'. The choice led to instant notoriety. In the chapter he argued that no reasonable person should believe in miracles, particularly not the miracles described in religious scripture. (To his regret, few at the time bothered to read the other parts of the *Enquiries*.)

As a result of that chapter, along with several later essays, Hume became infamous in his day as a critic of 'religious superstition'. His views on religion were rarely published openly, but this did not prevent them becoming known (and often distorted). In 1755 he nearly went too far. In an essay called 'Of the immortality of the soul' he cast doubt on a doctrine that was, and is, central to most religions: that we survive the death of our bodies. After consulting with some eminent reviewers, his publisher withdrew the essay from the printers. A few pre-publication copies escaped into the public arena all the same, and Hume's scandalous reputation was sealed. The reason people gathered at his home in 1776 was to see if 'the great infidel' would succumb to the promise of an afterlife by recanting his unpopular views.

Samuel Johnson (1709–84) was a defender of the solace provided by thoughts of an afterlife, and had anticipated this moment as early as 1768. His biographer James Boswell (1740–95) reports the following exchange:

> *Boswell:* David Hume said to me he was no more uneasy to think he should *not be* after this life, than that he *had not been* before he began to exist.

> *Johnson:* Sir, if he really thinks so, his perceptions are disturbed; he is mad. If he does not think so, he lies. He may tell you he holds his finger in the flame of a candle, without feeling pain; would you believe him? When he dies, he at least gives up all that he has.

Figure 4.1   (see caption facing page)

Figure 4.1   Joseph Wright of Derby, The Old Man and Death, 1773, oil on canvas, 101.6 x 127 cm, Wadsworth Atheneum, Hartford. Photo: reproduced by courtesy of Wadsworth Atheneum, Hartford, CT, Ella Gallup Sumner and Mary Catlin Sumner Collection.

Many would regard fear at his approaching death as indicating Hume to be disingenuous in his scepticism about religion: to deny God was to risk damnation. But Hume had in fact dismissed many years earlier the supposition that mortal fear indicated belief in an afterlife (see section 4 below), claiming it should properly be seen as attachment to one's present and only existence.

Fear of death is the theme of this painting by Wright of Derby (1734–97). The skeleton, presumably taken from an anatomical print, would have been more alarming, or at least less funny, two centuries ago, but the fear on the man's face is clear enough. The painting is based on a fable by Aesop called Death and the Woodsman, as adapted in one of a popular series of poems by Jean de la Fontaine (1621–95). The moral of the painting is expressed in the final lines of the poem:

A poor woodsman, covered in foliage,
Burdened by branches and years,
Groaning and bent, walks in heavy steps,
Struggling to reach his smoky cottage.
Finally, out of energy and in great pain,
He lays down his load and ponders his misery.
'What pleasure have I had since entering this world?
Is anyone on this globe worse off?
So often without bread, never any rest!'
His wife, his children, soldiers, tax officers,
Debt, and drudgery
Complete for him this image of misfortune.
He calls on Death, who comes without delay,
Asking what is required.
'I want you', he says, 'to help me
Reload this wood. Then you can go.'
Death cures all;
But let us not hurry things along.
Sooner to suffer than to die,
That is the maxim of men.

(Fontaine, 1946, pp.19–21; trans. Barber and Poirier)

Boswell: Foote,[29] Sir, told me that when he was very ill he was not afraid to die.

Johnson: It is not true, Sir. Hold a pistol to Foote's breast, or to Hume's breast, and threaten to kill them, and you'll see how they behave.

(Boswell, 1986, p.148)

Eight years later, Boswell travelled to Hume's house with 'a strong curiosity to be satisfied if he persisted in disbelieving a future state even when he had death before his eyes' (Wain, 1990, p.247).

Boswell found Hume to be:

> lean, ghastly, and quite of an earthy appearance. He was dressed in a suit of grey cloth with white metal buttons, and a kind of scratch wig. He was quite different from the plump figure which he used to present ... He seemed to be placid and even cheerful ... He said he was just approaching to his end ... He then said flatly that the morality of every religion was bad, and, I really thought, was not jocular when he said that when he heard a man was religious, he concluded he was a rascal ... I asked him if it was not possible that there might be a future state. He answered it was possible that a piece of coal put upon the fire would not burn; and he added that it was a most unreasonable fancy that we should exist for ever ... I left him with impressions which disturbed me for some time.
>
> (Wain, 1990, pp.247–50)

The economist Adam Smith (1723–90) was a close friend and colleague of Hume, and reported the same high spirits in letters first to Hume himself (22 August 1776):

> You have, in a declining state of health, under an exhausting disease, for more than two years together now looked at the approach of death with a steady cheerfulness such as very few men have been able to maintain for a few hours, though otherwise in the most perfect health.
>
> (Mossner and Ross, 1987, p.206)

and later to Hume's literary executor, William Strahan (9 November 1776):

> His symptoms, however, soon returned with their usual violence, and from that moment he gave up all thoughts of recovery, but submitted with the utmost cheerfulness, and the most perfect complacency and resignation. Upon his return to Edinburgh, though he found himself much weaker, yet his cheerfulness never abated and he continued to divert himself, as usual, with

---

[29] Samuel Foote (1720–77): English satirical actor and playwright.

correcting his own works for a new edition, with reading books of amusement, with the conversation of his friends; and, sometimes in the evening, with a party at his favourite game of whist. His cheerfulness was so great, and his conversation and amusements run so much in their usual strain, that, notwithstanding all bad symptoms, many people could not believe he was dying. 'I shall tell your friend, Colonel Edmondstone,' said Doctor Dundas to him one day, 'that I left you much better, and in a fair way of recovery.' 'Doctor,' said he, 'as I believe you would not choose to tell anything but the truth, you had better tell him that I am dying as fast as my enemies, if I have any, could wish, and as easily and cheerfully as my best friends could desire.' ...

I told him that, though I was sensible how very much he was weakened, and that appearances were in many respects very bad, yet his cheerfulness was still so great, the spirit of life seemed still to be so very strong in him, that I could not help entertaining some faint hopes. He answered, 'Your hopes are groundless. An habitual diarrhoea of more than a year's standing, would be a very bad disease at any age: at my age it is a mortal one. When I lie down in the evening, I feel myself weaker than when I rose in the morning; and when I rise in the morning, weaker than when I lay down in the evening. I am sensible, besides, that some of my vital parts are affected, so that I must soon die.'

'Well,' said I, 'if it must be so you have at least the satisfaction of leaving all your friends, your brother's family in particular, in great prosperity.' He said that he felt that satisfaction so sensibly, that when he was reading, a few days before, Lucian's *Dialogues of the Dead*, among all the excuses which are alleged to Charon[30] for not entering readily into his boat he could not find one that fitted him; he had no house to finish, he had no daughter to provide for, he had no enemies upon whom he wished to revenge himself. 'I could not well imagine', said he, 'what excuse I could make to Charon in order to obtain a little delay. I have done everything of consequence which I ever meant to do, and I could at no time expect to leave my relations and friends in a better situation than that in which I am now likely to leave them; I, therefore, have all reason to die contented.' He then diverted himself with inventing several jocular excuses, which he supposed he might make to Charon, and with imagining the very surly answers which it might suit the character of Charon to return to them. 'Upon further consideration', said he, 'I thought I might say to him: "Good Charon, I have been correcting my works for a new edition. Allow me a little time, that I may see

---

[30] Charon is a character in Greek mythology (later recorded and satirized by the Greek writer Lucian) who ferries often reluctant souls across the river Styx to Hades on their journey to an afterlife.

how the public receives the alterations." But Charon would answer, "When you have seen the effect of these, you will be for making other alterations. There will be no end of such excuses; so, honest friend, please step into the boat." But I might still urge, "Have a little patience, good Charon. I have been endeavouring to open the eyes of the public. If I live a few years longer, I may have the satisfaction of seeing the downfall of some of the prevailing systems of superstition." But Charon would then lose all temper and decency. "You loitering rogue, that will not happen these many hundred years. Do you fancy I will grant you a lease for so long a term? Get into the boat this instant, you lazy loitering rogue.'"

(Mossner and Ross, 1987, pp.217–21)

Hume died shortly after this reported exchange.

See Plate 4.1 in the Illustrations Book (portrait of David Hume by Allan Ramsay, 1713–84), which relates to the comment below.

Lord Charlemont said of Hume: 'Nature, I believe, never formed any man more unlike his real character than David Hume ... The powers of physiognomy were baffled by his countenance; neither could the most skilful in that science pretend to discover the smallest trace of the faculties of his mind in the unmeaning features of his visage. His face was broad and fat, his mouth wide and without any other expression than that of imbecility. His eyes vacant and spiritless, and the corpulence of his whole person was far better fitted to communicate the idea of a turtle-eating alderman than of a refined philosopher' (quoted in Warburton, 2002, p.41).

*Spiritless though his eyes may have been, his vacant stare had disturbing effects. The **philosophe**[31] d'Alembert advised him in 1766: 'It is not necessary to gaze intently at the people you are speaking to ... it might play you a nasty trick'. It did. After a collapse in their friendship (to be related in Unit 5), Rousseau wrote of Hume: 'The external features and the demeanour of le bon David denote a good man. But where, Great God, did this good man get those eyes with which he transfixes his friends?' Hume's 'ardent and mocking' stare so unnerved Rousseau on their last evening together, he claimed, that he attempted to stare back but fell into a 'giddy and confused state', leading to their split. Hume claimed to be unaware of his habit (quotations in this paragraph Mossner, 1980, pp.477, 529, 522 respectively).*

---

[31] One of a number of participants in the French Enlightenment. The term *philosophe* was used because a preparedness to engage with philosophical topics was a hallmark of the movement in France. Prominent among the *philosophes* were Diderot, Voltaire, d'Holbach and d'Alembert. See also Unit 1.

Hume's reportedly high spirits in the face of death struck a dissonant chord with many of his religious opponents. Johnson insisted to Boswell that Hume must have been pretending to be cheerful (Boswell, 1971, p.155). The following comment on Adam Smith's letter to Strahan was sent anonymously to the *Weekly Magazine, or Edinburgh Amusement* (1777, vol.36, pp.139–41):[32]

> Doubtless the doctor [i.e. Smith] intends a panegyric upon his friend; but in truth the publication of his frolicsome behavior in dying is a satire which must expose Mr Hume's memory to the pity, if not to the contempt, of the truly wise ... From the doctor's narrative of Mr Hume's dying behavior, a Christian cannot easily allow that the concluding eulogy of his character fairly follows. [In his letter, Smith had described Hume as 'approaching as nearly to the idea of a perfectly wise and virtuous man, as perhaps the nature of human frailty will permit'.] ... It is an affecting picture the doctor exhibits to view. A man of distinguished intellectual powers acting the fool at his end – dying indecently humorous – ... dying in a manner that betrayed the darkest ignorance of an *Indian savage* ... Can anything be more frivolous, more childish, more indecently wanton and presumptuous in a dying man, perceiving himself on the verge of time, than Mr Hume's sportful dialogue with Charon? ... We are told that Mr Hume was quite resigned. Resigned! To what? Not to the will of God ... How miserable the comforter, who could minister no other consolation to his dying friend, than that he was to leave his friends in great prosperity!... Compare together a sceptical philosopher and a scripture saint in dying, and see the abject meanness into which the one sinks, the grandeur, in hope of everlasting glory, to which the other rises.

Reacting to the same letter by Smith, the Bishop of Norwich, George Horne (1730–92), wrote anonymously to Adam Smith in 1777. Though addressed to individuals, such letters were in effect public statements (this one was eventually published in Horne, 1806, pp.xvii–xxi):

> You have been lately employed in embalming a philosopher – his *body*, I believe I must say, for concerning the other part of him, neither you nor he seem to have entertained an idea, sleeping or waking ...

> Sir, friend as I am to freedom of opinion, ... I am rather sorry, methinks, that men should judge so *variously* of Mr Hume's philosophical speculations. For since the design of them is to banish out of the world every idea of truth and comfort, salvation and immortality, a future state, and the providence and even existence of God, it seems a pity that we cannot be all of a mind about them, though we might have formerly liked to hear the

---

[32] Smith's letter to Strahan was published in Hume, 1777.

author crack a joke, over a bottle, in his lifetime. And I would have been well pleased to have been informed by you, Sir, that, before his death, he had ceased to number among his happy effusions tracts of this kind and tendency ...

Are *you* sure, and can you make *us* sure, that there really exist no such things as a God, and a future state of rewards and punishments? If so, all is well. Let us *then*, in our last hours, read Lucian, and play at whist, and droll upon [i.e. joke about] Charon and his boat; let us die as foolish and insensible, as much like our brother philosophers, the calves of the field and the asses of the desert, as we can ... But if such things *be* [i.e. if God and a future state exist], as they most certainly are, is it right in you, Sir, to hold up to our view, as 'perfectly wise and virtuous', the *character* and *conduct* of one who seems to have been possessed with an incurable antipathy to all that is called religion; and who strained every nerve to explode, suppress, and extirpate the spirit of it among men, that its very name, if he could effect it, might no more be had in remembrance? Are we, do you imagine, to be reconciled to a character of this sort, and fall in love with it, because its owner was *good company*, and knew how to manage his *cards?* Low as the age is fallen, I will venture to hope it has grace enough yet left to resent such usage as this.

The vehemence and explicitness of these and other attacks on Hume's character is at odds with the charity often extended to those who have recently died. Ten years later Smith expressed his amazement at the reaction to Hume's temperament before his death, and to his own description of it in the letter to Strahan:

A single, and as I thought, a very harmless sheet of paper which I happened to write concerning the death of our late friend, Mr Hume, brought upon me ten times more abuse than the very violent attack I had made upon the whole commercial system of Great Britain [i.e. Smith's *The Wealth of Nations*, 1776, a groundbreaking work in economics].

(Quoted in Scott, 1937, p.283)

2   Introduction

This unit and the next examine Hume's reasons for being complacent in the face of death, as these are laid out in his suppressed essay of 1755, 'Of the immortality of the soul'. More generally, they examine some of the shifts in attitude concerning death and religious belief that were taking place in Europe at the end of the eighteenth century, through examination of this and other short essays.

These changes were wide ranging and driven by many factors. Religion touched every aspect of cultural life, as you will witness throughout the course. In Units 10–11, for example, you will study the growth of Evangelicalism in the period. The focus for the present two units will be on debates surrounding the existence of God and an afterlife and the moral permissibility of suicide. These discussions are as fascinating today as they were then, but beyond this they shed light on the altering shape of the commitment to **reason**. Commitment to a particular conception of reason came under increasing strain as the century progressed, and this strain shows up well in the present context.

Working through the units

You will be looking at four short texts by three writers: two by David Hume (1711–76) in Unit 4, then one each by Jean-Jacques Rousseau (1712–78) and the Marquis de Sade (1740–1814) in Unit 5. In the next section I will provide some information on the intellectual background against which the four readings for these units were written. This should help you to understand the claims made by the writers more readily.

Unlike the letters seen in the prelude, the authors of these four pieces do not address one another explicitly. That said, many of the notions, arguments and assertions discussed were in the air at the time, and at a number of points they offer what are in effect replies to one another. Such disagreements will be highlighted in my commentary.

Opinions and disputes are as much a part of the cultural life of a society as paintings, music and literature. Just as portraits, operas and novels can be interpreted and evaluated, so can contributions to a debate. This was especially true during the mid-to-late eighteenth century, the culmination of the Age of Reason. At no time in European history has the importance of reasoned opinion been given greater recognition than it was then, save perhaps in classical antiquity, a period looked back on at the time with such admiration precisely because of this fact.

It was in the written medium that the precision required for these particular debates could be most readily achieved, so written texts will be our primary focus. But the images accompanying these units indicate the extent to which intellectual debates were given vivid expression in media other than the written word. If nothing else, they served to carry certain messages home. That is one way in which they will be used here, and you should not treat the images and the associated comments as mere decoration. These comments will occasionally offer interpretations of the images that are tentative or that do not necessarily capture what was central to the painter's intentions; their main purpose will be to supplement my commentary.

One of the few commitments all three writers had in common was to the need to persuade their reader, not merely through the use of elegant turns of phrase but through transparent and effective reasoning. In view of this, any proper engagement with these texts must involve a suitable response to these attempts at reasoned persuasion. In several of the exercises I encourage you to enter the fray and develop your own opinion of the matter under discussion. By the end of your work on these units you ought to be in a better position to understand, compare and assess the views presented and defended in the readings. In other words, you should have become a participant in the discussion.

The readings have not been selected as typical for their time and context. On the contrary, each departs from the prevalent norms in unpredictable and often surprising ways, and always at personal cost to the author. Hume's deviation from religious norms cost him dearly in his professional life in Scotland, which was heavily Calvinist. Rousseau was spurned by his Enlightenment peers for the highly personalized religious sentiments expressed in the first half of his 'Profession of faith of a Savoyard vicar', and he spent long periods in exile because of the hostility to organized religion expressed in the second half of the same work. The Marquis de Sade spent most of his adult life in the prisons and mental asylums of both pre- and post-revolutionary France, in part for writing or acting out lascivious and vicious anti-clerical dramas, of which the dialogue we will be looking at is an instance.

Their atypicality does not prevent the readings from being used as vehicles for the appreciation of tendencies in that period. Studying cultural history would be a dull process if it consisted of being given a checklist of themes to mark off against a series of typical cultural artefacts. The pieces you will be reading have been chosen because of their enduring value as contributions to a discussion; their service in the illustration and explanation of cultural trends would have been a happy by-product from their authors' perspectives.

Because our authors were writing more than 200 years ago, their style is likely to be unfamiliar. Eighteenth-century prose had different punctuation, spelling and grammatical rules, and sentences could be long, complex and mannered. Punctuation and spelling have been modernized in the anthology, but there is no getting around the other factors.

EXERCISE   You have been exposed to eighteenth-century English already, in the letters in the prelude and in the previous units. Reread the letter from George Horne to Adam Smith (pp.165–6 above). Aim to appreciate the prose itself and not merely to pick up the general drift of his remarks. A good test of your having done this is if you can read it out aloud as if saying it yourself, putting the stress in the appropriate places.

Hopefully you will come to enjoy this elegantly expressed diatribe (without necessarily agreeing with its claims). You would not be alone if you found it takes time to come to terms with stylistic conventions of the eighteenth century. You will have further practice.

You should eventually expect to become practised at confronting and interpreting historical documents without the crutch provided by a running commentary, but at this early stage in the course the strategy will be to ask you to read the original documents only *after* you have been told what to expect to find contained within them. This strategy may give rise to a temptation to rely on the commentary and read the primary material less thoroughly than you otherwise would. If you ever feel the force of such a temptation, do not succumb! It is your engagement with the texts themselves that matters; the commentary matters only to the extent that it helps you to do this in a rewarding way. The exercises are designed with this in mind, and can normally be tackled only after the relevant portion of text has been read.

3   The intellectual background

Hume, Rousseau and Sade often assume familiarity with views that were popular at the time of writing. To have done otherwise would have been tedious for their original readership. Many of these views are no longer so widespread, so in this section I want to describe three features of the eighteenth-century intellectual backdrop against which all the readings were written. The three features are: **empiricism** (a view about knowledge), **deism** (a view about religious belief), and the main **arguments for the existence of God**.

Empiricism

The Enlightenment is also known as the Age of Reason, but it was a very specific conception of reason that held sway. Seventeenth- and eighteenth-century Europe had seen a boom in knowledge brought about by the birth of modern science. This boom was accompanied by both optimism and a wish to identify what it was that investigators were suddenly getting right. What was it about science that made it so reasonable, and hence so successful?

See Plate 4.2 in the Illustrations Book *(Lecture on the Orrery in which a Candle is used to create an Eclipse by Joseph Wright of Derby), which relates to the comment below.*

This painting shows a scientist (who perhaps intentionally resembles the physicist Isaac Newton, 1642–1727) giving a lecture using an orrery, a model of the solar system. Reverence for science is manifest in several ways. First, the demonstration, surrounded by the darkness of ignorance and prejudice, is giving off the light of knowledge. This distribution of light expresses what was seen as positive about science: its capacity to fight against ignorance and prejudice. (The metaphor of light was eventually adopted in the labels for the Age of Reason in all the main European languages, e.g. le siècle des lumières *in French,* Aufklärung *in German,* illuminismo *in Italian, and* Enlightenment *in English.) Second, the heads of the characters are themselves like planets rotating around the sun. This is perhaps intended to suggest optimism about the progress being made in the early scientific study of humanity itself. And third, the variety in age and sex of the people in the picture suggests that science could infiltrate and benefit the whole of society.*

In many of Wright's paintings, including his An Experiment on a Bird in the Air Pump *(1768), admiration of science was tempered by a fear of the power of this new knowledge, and uncertainty about the unquenchable thirst it could give rise to. In this instance, however, his representation seems to be wholly favourable. (Wright's* Air Pump *painting is discussed in Block 5.)*

Many hoped to be able to classify *all* opinion as either reasonable or unreasonable according to how it compared with scientific opinion. An opinion would be classified as reasonable if arrived at in the same fashion as scientific opinions; it would be classified as unreasonable if arrived at in some other, less reputable fashion (e.g. superstition, reliance on tradition, idle speculation, etc.). But before this splitting of opinions into the reasonable and the unreasonable could be achieved, an explanation was needed of scientific success. The hunt was on for the magic ingredient that constituted the essence of the scientific attitude.

The most popular account of what set this new scientific age apart from the pre-Enlightenment era was and is *empiricism* (a nineteenth-century term). The backbone of empiricism is a simple claim:

> *Empiricism (roughly characterized):* opinions are reasonable if, and only if, they are supported by evidence that is ultimately grounded in experience.

'Experience', here, can mean everyday observation using one or more of the five senses, but it is also meant to include rigorous scientific experimentation. Respect for this principle is what supposedly sets the

Figure 4.2   Louis-Léopold Boilly, Les Cinq Sens (The Five Senses), *1823, colour lithograph, 21 x 18cm. Photo: © Leonard de Selva/CORBIS.*

Empiricists claimed that experience was the source of all genuine knowledge; claims that didn't ultimately spring from the senses were to be dismissed as fanciful. This caricatured personification of the senses reveals how not everyone was so convinced of the effectiveness of scientific methods at yielding all the truth and only the truth.

As mentioned in the main commentary, empiricism was proffered as an account of why Newton and other scientists had been so successful in their investigations of the physical world. But it also embodied a 'science of the human mind' in its own right. The English empiricist philosopher John Locke (1632–1704), for example, was heralded by many as having achieved for our understanding of human nature what Newton had achieved for our understanding of the nature of the physical universe (see Locke, 1975).

scientific age apart from the pre-scientific age. In that earlier age, unsupported speculation was purportedly rampant; since the scientific revolution, experience served to constrain such speculation.

Expressed more negatively, empiricists are claiming that we should refuse to accept as true anything that has not been observed to be true. By this criterion, many religious doctrines are no more than unsupported speculation. Empiricists often denounced them as such in the period under discussion.

Empiricism as expressed in the simplified statement above has some embarrassing consequences. Moral and mathematical platitudes (e.g. that torturing people for fun is morally objectionable, or that 55 plus 55 necessarily equals 110) do not seem to require observational support, yet few would be prepared to denounce these judgements as unreasonable. The evidence for these and other reasonable opinions must come from some other source than the senses.

Empiricists tried to get around this difficulty in a variety of ways. They were anxious not to create any excuses for a return to the unscientific guesswork of previous eras, but were forced to acknowledge a limited role for reasoning that was not simply a response to experience. Though it would be interesting to look at the details of their efforts, this would take us too far afield. For our purposes it will be enough to sum up the empiricist agenda as follows: all opinions should be rejected unless backed up with evidence that is grounded *either* in experience *or* in one of some small number of permitted principles of abstract reasoning (e.g. mathematical principles).

Hume was empiricism's most eloquent advocate, as these uncompromising closing words of his *Enquiry Concerning Human Understanding* (1748) show:

> When we run over libraries, persuaded of these [empiricist] principles, what havoc must we make? If we take in our hand any volume, of divinity or school metaphysics[33] for instance, let us ask: *Does it contain any abstract reasoning concerning quantity or number?* No. *Does it contain any experimental reasoning concerning matter of fact and existence?* No. Commit it then to the flames, for it can contain nothing but sophistry and illusion.

(Hume, 1975, p.165)

---

[33] School metaphysics: philosophy in the scholastic tradition that was dominant in the first half of the last millennium. Hume was hostile to this tradition, which is sometimes lampooned as being obsessed with how many angels could dance on the head of a pin. This is unfair, but the scholastics did look to scripture and logic rather than solely to experimentation and experience.

The reference to flames, here, is almost certainly just a dramatic device. Enlightenment thinkers were or ought to have been hostile to censorship of opinion. For one thing, they held that reason and not force should be what determines public opinion. For another, most of them had themselves suffered censorship or repercussions for having published unpopular ideas. In actual fact, Hume did on at least one occasion seek to suppress material he found objectionable: in 1764 he tried and failed to prevent the publication of a mocking review of a friend's book by Voltaire (Mossner, 1980, p.412). But whether he really wanted to burn library books for failing to pass his test is not relevant to our concerns. What is relevant is just that, in Hume's view, such books are entirely without value.

The empiricists' uncompromising attitude had risks as well as benefits. The benefits were evident in the explosive growth in scientific knowledge of the world about us and increasingly of ourselves. The main risk was that, by setting such high standards on what can permissibly count as a reasonable belief, empiricists would end up having to abandon many dearly held beliefs. Opinions on topics that weren't susceptible to empirical (i.e. scientific, experience-based) investigation would need to be dropped, leaving us floundering in ignorance on many important matters.

Hume claimed that such scepticism is really just realism about our predicament. On a wide number of topics – whether the sun will rise tomorrow, whether we have souls, whether these souls survive the death of our bodies, whether the external world exists – he insisted that, though we are unable to stop ourselves holding opinions, these opinions are not ones to which we are properly entitled. Hume's philosophy was a high water mark for classical empiricism. Rightly or wrongly, most of those who came after him were not prepared to embrace his resulting scepticism. They began instead to search for and defend alternative sources of evidence – alternative to the evidence of the senses, that is. By the late eighteenth century, the empiricists' rigidity on this matter was beginning to unravel. That unravelling is a thread running through these units and beyond.

Deism

In the readings you will often come across allusions to the contrast between **revealed religion** and **natural religion** (or deism). The distinction turns on what the nature of the evidence is for a particular religious outlook. Deism is a form of natural religion that was prevalent in eighteenth- and nineteenth-century Europe.

The evidence underpinning revealed religion typically consists of a god supposedly revealing himself (or herself or itself) to an individual or small number of individuals, perhaps on a unique occasion. The report in scripture of, for example, a burning bush speaking to Moses, where the voice is said to have had a divine source, is revelatory evidence.

Natural religion, by contrast, is based exclusively on non-revelatory evidence. In particular, it does not call for acceptance of the testimony of a single individual, an organization or a religious text. It is 'natural' in the sense that the evidence for it is available to all of us as reasoning and experiencing human beings; it is not a special privilege of some subset of humanity.

A helpful way to think of the difference is to imagine what it would be like if all bibles, all priests, all mullahs, all torahs and all holy relics, etc. disappeared overnight, along with all our memories of their ever having existed. Any evidence of God's existence and character that would survive such a disappearance is natural evidence, not revelatory evidence. Natural religion consists solely of doctrines that are supposedly supported by natural evidence. You may be wondering what evidence for God's existence would remain once mosques, churches, popes, rabbis, and so forth are set to one side. As it happens there are several traditional arguments for the existence of God that do not appeal to the trappings of established religion (see below). It is to these that deists looked in defending their views.

For our purposes we can divide the main religious perspectives available at the time into four:

1   *Atheists* denied that there was any god.

2   *Agnostics* denied that there is sufficient evidence for or against God's existence; they abstained from believing either in his existence or in his non-existence. Hume insisted he was an agnostic rather than an atheist.

3   *Deists* believed that we have natural, non-revelatory evidence of God's existence and nature. Several of the *philosophes* had deist leanings, Voltaire, d'Alembert, and Rousseau being the most notable among them. None had anything but scorn for revelatory evidence.

4   *Revealed religion* was adopted by those who accepted the testimony of scripture, and in particular of the Bible as interpreted by the established churches.

The Enlightenment movement as a whole was an accelerated part of a drift away from appeals to authority that has continued in western culture to this day. Entrusting oneself and one's opinions to the dictates of an institutional religion was anathema to such thinking. All the old authorities, including the Church, were held to be subject to the authority of reason tempered by experience. Inevitably, there were exceptions such as Samuel Johnson, quoted above, but it is undeniable that pressure on the Church was growing in this period.

Proving God's existence

Deists had at their disposal three traditional ways of arguing for the existence of God.

The most popular in the late eighteenth century was the **argument from design** (also known as the *teleological argument*, from the Greek word *telos*, meaning end or purpose). This argument begins with an observation: the world around us is not chaotic but ordered and harmonious. Some examples: whenever the tide comes in it goes out again shortly after; without an ability to inhale air we could not survive, but we have lungs so we can; plants need to be pollinated to survive, and bees do it for them, benefiting in turn from the nectar. According to proponents of the argument from design, the only plausible explanation of all this observable order and harmony involves supposing that an intelligent, benign and all-powerful being – God, in other words – created the universe.

Notice that this argument does not depend on accepting the Gospels as true. This is what makes it useable by a deist. Someone who used it enthusiastically was Voltaire. In the following passage from a book introducing Newton's empirical discoveries to the French world (*Éléments de la philosophie de Newton*, 1738), he suggests that Newton's law of gravitation was proof of God's presence in the world:

> The whole philosophy of Newton leads of necessity to the knowledge of a Supreme Being, who created everything, arranged all things of his own free will ... If matter gravitates, as has been proved, it does not do so by virtue of its very nature, as it is extended by reason of its nature. Therefore it received gravitation from God. If the planets rotate through empty space in one direction rather than another, their creator's hand, acting with complete freedom, must have guided their course in that direction.

(Quoted in Hampson, 1968, p.79)

Voltaire's thought here is that God's will is evident in the fact that all of nature, without exception, obeys the simple laws discovered by Newton.

A second popular argument for God's existence was the **cosmological argument**. As with the argument from design, the hypothesis that God exists is adopted as the only plausible explanation of an observable phenomenon. This time the observable phenomenon is not order and harmony but motion in the material universe (or the 'cosmos'). Something must have made things move in the first place, and God is an obvious suspect. In this guise he is sometimes referred to as the 'first mover'.

According to a variant of the cosmological argument, God is needed to explain not only motion in the universe but the very existence of the universe. God, conceived of as the all-powerful creator, once again fits the bill.

The third traditional argument for the existence of God, known as the **ontological argument**, was out of fashion at this time, perhaps because it did not rest upon empirical observation. It will not figure in these units, but for the sake of completeness it goes like this: God is, by definition, a perfect being. He is 'that being than which no more perfect being can be conceived'. So he cannot possess anything but perfect properties. Since the property of not existing would be an imperfection, God cannot possess it. Therefore he must exist.

See Plate 4.3 in the Illustrations Book (portrait of Isaac Newton by William Blake, 1757–1827), which relates to the comment below.

Painted a decade or more after the period with which these units are concerned, Blake's portrait shows Newton at work modelling the cosmos, and unlike Wright's Orrery *painting (Plate 4.2) is filled with religious intent. But this is not an easy work to interpret, and indeed there is no agreed way of reading Blake's intentions here.*

On first examination it seems as though Blake is following Voltaire in claiming that we can discover God through Newton's laws using the argument from design. Nature, behind Newton, is more powerful than he is, seeming to embody a higher being; this higher being is then represented on the page with Newton serving almost as a kind of magnifying glass. And on the page we see, in place of Newton's laws, a graphical representation of the Trinity.

But Blake is known to have been hostile to the widespread lionization of Newton as the man who has revealed the underlying nature of reality. This suggests we should look for a different interpretation. A possible clue is in the way Newton is made to resemble Adam in Michelangelo's Creation of Adam *(1508–12). As Newton is creating a diagram on the page, so God is creating Newton. But Newton is oblivious to all of this as he peers at his page; he is looking the wrong way. Were he to turn around and use his imagination, he would see his creator in nature. Instead he is reason's slave. Using his intellect and outer senses alone, he has sought to regiment nature into a tiny number of laws and measurements, erasing all trace of God in the process; and yet from his relatively puny 'Laws of Nature' he is desperately attempting to reproduce religious knowledge. Blake himself made the same claim in a related text: 'He who sees the Infinite in all things, sees God. He who sees the Ratio only, sees himself only' (There is no Natural Religion, 1788, quoted in Butlin, 1983, p.7). Blake's position is the precise opposite of Voltaire's.*

4 Hume on life after death

Why was our immortality an issue?

When reading about Hume's death you may have been puzzled as to why people became so worked up about Hume's attitude. The question of what, if anything, happens after death is something most of us are at least curious about, just as most of us are curious to know what we will be doing in a few years' time. But curiosity cannot explain the venom evident in the condemnations of Hume.

The reason for the hostility can be approached by revisiting the opera you studied in the previous two units. *Don Giovanni* is, on the surface at least, a morality tale. The bulk of the opera consists of Don Giovanni refusing to acknowledge an unwelcome implication of his actions: eternal damnation. The narrative of the opera would be meaningless without the scene in which he is made to recognize his lifelong selfishness through confrontation with its consequences. The statue of Donna Anna's father is chosen as the symbol of his entrance into hell precisely because it is also symbolic of his reckless existence. This aspect of the story brings out what was so important about the assumption of an afterlife in a Christian context: the afterlife plays an important moral role. It is where accounts are settled and justice is done. Don Giovanni is made to pay for his sinful existence. If there were no afterlife, justice could not be done.

The mortality of the soul – the failure of the individual to survive beyond the demise of her or his body – would have been an intolerable supposition for many at the time because it would remove this scope for justice's execution. No longer could those who behaved wickedly in this life be made to suffer in the next; no longer could those who behaved well or who suffered in this life be rewarded or compensated in the next.

The disappearance of justice would be bad enough, but the perceived consequences of such a disappearance are likely to have compounded the anxiety and animosity of Hume's critics. For example, belief in the soul's mortality, were it to become widespread, would lead to a breakdown in the moral order as people lost the incentive to behave morally. Few would be willing to put up with suffering on earth without the prospect of reward in heaven. Another feature of Hume's position is that a less than perfectly just universe reflects poorly on God the creator. Hume's claim that when his body dies he would die with it was taken to suggest that God himself was incapable of acting justly.

Hume did not take himself to be insulting God's design, for the simple reason that he saw no reason to suppose God exists in the first place. This agnostic stance was argued for elsewhere by Hume, notably in *Dialogues Concerning Natural Religion* (1750) and 'Of miracles' (in *An*

Enquiry Concerning Human Understanding, 1748). The first of these has become the classic statement of the case against the argument from design and the cosmological argument. We will not be considering Hume's broader **agnosticism** here, since it is not presupposed in 'Of the immortality of the soul' (Anthology I, pp.17–24). In this essay Hume takes the unusual approach of granting that God exists, and then arguing that *even so* there are no grounds for the assumption that we survive bodily death.

EXERCISE   Read the short opening paragraph of this essay (Anthology I, p.17). The essay has three subsections. Try to predict from this paragraph what the structure and conclusion of the essay will be.

DISCUSSION   Hume distinguishes and names three potential reasons for assuming that individuals survive the death of their bodies: a 'metaphysical' reason, a 'moral' reason and a 'physical' reason. He will present and refute these three reasons in turn, one per section. A fourth reason for assuming the existence of an afterlife is that this is what it says in the Bible. Hume's explicit conclusion, then, is that we should be grateful to the Gospels for revealing to us something that otherwise we would be ignorant of. You can confirm this by looking at the final paragraph.

Hume's explicit conclusion and what he *really* wants to claim – his implicit conclusion – are not the same thing. To understand what the implicit conclusion is, recall again how the Enlightenment was characterized by a shift away from revealed religion and towards either natural religion (especially deism) or outright agnosticism/**atheism**. It is against this background that Hume's essay should be read. Hume argues explicitly that there are no reasons *save those given to us by revelation* for believing in the immortality of the soul. To Hume's readership, many of whom would have shared his assumption that the only real competition is between natural religion and no religion, this is tantamount to saying that there are in fact no reasons at all for believing in life after death.

Hume pays no more than lip service to the possibility that we should take it on trust from the Bible that the soul is immortal, once in the opening paragraph and again in the final one. Readers of the final paragraph would have detected the ironic tone in Hume's claim that we are infinitely indebted to divine revelation (i.e. religion as revealed in the Bible) for letting us in on the 'great and important truth' of our immortality, which 'no other medium could ascertain'.

With this subtlety recognized, Hume's essay can be read as an attempt to demonstrate our lack of evidence for the soul's immortality, or at least our lack of natural evidence, the only kind of evidence worth bothering with. Hume shows this, he thinks, by dividing the potential evidence into three kinds and refuting each in turn, one per section. We will be looking at sections II and III only.

EXERCISE   Begin reading section II. (Do not read section I, which is on 'metaphysical reasons' and concerns arguments based on the supposed independence of the mind from the body.) You will almost certainly find it difficult and obscure at this stage. The sole point of this exercise is for you to take note of this difficulty and obscurity. After five minutes, stop reading and go to the discussion below.

DISCUSSION   Hume was both a philosopher and a historian. In this essay he is being a philosopher. Philosophy is not written to be read as a novel is read. It can take the same time to work effectively through five pages of philosophy as it takes to read fifty or more pages of a novel. Hume's essay cannot be described as a poem, but it is similar in respect of its density and the level of concentration it calls for from its readership. This is one reason why these readings are short. We will be working through them with considerable attention to detail, paragraph by paragraph. Afterwards you will be asked to reread the essay from the beginning (again skipping section I) so as to get a sense of the whole.

It is common for those who are relatively new to philosophy to think that finding it difficult reflects somehow on them. Philosophy never gets easy, even for those who have spent an entire life at it. It is important not to let the difficulty everyone experiences stand in the way of your progress and enjoyment. Remember that you are at the very beginning of a process in which Hume's essay will appear to transform itself from an unstructured and barely comprehensible string of words into an articulate, well-organized and lucid discussion! That, at least, is the hope.

A final tip: you are advised when working through these two units to take detailed notes, and to have a pen and a jotting pad for the exercises.

Moral grounds for thinking we are immortal

The moral reason (as Hume calls it) for thinking that there is an afterlife has already been touched on. God, being just, would surely see to it that we are punished or rewarded for our aberrant or commendable actions; this punishment or reward doesn't take place in this life, so it must take place after our body's demise. Here is a simple statement of the reasoning:

> *The moral argument for supposing there is an afterlife:* the universe as created by God is a just universe; in a just universe, actions are rewarded or punished adequately, but actions are not rewarded or punished adequately in this life; therefore, there must be some other life in which actions are rewarded or punished.

The final clause of this argument expresses the claim that Hume wishes to reject. So he must find a fault with the reasoning that leads to it.

Hume would have been happy to reject this reasoning by rejecting the assumption of God's existence that lies at his heart. But as already mentioned, he does not want to adopt this strategy in this essay. Instead he seeks to persuade those sympathetic to natural religion that even they should reject this argument for the immortality thesis.

EXERCISE (a) Go to paragraph 7 and notice how little time Hume spends laying out the position he is about to criticize. This position would already have been familiar to his readership.

(b) How impressed are you by the moral reason for believing in an afterlife? Can you think of an objection to it that does not involve simply denying the existence of God?

DISCUSSION The point of (b) is merely to help you appreciate the task that Hume has set himself. The reasoning is, at first sight, quite persuasive. If you came up with your own objections to it, compare them to Hume's own objections, to which we now turn.

Our task now is to interpret and assess Hume's objections to this attempt to justify a belief in an afterlife. He offers three distinct replies, though he does not number them as such.

His first objection is very short, and is set out in paragraph 8, just after he has given the truncated statement of the moral reason. It draws heavily on his empiricist assumption that one ought not to make judgements that go beyond what we can infer from experience. We should not make claims about God's attributes – such as that he is just – without evidence, and that evidence must come from experience. But what experience do we have of the justice of God?

Our experience of God's justice, confined as it is to our experiences in this life, is not particularly persuasive, Hume implies. Experience contains plenty of instances of what to us seem to be *in*justices. Though he does not give examples, he could have had in mind catastrophic events such as the Lisbon earthquake of 1755, ironically on All Soul's Day. On that day some 60,000 people died as a modern European capital was flattened, then swamped beneath a tidal wave, and finally engulfed in flames. 1755 was also the year Hume was writing his essay.

EXERCISE   Read paragraph 8. Which clause of my representation of the moral argument (p.180 above) is Hume calling into question, and how?

DISCUSSION   Hume is challenging the first clause by asking for evidence to support the assumption that God is just. God may well manifest his justice in an afterlife, but this is not something we have any experience of, and so not something we have a right to assume – and nothing we see in *this* life supports the assumption either.

Hume does not develop this first objection to the moral argument. Instead he moves quickly on to an independent and more developed response that does not call God's justice into question (paragraphs 9–11). In rough outline, this second objection is that almost everything about us seems to be directed towards this life and not a next life. In particular, the 'structure of ... [our] mind and passions' make us ill-prepared for an afterlife in which we are punished or rewarded for our earlier actions. Hume infers, from these supposedly observable design flaws, that there is no afterlife.

To understand and evaluate this more developed response, we need to understand and evaluate his claim about our apparent design flaws, and his inference from this claim to the non-existence of an afterlife. We can begin with the claim, before looking at the inference.

In paragraph 9 Hume seeks to establish the truth of the claim that our minds and passions are ill-adapted to the existence of any afterlife. He asks us to notice how less persuaded we are by the 'floating idea' of a post-death existence than we are even by 'common life' facts (by which he could mean, perhaps, some trivial memory of what we did last week). So if there really is an afterlife, our minds are manifestly not equipped to recognize this fact. Moreover, our everyday concerns – our 'passions' – are not the concerns we ought to have if this life is but a preparation for eternity. We constantly let 'worldly' considerations govern our actions. Don Giovanni does not let the prospect of eternal damnation guide his actions. Instead he is guided by lust.

But, you may be thinking, some people *are* quite strongly persuaded of the existence of an afterlife, and seek to behave accordingly in this life. Perhaps you yourself are such a person. Hume acknowledges this fact and attempts to accommodate it. Such people, he says, have been effectively brainwashed (to use modern terminology) by the clergy. He even suggests, with some cheek, that the 'zeal and industry' of the clergy in seeking to gain 'power and riches in this world' by perpetrating their unsupported ideas prove that *even they* do not have much expectation of an afterlife.

Having established (he thinks) that our minds and passions could be counted as well designed only if there is no life beyond the present one, Hume goes on to infer from this that there *cannot be* an afterlife. He offers us two quite independent ways of making this inference, in paragraph 10 and paragraph 11 respectively.

In the moral argument, God's justice is used to show that there is an afterlife. In paragraph 10 Hume suggests that God's justice would really require the exact opposite: that there isn't an afterlife. A just god would only have designed our minds and passions to be the way they are if

Figure 4.3   Johann Friedrich Bolt, after Vinzenz Kininger, title page from the printed music score of Don Giovanni*, 1801, engraving, Gesellschaft der Musikfreunde, Vienna.*

Hume criticizes the moral argument according to which there must be an afterlife so that people like Don Giovanni, who is not punished in this life, receive their just deserts. Don Giovanni eventually realizes he is going to have to pay for his sinful past. But up to that point he does not let the prospect of eternal damnation guide his actions at all, showing (Hume would say) what poorly designed creatures we would be if eternal damnation were a genuine prospect and not just the final scene of an opera.

there is no afterlife. Doing otherwise would be cruel and deceptive. It would be unfair on Don Giovanni and the rest of us to be held so much to account for our God-given inclination to act as if there is no afterlife.

The second version of the inference (paragraph 11) starts with the same assumption – that we are ill-equipped for an eternal existence – and reaches the same conclusion – that there is no afterlife – but it does so via a different route. The bridging assumption this time is that a creature's abilities are matched ('proportionate') to the tasks facing that creature. This is an observably true generalization, showing up once again Hume's empiricist leanings. Hume notices that, for example, the tasks facing 'foxes and hares' are well served by these animals' abilities. Hares have no capacity to appreciate opera, but such appreciation would be superfluous to the requirements of a life as a hare. Since a match between tasks and abilities is true of all other creatures, it is reasonable to infer ('from parity of reason') that we humans, too, have abilities that are matched to the tasks facing us. The existence of an afterlife would be in violation of this observable truth, since the task of preparing for this afterlife would far outstrip our ability to carry it out effectively – something shown once again by the recklessness of Don Giovanni.

Softly spoken, intelligent, witty, kind and unpretentious, Hume was reportedly 'the darling of all the pretty women' of the Parisian *salons* in which much of the Enlightenment took place (Mme de Verdelin to Rousseau, quoted in Dufour and Plan, 1924–34, vol.11, p.106). This did not stop him being – as we would put it today – sexist in his writing. You will find evidence of this in the second half of paragraph 11. He attempts to draw out still further the significance of the fact that abilities are generally suited to requirements. Women are less able than men, he asserts. This can only be because the demands placed on women are lower than those placed on men. An inequality of skills between the sexes is to be expected if the only life is this life, since women are well suited to the less onerous domestic sphere. But an inequality of skills makes no sense if both sexes have the same task to perform: to prepare for eternity. Once again, an 'observable truth' (inequality between the sexes in respect of capacities) is used to argue for the absence of an afterlife.

EXERCISE   Read paragraphs 9–11. Does the sexism of Hume's remark, noted above, undermine this second objection to the moral argument?

DISCUSSION   In my opinion it does not. Here are my two reasons. First, the expression of sexism may affect our assessment of Hume as a likeable fellow, but his likeability is entirely irrelevant to the quality of his arguments. Second, though Hume asserts that women are suited to the domestic sphere but otherwise less able than men, these assertions are not essential to his argument about capacities in nature matching the demands placed on them. They are merely part of a misguided effort to extend his argument. So the fact that these assertions are (I would argue) mistaken leaves his objection to the moral argument more or less intact.

In the remainder of section II (paragraphs 12–17), Hume presents the third and final objection to the moral argument. He proposes in paragraph 12 that we be guided by *our* conception of justice, not the imagined preferences of a deity, when we make judgements about what would count as appropriate punishment or reward. His point is simply that our conception is the only one we have. If God's conception of punishment is different from ours, then all bets are off since we would be ignorant of what that conception is. He makes the same point later (paragraph 17):

> To suppose measures of approbation and blame different from the human confounds every thing. Whence do we learn that there is such a thing as moral distinctions, but from our own sentiments?

Again and again, Hume reminds us that we must assess God's justness *by our own lights* or, as he often puts it, *by the lights of our own sentiments*. To do otherwise – to say that God's ways are a mystery – is to abandon the perspective of natural religion and move to mysticism. Mysticism is, if anything, even worse than revealed religion in Hume's eyes.

In paragraphs 13–16 he presents four features of just punishment (i.e. punishment that our sentiments regard as just), each of which is incompatible with a traditional Christian conception of an afterlife: that is, an afterlife equipped with facilities for eternal damnation for those of us who have been wicked in our first life, and eternal bliss for the rest. In the next exercise you are asked to extract these four features.

EXERCISE   Read paragraphs 12–17. In paragraphs 13–16, what are four features of punishment and reward that, according to our sentiments, speak against the existence of an afterlife as conceived in the Christian tradition, according to Hume? (Warning: paragraph 13 is quite elliptical and possibly confused; you may wish to come to it last.)

DISCUSSION   According to Hume, our sentiments tell us that:

1   Paragraph 13: the Christian virtue of unconditional love for one's God and neighbours is not the only virtue there is. There is also value in being a good poet or brave soldier. Yet it would be contrary to common sense to suppose that good poets or brave soldiers have their own special kinds of heaven.

2   Paragraph 14: punishment should serve a purpose; no purpose is
     served by punishing people after they have left this life.

3   Paragraph 15: punishment should be kept in proportion. Eternal
     damnation can never be in proportion to an offence committed in
     the present life. He makes the same point in paragraph 17: 'The
     [eternal] damnation of one man is an infinitely greater evil in the
     universe, than the subversion of a thousand millions of kingdoms.'

4   Paragraph 16: punishment in the Christian tradition divides everyone
     up into the good and the bad without distinguishing degrees of
     desert within each group.

Figure 4.4   William Blake, Capaneus the Blasphemer, *illustration to Dante's* Divine
Comedy, *Hell Canto 14, 1824–7, pen, ink and watercolour, 37.4 x 52.7 cm, National
Gallery of Victoria, Melbourne, Australia (Felton Bequest, 1920).*

In Dante's Inferno *(part of the* Divine Comedy, *c.1314), for which this image is an
illustration, Dante (1265–1321) and Virgil (70–19 BCE) travel through the different circles
of hell and meet those who have committed a variety of sins. In the seventh circle they meet
Capaneus, who boasted in his mortal life that even the great God Jove could not defeat him
in war. For this he is now receiving his punishment: 'Eternal fire descended in such
profusion [that] sand kindled like tinder under flint, and made the pain redouble' (Pinsky,
1994, p.113). Hume claims (paragraph 15) that, according to our ordinary sentiments, an
eternity of extreme pain is an overly harsh punishment for most human sins.*

Classical allusions aside, paragraph 17 is mostly repetition, but in its closing sentence Hume notes a final aspect of our ordinary attitude towards punishment. We do not punish people if they are not responsible for their actions. Infants could not really be said to be responsible for their actions, and yet those that die – 'half of mankind' in those days – are supposedly assessed and either condemned or saved. The death of infants is, he thinks, an especially vivid illustration of why the moral argument fails.

Physical grounds for thinking we are immortal

In section III Hume discusses what he calls *physical* reasons for thinking there is an afterlife. A sensible guess as to what he means by a physical reason is that it is one based on observation and experience of the physical world. He begins by asserting that physical reasons are the ones he has most respect for. (This assertion is unsurprising: his objections to moral reasons, and the metaphysical reasons we skipped, turn on the allegation that they depend on claims that go beyond what is observable.) He goes on to claim, further, that all evidence that *is* based on observation – all 'physical' evidence – points not towards there being an afterlife, but rather towards our being fully mortal.

Before looking at how Hume seeks to vindicate this further claim, it will help to have a better appreciation of how he thinks we reason from experience. For although I have stressed the importance to Hume and his contemporaries of treating experience as the sole source of evidence, I have not said much about how reasoning from observation is supposed to work.

Consider how, whenever we have touched snow in the past, we have felt coldness. These past experiences tell us that the next time we touch snow, it will once again feel cold. Or at least that is what we think they tell us. That is because we are tacitly using what Hume calls the **rule of analogy**. (It later came to be called a *principle of induction*, but I will keep to Hume's terminology.) The rule of analogy is named but not explicitly stated by Hume in this essay. According to it:

> If all experiences of one type (e.g. seeing snow) have been followed by an experience of another type (e.g. feeling it to be cold) *in the past*, then experiences of the first type will be followed by experiences of the second type *in the future*.

It is thus a rule of reasoning that allows us to infer from what we observed already to what we have not yet observed.

It is no exaggeration to say that early empiricists held this rule of analogy, or some variant of it, to be the golden gateway to all genuine knowledge. The legitimacy of analogical reasoning is what, according to many, lay at the heart of the success of the scientific method. By conducting experiments and observing the results, scientists were able to make accurate predictions about the future, building theories on that basis. Hume too takes this rule of reasoning to be central to scientific advancement. He doesn't think rules of reasoning can get any more basic than this one. What we must now turn to is Hume's application of the rule to the question of our immortality.

In paragraphs 18–19, Hume makes his first application of the rule to the question of our mortality. It is also the most complex; be prepared to skip to the second application rather than become bogged down in this first application. The key passage is:

> Where any two objects are so closely connected that all alterations which we have ever seen in the one, are attended with proportionable [i.e. proportional] alterations in the other, we ought to conclude by all rules of analogy, that, when there are still greater alterations produced in the former, and it is totally dissolved, there follows a total dissolution of the latter.

The relevant 'two objects' are the mind and the body. Hume's basic idea is this. The mind and the body show 'proportionable' alterations: as the body grows feeble so does the mind (or soul), and so they can also be assumed to 'dissolve' (by which Hume appears to mean 'to cease to exist') together. From this he concludes that when the body ceases to function entirely, or 'dissolves', so does the mind. The complexity comes with trying to see how this is an application of the rule of analogy as I have stated it above.

To see that it is, consider what the relevant previous experiences are. Hume does not bother to say what he has in mind, but we can help him out here:

> The forward acceleration of a bicycle is proportional to the force applied to its pedals; elimination of this force leads to elimination of acceleration.

> The population size of the fish in a pond varies in proportion to the quantity of water; elimination of water leads to elimination of fish.

In all our previous experience, Hume is claiming, whenever alterations between two objects are 'proportionable', it is also the case that total dissolution of the one object is accompanied by total dissolution of the other. And now the rule of analogy tells us to infer that this will be the case in the future too. Thus, if all experiences of one type (e.g. alterations between two objects being proportional) have been followed by an experience of a second type (e.g. total dissolution of the one object being accompanied by total dissolution of the other) *in the past*, then experiences of the first type will be followed by experiences of the second type *in the future*.

The future case he has in mind is that of the soul when the body 'dissolves'. The proportionality or close interconnection observable between soul and body must mean that the dissolution of the body will be accompanied by the dissolution of the soul.

EXERCISE   Read to the end of paragraph 19. (*The next question is optional; you may prefer instead to jump straight to Hume's second application of the rule of analogy in paragraph 20, which I examine below.*) Why in paragraph 19 does Hume list some ways in which deterioration in the functioning of the body is often accompanied by deterioration in the functioning of the soul (or mind): in sleep, in infancy, in sickness and in ageing?

DISCUSSION   The sharpness of the human mind is observed always to match or be proportional to the robustness of the human body, he claims. By the rule of analogy, based on other examples that he doesn't make explicit (such as the bicycle or fish examples above), he thinks it reasonable to conclude that when the body declines completely, the mind (or soul) ceases to exist as well.

A second and more straightforward application of the rule of analogy can be found in paragraph 20. There are many observable situations in which transplanting something into a new and alien environment tends to kill it. We don't see fishes surviving away from water or trees thriving beneath water. In other words, a change to an organism's environment is always associated with a change in its capacity to thrive. The bigger the change in the environment, the more likely it is that the organism will cease to exist. Given this, says Hume, why should we expect the soul to be able to survive without its body? Loss of our bodies is the biggest change we could possibly undergo, making it more likely that we simply cease to exist entirely.

EXERCISE   Read up to the end of paragraph 20. (*The following question is optional unless you skipped the optional question in the previous exercise.*) Hume suggests in paragraph 20 that a purely spiritual, bodiless afterlife is even less plausible than metempsychosis, the transmigration of the soul from one body to another, perhaps across species boundaries. What are his grounds for this claim?

DISCUSSION   A change of environment is always detrimental to the thing moved. Moving to a new body is less of a change than ceasing to have any body at all. So it is more plausible that we could survive migration to another body than that we cease to be embodied at all. This is true even if the new body is an animal's, since animals' bodies bear many similarities to our own.

Figure 4.5   Jean-Baptiste Greuze, The Paralytic, *1763, oil on canvas, 115.5 x 146 cm, The State Hermitage Museum, St Petersburg. Photo: Scala.*

Metempsychosis (mentioned jestingly by Hume), in which souls migrate from body to body across species boundaries after each successive death, was one of several popular secular alternatives to Christian conceptions of the afterlife. Another is expressed in this painting: that we can live on in our children. The presence of the Bible on the left of the painting is swamped by the presence of the children. This doctrine of filial piety was even associated with a moral injunction: if you are good in this life (i.e. raise your children well), your survival into posterity will be all the more assured. This is explicit in the title Greuze gave to a preparatory study for the painting, 'The fruits of a good education'.

The remainder of section III contains three diverse objections to the theory that we survive beyond our death. The relation of these to the rest of the essay is slim, and Hume is occasionally only half-serious when he presents them. We can proceed through them quite quickly.

In paragraph 21 Hume asserts that supporters of the thesis that we have an afterlife have an accommodation crisis: the place where souls go will be populated by an ever-growing number of individuals. Ready replies to this thought were available at the time. Since souls are supposedly immaterial, by definition this means they do not occupy space so there would be no danger of overcrowding. Moreover, what justification had Hume for supposing that heaven or hell had a limited size?

In a different objection (paragraph 22), he suggests that our soul's non-existence prior to birth increases the probability of its non-existence after death. This is the opinion attributed to him by Boswell, as quoted above ('David Hume said to me he was no more uneasy to think he should *not be* after this life, than that he *had not been* before he began to exist.'). Hume offers some discussion of this in section I of his essay (paragraph 5), which we are not focusing on. No further support is provided in the present paragraph, just a quotation from a classical source.

In paragraph 23 Hume is implicitly responding to an attitude that would have been common. Fear of death in a person was assumed to be evidence in favour of their belief in an afterlife in which non-believers are damned. Fear of death could therefore reveal a profession of agnosticism to be disingenuous. This, in part, is why people were so curious about whether Hume would recant his views on his deathbed.

Hume makes the point that belief in an afterlife is not the only available explanation of fear of death. This fear could be accounted for easily enough as attachment to happiness in this, the only, life. (In fact, he says, many of those who *do* believe in an afterlife should be placid, since for them our mortal death is not really the end of our existence.) In view of this claim, Hume went beyond the call of duty in dying with:

> great cheerfulness and good humour and with more real resignation to the necessary course of things than any whining Christian ever died with pretended resignation to the will of God.
>
> (Adam Smith, letter to Alexander Wedderburn, 14 August 1776, quoted in Mossner and Ross, 1987, p.203)

Paragraph 23 ends with a speculation: it is a passionate *hope* to live on that irrationally gives rise in us to a belief that we *do* live on. Paragraph 24 merely repeats earlier material, and the ironic final paragraph has been discussed already.

EXERCISE   Finish reading to the end of the essay. How persuaded are you by his discussion of fear of death in paragraph 23?

DISCUSSION   You will almost certainly have come up with your own conclusion, but here is mine: Hume is unfair in suggesting that fear of death is incompatible with belief in an afterlife. Fear of death could easily be explained as fear of the possibility of an eternity of pain. It needn't be put down to an irrational attempt to match false hopes with false beliefs.

You should by now appreciate just how careful a writer Hume was. Aside from one or two light-hearted paragraphs near the end, not a single sentence is included that doesn't have an important purpose. Every paragraph develops his case in some unpredictable but thoughtful way. Repetition is minimal. That is why we have gone through the essay in such a painstaking way, paragraph by paragraph. All the same, it helps to step back and gain an appreciation of the whole essay, and in the next exercise you are asked to read it through in a single sitting.

EXERCISE   Reread 'Of the immortality of the soul' from beginning to end (omitting section I). Look out for the three objections to the moral reasoning in section II, and the role of Hume's appeals to experience as the final arbiter throughout the essay.

It is unlikely you will understand the point Hume is trying to make in every paragraph. But do make a mental note of how much of the essay you now more or less understand. When you have finished, recall your reaction to the exercise on p.179. I hope this will reveal the extent to which an apparently obscure piece of writing may in fact contain a carefully constructed discussion, which careful study can render accessible.

---

5   Hume on suicide

The reception of Hume's views

'Of suicide' was received with the same degree of public hostility as his essay on immortality. Here is what an anonymous reviewer of the 1777 posthumous edition of both essays had to say in the *Monthly Review* (1784, vol.70, pp.427–8):

> Were a drunken libertine to throw out such nauseous stuff in the presence of his Bacchanalian[34] companions, there might be some excuse for him; but were any man to advance such doctrines in the company of sober citizens, men of plain sense and decent manners, no person, we apprehend, would think him entitled to a serious reply, but would hear him with silent contempt.

---

[34] Worshippers of Bacchus, Greek god of wine; drunken revellers.

This reviewer, unfortunately, is true to her or his word and does not provide a serious reply to Hume, preferring instead to hold up one or two statements in the essays and jeer:

> Mr Hume affirms that it is as clear as any purpose of nature can be that the whole scope and intention of man's creation is limited to the present life, and that those who inculcate the doctrine of a future state have no other motive but to gain a livelihood and to acquire power and riches in this world ... The life of a man, he says, is of no greater importance to the universe than that of an oyster. It would be no crime, we are told, in any man, to divert the Nile or Danube from their courses, were he able to effect such purpose. Where then is the crime, Mr Hume asks, of turning a few ounces of blood from their natural channel?

The first sentence of this passage alludes to remarks made in 'Of the immortality of the soul' (paragraph 9), remarks that in fact play a relatively marginal role in the essay. The remainder of the passage cites claims in 'Of suicide' that are similarly peripheral.

Other commentators were equally disrespectful towards Hume the person, but more respectful of the need to respond at greater length to Hume's reasoning. In his lengthy tome, *A Full Inquiry into the Subject of Suicide*, Charles Moore describes Hume as 'a more pernicious and destructive member of society than even the profligate and abandoned liver' (1790, vol.2, p.54). In *The Dreadful Sin of Suicide: A Sermon*, George Clayton calls him a 'source of incalculable evil' (1812, p.48n).

In the essay Hume claims that the act of taking one's own life should be 'free from every imputation of guilt or blame' (paragraph 4). Suicide, he argues, can be morally unobjectionable or even admirable. As the reviews suggest, this was a controversial claim: to commit suicide was generally regarded as sinful, and to attempt suicide was a criminal act. What was peculiarly unsettling about Hume's perspective was that he did not bother to reject the core religious assumptions from which hostility to suicide more commonly sprang. Hume was, we know, an agnostic, but his agnosticism does not figure in this essay. His claim is that suicide can be shown to be morally permissible *even after granting God's existence*. In this respect the present essay resembles the one we have already studied: admitting suicide to be morally permissible, like rejecting the doctrine of immortality, will not depend on denying the existence of God.

The essay does not have explicitly numbered sections as did the previous essay. This does not mean it lacks a structure. Rather, the structure is something for us to uncover as we study it. As before, we will be working through the essay stage by stage. You will then be asked to read it through as a whole.

Philosophy, religion and everyday life

Perhaps because he is aware he will be stirring up trouble by publishing his views on this topic, Hume warms to his theme by talking in paragraphs 1–4 about how he conceives of the relation between philosophy, religious 'superstition' and ordinary life. The rest of the essay can be read independently of this opening, but these early ruminations are worth pausing over. They reveal subtleties in Hume's sceptical outlook that are drowned out in the more polemical parts of the two essays.

Hume is concerned with which of these three elements – philosophy, superstition, ordinary life – is most effective at dominating the other two. He is especially vocal about how philosophical reason is an 'antidote' to superstition, where this is clearly meant to include religious belief. But he also discusses the relation of both religion and philosophy to the views and emotions ('passions') that serve us so well in ordinary life – what he describes as 'plain good sense and the practice of the world'.

He notes with regret that religious superstition can and does distort our ordinary outlook, and in a 'pernicious' way. He gives one or two examples, including the example of superstition surrounding death and suicide. A clear statement of what he sees as the negative effects of religious beliefs on human happiness is found later in the essay (paragraph 12):

> It is impious, says the old Roman superstition, to divert rivers from their course, or invade the prerogatives of nature. It is impious says the French superstition, to inoculate for the smallpox, or usurp the business of providence by voluntarily producing distempers and maladies. It is impious, says the modern European superstition, to put a period to our own life and thereby rebel against our Creator.

The result of this pernicious influence of superstition on common sense is that dams don't get built, smallpox doesn't get eradicated, and those for whom it is rational to do so do not commit suicide. (Women in particular, he remarks, are particularly susceptible to superstition. It is not clear whether he is recommending they study philosophy, given that, as we saw earlier, he thought women have relatively poor powers of reasoning.)

Hume's position can be summarized as: *religious superstition can triumph over our ordinary views and emotions.* And since philosophy is a 'sovereign antidote' to religion, *philosophy can triumph over religious superstition.* We might therefore expect Hume to think that philosophy triumphs over the views and emotions that ordinarily serve us so well in life, as and when these fall short. But Hume surprises us here. Our emotions are curiously immune to the influence of reason, he says; and in other writings he insists that our ordinary views and expectations, the habits or customs of our minds, will not bend to accommodate philosophical reasoning (*A Treatise of Human Nature*, I.IV.1). The relationship between the three elements – philosophy, religious superstition, ordinary views and emotions – is not hierarchical after all. None of them dominates the other two. The situation is closer to the children's game in which each participant simultaneously brings a hand out from behind her or his back in the shape of either scissors, paper or stone. Scissors shred paper; paper smothers stone; and stone blunts scissors. Hume's view is that philosophy cuts through religion; religion distorts ordinary views and emotions; and ordinary views and emotions are immune to revision through the application of reason.

Hume does not offer any lengthy reasons here for supposing that ordinary life is impermeable to philosophy. It is, however, a salient feature of his other work. Far from being a straightforward supporter of Enlightenment rationality, he was notoriously sceptical of the power of reason. For example, although you would never be able to guess it from the previous essay, he did *not* think the rule of analogy could be defended using reason. He thought this rule was simply something we blindly follow out of 'habit'; the philosophical indefensibility of the rule can never alter this habit. So his appeal to this rule is actually an appeal to our common sense, which he thinks incapable of being grounded in reason. Hume is a celebrator of ordinary life, which is perhaps why he is so keen to defend it against the perceived threat of religion.

Evidence of this fondness for ordinary life was reflected in his personality. Famously, he enjoyed recovering from philosophical reflection by playing cards or board games. In *A Treatise of Human Nature* Hume describes how playing games allows him to 'dispel the clouds' of scepticism, cure himself of 'philosophical melancholy and delirium', and 'obliterate the chimeras' that abstract reflection has led him to conjure up (I.IV.7; Hume, 1978, p.269):

> I dine, I play a game of backgammon, I converse, and am merry with my friends; and when after three or four hours' amusement I would return to these speculations, they appear so cold and strained and ridiculous that I cannot find [it] in my heart to enter into them any farther.

This aspect of his personality divided those commenting on his death in the letters you read earlier. Adam Smith described the dying Hume as 'continu[ing] to divert himself, as usual, with ... a party at his favourite game of whist' (quoted in section 1 above). The Bishop of Norwich lamented how low the age has fallen that we are to admire someone because he 'knew how to manage his *cards*' (also quoted above). The symbolism of backgammon and whist is that just as philosophy is an antidote to religion, ordinary life is an antidote to philosophy, and to sceptical paralysis in particular.

EXERCISE   Read paragraphs 1–2 of the essay on suicide in Anthology I. Identify sentences that express Hume's view that (1) philosophy cuts through religion, (2) religious superstition distorts ordinary views, and (3) ordinary emotional reactions are immune to philosophical reason.

DISCUSSION   There are several alternatives, but the following get his message across:

1   'One considerable advantage that arises from philosophy consists in the sovereign antidote which it affords to superstition and false religion.'

2   'History as well as daily experience afford instances of men endowed with the strongest capacity for business and affairs, who have all their lives crouched under slavery to the grossest superstition.'

3   'Love or anger, ambition or avarice, have their root in the temper and affection, which the soundest reason is scarce ever able fully to correct.'

Paragraph 5 is where the essay really gets underway. In it Hume indicates the aim and structure of his argument and of the essay as a whole. Hume's stated aim is to persuade his reader that suicide is not 'criminal', i.e. is not morally objectionable. If suicide is morally objectionable, he insists, it must violate ('transgress') some duty we owe, either to God, to other people, or to ourselves. So the essay considers in turn our duties to (i) God, (ii) to others, and (iii) to ourselves, finding in each case that the act of suicide violates no such duty. Most of his energy is directed towards considering our duties to God. Duties to others and to ourselves receive relatively short shrift near the end.

EXERCISE   Find and read the brief fifth paragraph. Although they are not numbered as such, there are three further subsections. Duties to God are discussed in paragraphs 6–14, duties to others in paragraphs 15–17, and duties to ourselves in paragraphs 18–19. Find and make a note of these boundaries.

Do we have a duty to God not to commit suicide?

Why, you may be wondering, would anyone think that we have a duty to God not to take our own lives? Because it would have been so familiar to his original readership, Hume barely bothers to state the position he is opposing before criticizing it. His concern is to refute the charge that in taking our own lives we would be 'encroaching on the office of divine **providence**, and disturbing the order of the universe' (paragraph 8). This position can be expressed less elegantly but more transparently as follows:

> *The sanctity-of-life argument against suicide:* life ought not to be taken by anyone save God; so one ought not to take one's own life.

In a later idiom, the charge against suicide is that it involves *playing God*, i.e. making and acting on a decision that properly belongs to God and God alone. The phrase 'playing God' is often used even in a non-religious context to describe any action that involves the agent going beyond their proper station in the universe. In the Second World War some military strategists declared themselves uncomfortable at being called on to make decisions that would determine which of two cities would be heavily bombed. Their discomfort did not necessarily have a religious basis, and their use of the phrase 'playing God' in that context would often have been metaphorical. But the origins of the idiom lie in a genuine worry about literally taking God's decisions for him.

Without seeking to undermine the arguments for God's existence, Hume sets out to show that taking one's own life is unobjectionable. The thought that we have a duty not to take God's decisions for him, and in particular not to take the decision to end our own life, is, Hume suggests, preposterous *even from the most reasonable theological perspective.*

In order to show that from the most reasonable theological perspective available we should not condemn suicide, Hume must first establish what the most reasonable theological perspective available actually is. This task occupies him in paragraphs 6–7. At the very least, he suggests, the most reasonable theological perspective will assume the legitimacy of the argument from design (see the glossary if you need a reminder); this is the only argument for the existence of God that he believes is even remotely plausible.

Central to the argument from design is the assumption that order and harmony are evidence of a benign and powerful creator. Anyone who accepts the argument – in other words, anyone with a reasonable theological perspective – is committed to seeing order and harmony as God's handiwork. Any denial of the inference from order and harmony to divine influence would undermine the only plausible reason for accepting that God exists at all.

If the first component of any reasonable theological perspective is a commitment to the argument from design, the second is a recognition that order and harmony permeate every aspect of the universe. Each is observable within nature, within us, and within our relation to our environment. Since harmony and order are to be regarded as evidence of

God's handiwork, this must mean that no part of the universe is free from God's influence.

The all-pervasiveness of harmony and order throughout the universe is something we can easily observe, says Hume (paragraph 6):

> [A]ll bodies, from the greatest planet to the smallest particle of matter, are maintained in their proper sphere and function.

Hume is insistent on this point about the all-pervasiveness of harmony and order, and hence of God's influence (paragraph 6):

> These two distinct principles of the material and animal world, continually encroach upon each other, and mutually retard or forward each other's operation.

In other words, all entities, including both inanimate and animate, appear subject to a single system of interlocking laws.

The significance of this is reached in paragraph 7:

> When the passions play, when the judgement dictates, when the limbs obey, this is all the operation of God ...

Consider the last of these three phenomena, the 'obedience' of our limbs to our decisions to move them. What he seems to have in mind here is that when you act – to scratch your ankle, for example – you are usually able to do so because the physical world accommodates your mental decision. In a non-harmonious world, your decision to scratch could just as easily be followed by your hand flying up towards the ceiling as its moving down towards your ankle. The fact that your hand moves down towards your ankle is a sign that human decision making is just as permeated by harmony as any other event in the universe, and so equally subject to God's benign influence as the rest of the universe.

A useful term to know here is 'providence'. Divine providence includes all goings-on in the universe that are the direct result of God's influence. Many theologians have held that human action falls outside of divine providence, that our individual choices are not part of God's plan at all, and that we alone bear responsibility for them. Hume is arguing to the contrary that the entire universe, including each of our actions, falls within God's providential reach. His ground for thinking this, to repeat, is that harmony and order are manifest in human action just as they are manifest in the non-human sphere, and harmony and order are the surest sign there is of God's presence.

In paragraph 7 Hume addresses the thought that some of our actions do not really seem to be anyone's but our own. We cannot see God's hand at work in our actions looked at in isolation, he acknowledges. But seen as part of a harmonious system, our actions are as much permeated by God's influence as is the rest of the universe.

Figure 4.6 (a)   (top)
Figure 4.6 (b)   (bottom)

Figure 4.6 (a)   J.P. Le Bas, Ruins of the Opera House *(after the Lisbon earthquake of 1755), 1757, from the Le Bas series, Bibliothèque Nationale de France, Paris. Photo: courtesy National Information Service for Earthquake Engineering, University of California, Berkeley.*

Figure 4.6 (b)   J.P. Le Bas, Ruins of the Praca de Patriarchal (Patriachal Square) *(after the Lisbon earthquake of 1755), 1757, from the Le Bas series, Bibliothèque Nationale de France, Paris. Photo: courtesy National Information Service for Earthquake Engineering, University of California, Berkeley.*

*The Lisbon earthquake was mentioned earlier in a different connection. This event gave rise to debates that reflected issues salient at the time. Many focused on trying to understand the disaster as a natural phenomenon, and the science of seismology began in earnest around that time. Others were more concerned with reconciling such a cataclysmic event with their preferred conception of divinity. In particular, theologians struggled with the so-called **problem of evil**: if God is all-powerful and benevolent, why does he let terrible things happen?*

A popular answer to this problem prior to the Lisbon earthquake was that evil is brought into the world by human weakness. This was one reason why many, unlike Hume, thought that human action fell beyond God's providence. But while political corruption, murder and war could be understood in this way, earthquakes were clearly a different matter. A few tried to account for the earthquake as God's punishment for the sinfulness of Lisbon, which was perceived as a decadent city. But this was hard to reconcile with the fact that the 'decadent' opera house (Figure 4.6(a)) was joined in ruin by the cathedral and other religious buildings. In fact, five of Le Bas's six etchings contain one or more religious buildings. Figure 4.6(b) shows the patriarchal palace, which was the only major religious building to survive the tremor and the tidal wave. It served as an impromptu prayer centre before it too was lost in the fires that followed.

EXERCISE Read paragraphs 6–7. Their meaning is occasionally quite elusive. A useful maxim to adopt when this happens is to aim to get the author's basic gist, then move on, coming back later if you have to. With this in mind, what is the basic gist of these two paragraphs?

DISCUSSION Hume is attempting to set out what the most reasonable theological perspective is; he has yet to say anything about suicide from this perspective. The first component of this perspective is a commitment to the argument from design. This is left largely implicit by Hume, save where he announces that 'sympathy, harmony, and proportion, ... [afford] the surest argument [for] supreme wisdom' (paragraph 6). The second component is recognition that harmony and order permeate every aspect of the universe, including the human sphere. Putting these two components together, even events taking place in the human sphere – our own actions – must be regarded as part of God's plan (i.e. as 'belonging to divine providence'). Or, if you like, our actions are also God's actions. This is true of all actions, so there are no grounds for distinguishing between actions that are our own and those that belong to God.

Having established that, on pain of having to reject design as a sign of God's existence, *all* our actions need to be treated equally as a part of God's plan, Hume unveils the relevance of this for the morality of suicide (paragraph 8).

It is absurd, he claims, to condemn an act of suicide as 'encroaching on the office of divine providence', that is, as doing what God and only God may do. Such condemnation would be absurd because every action would then have to be condemned for the same reason. If we condemn acts of suicide for encroaching on God, we would also need to condemn acts of ankle scratching. Both actions fall inside the scope of divine providence. Both have equal status as part of God's grand design.

Hume is criticizing any attempt to establish a division between ordinary decisions and sacred decisions. Decisions of the first kind would belong to us alone; decisions of the second kind would belong to God alone. His long discussion of divine providence is meant to have shown that such a division is misguided. 'Shall we assert', asks Hume in paragraph 8,

> that the Almighty has reserved to himself in ... [some] peculiar manner the disposal of the lives of men, and has not submitted that event [i.e. the disposal of human life], in common with others, to the general laws by which the universe is governed? This is plainly false.

It is 'plainly false' because having a specially reserved sphere of influence is incompatible with the *universality* of divine providence. All types of action, from ankle scratching to suicide, are on the same footing; indeed, they are on the same footing as every event in the universe. All are subject to the universal laws of nature. These regular, ordered and harmonious laws of nature are our only assurance that God exists at all, so *must* be taken as a sign of God's influence.

EXERCISE   Read paragraph 8. How does Hume's view of providence bear on his views on the moral acceptability of suicide?

DISCUSSION Hume holds that no distinction can be drawn between those decisions that belong to God and those that do not: God's providence is total. So ending life cannot be treated as unique in belonging exclusively to God.

By the end of paragraph 8 Hume has stated the main argument of his essay. The principal value of the essay lies in this discussion of the all-pervading presence of divine providence, and its relevance for the morality of suicide. The remainder is repetition or else it introduces some short and relatively easy-to-grasp theological considerations. So now would be a good time to state Hume's reply to the sanctity-of-life argument in as simple a way as possible:

> *Hume's reply to the sanctity-of-life argument:* any reasonable theology will see order and harmony as a sign of God's influence; order and harmony are present equally in all human actions; so there is no distinction to be made between actions (e.g. suicide) that belong to God and actions (e.g. ankle scratching) that do not.

EXERCISE   Read paragraphs 9–14. Paragraphs 11–14 recapitulate the core 'providence' argument discussed already, so treat this as an opportunity to cement your understanding of his position. Before that, jot down a sentence capturing the objection Hume is *responding* to in paragraph 9. Then do the same for paragraph 10.

DISCUSSION Paragraph 9: the huge significance of the decision whether to end a human life should lead us to regard it, unlike other decisions, as one that only God may take. Paragraph 10: to take one's life is to insult God by destroying his creation. (You may have come up with a different emphasis.)

You may have recognized in Hume's reply to the objection in paragraph 9 the comments that so annoyed the anonymous commentator for *Monthly Review* quoted earlier. Actually, Hume presents several different replies in quick succession. In the first of these he suggests that 'the life of a man is of no greater importance to the universe than that of an oyster'. It is not clear what Hume means by 'importance to the universe', but on the face of it this is a bizarre claim. He makes a similar-sounding claim in comparing diverting the Nile with diverting the flow of blood through human veins. This is a case where, as interpreters, we have to make a decision. Either Hume had a good but obscure point to make with these examples, and we should pause to work out what that point is. Alternatively he was just being sloppy, in which case we should ignore his remark and move on to his other responses. I am going to adopt the latter strategy.

A more promising reply (I suggest) is embedded elsewhere within paragraph 9. Hume points out that we don't condemn those who *save* their own lives by 'turn[ing] aside a stone which is falling upon ... [their] head' for stepping on God's toes. Yet deciding to save a life is just as significant as deciding to end one. Why then should we make this complaint when it is a matter of ending our lives? The same reasoning used to condemn those who take their own lives could be used to condemn those who save their own lives. Both the taker and the saver could be said to be acting 'presumptuously' in taking such huge decisions. Hume treats this as showing the reasoning to be equally absurd in each case.

In paragraph 10 Hume is responding to the thought that by killing oneself one is destroying God's greatest creation. This would be insulting to God, rather as destroying a watch would be insulting to the watch's maker. Hume, however, is concerned with acts of suicide that are motivated by inconsolable misery and incurable illness. So a better analogy would be with the act of destroying a watch that is already permanently broken down and useless. Throwing out such a watch is in fact an act of *respect* for the watchmaker.

EXERCISE   Remind yourself of the structure of the essay as stated in paragraph 5. Then read the remaining paragraphs of the essay. Paragraphs 15–16 deal with duties to society; paragraphs 17–18 deal with duties to self.

Assessing Hume's views

The main value of Hume's essay lies in its discussion of our duties to God. Here Hume's arguments initially seem quite convincing. But arguments almost always seem convincing when they are first heard and understood. The real test comes when we try to think of possible objections. Here is one such objection, based on what has become known as the *problem of evil*, the problem of reconciling God's benevolence and omnipotence with the fact that evil exists in the world:

> Hume thinks that divine providence extends to all human action. But how can this be true? If it were, we would have to say that God is responsible for the actions of every cruel or brutal ruler.

This would be incompatible with the assumption that God is a benevolent being. At least *some* human actions must fall outside of divine providence. Hume's claim that from the most reasonable theological perspective all actions belong equally to God's grand design looks suspect.

This matter, it turns out, is discussed by Rousseau and Sade, and we will return to it in the next unit.

EXERCISE   Reread 'On suicide'. Has Hume shown that suicide is not always wrong in principle? Try to come up with an objection, or reproduce in your own words the objection having to do with the problem of evil outlined above.

Unit 5
Faith and death in the late Enlightenment: Jean-Jacques Rousseau and the Marquis de Sade

Prepared for the course team by Alex Barber

Contents

1   Prelude: the friendship between Hume and Rousseau

Hume and Rousseau had a brief and intense friendship in 1766. In a few months Rousseau passed in Hume's eyes from being his 'nice little man' and a 'genius' with whom he could 'live all his life in mutual friendship and esteem' to being 'the blackest and most atrocious villain that ever disgraced human nature', a 'monster' and 'a lying ... ferocious ... rascal', and eventually to his being simply 'plainly delirious' (quoted in Mossner, 1980, pp.511, 522, 526, 528). The tale is a sad one, but it reveals differences in temperament that were also reflected in their different attitudes towards religion and much else.

EXERCISE　　Before reading about this friendship, read the AV Notes for, and then view, the 30-minute video, *Jean-Jacques Rousseau: The Retreat to Romanticism* (Video 1, band 3). The video gives an overview of Rousseau's life, his concerns and his influence.

Mention is made in the video of Rousseau's journey to England and his quarrel. Below are the details of that episode, which reveal something of the conditions under which Hume, Rousseau and others were writing: the ease with which they could pass between esteem and ridicule in the public's estimation, the thoroughly international yet gossipy and incestuous character of the intellectual community, and the human failings that occasionally got in the way of their work as philosophers.

The events

The story begins with Rousseau's publication of *Émile* in 1762, shortly before Hume arrived in Paris as an assistant to the British ambassador. Embedded within the book is a subchapter, 'Profession of faith of a Savoyard vicar' (Anthology I, pp.33–60). This gives expression to what was clearly Rousseau's own deist perspective. The second half of the 'Profession' contained a condemnation of established religion, and in particular of Roman Catholicism. More virulent challenges had been made to the authority of the Church, but this one was especially threatening for at least three reasons: it contained a passionate and reasoned denunciation of established religion without resorting to common abuse; it sought to engage the reader in an alternative and well-worked-out mode of religious experience; and it was published openly under the author's recognized pseudonym ('A Citizen of Geneva') so was not tarnished by the connotations of shame that come with truly anonymous publication. The gauntlet was picked up by the Archbishop of Paris. *Émile* was torn up and burned at the foot of the great staircase of the city's *parlement* (the main judicial body for France under the *ancien régime*).

Rousseau was forced into exile, not helped by the condemnations he suffered elsewhere, including his native Geneva. He fled to Neuchâtel in Switzerland, then a territory belonging to the enlightened King of Prussia, Frederick the Great (b.1712; r.1740–86). Things came to a head when he was attacked by peasants, and through the delicate promptings of the Comtesse de Boufflers, Rousseau's sometime sponsor and Hume's would-be lover, Rousseau accepted Hume's offer of refuge in London under the patronage of George III (b.1738; r.1760–1820).

It was Rousseau rather than Hume who needed persuading. Hume had admired Rousseau's work for a long while, whereas Rousseau was loathe to accept what he regarded as charity from anyone. He had recently spurned the further aid offered by Frederick the Great, and had gained a reputation for turning on those who tried to help him. Rousseau was also suspicious both of Hume's apparent enjoyment of the *salons* he himself despised and of the mutual adulation taking place between Hume and the *philosophes*, or 'd'Holbach's coterie' as he contemptuously referred to this group. Baron d'Holbach (1723–89) was a materialist and atheist, an admirer and friend of Hume, and a centrepiece of the social structure that Rousseau had over the years come to find repulsive. This hostility towards the *philosophes* was mutual: Rousseau was mistrusted and ridiculed by many of his peers even as he came to be exalted by the public. D'Holbach warned Hume against Rousseau after having listened unmoved to the Scot's excitement at the prospect of a new friendship with Rousseau:

> I am sorry to dispel the hopes and illusions that flatter you, but I tell you that it will not be long before you are grievously undeceived. You don't know your man. I tell you plainly, you are warming a viper in your bosom.
>
> (Quoted in Mossner, 1980, p.515)

Despite these premonitions, a friendship grew between the two that seemed set to last. Hume wrote to his friend and physician Joseph Blair in December 1765:

> The philosophers of Paris foretold to me that I could not conduct him to Calais without a quarrel, but I think I could live with him all my life, in mutual friendship and esteem.
>
> (Quoted in Mossner, 1980, p.511)

Rousseau was more circumspect at first, but when the two of them arrived in Dover he covered Hume's face in kisses and soaked him in tears. He had reached dry land after a bad crossing; he had reached a country renowned for its (relative) freedom; and he had at last found a friend of similar intellectual standing whom he could trust.

Rousseau drew a fascinated response from London society when they arrived shortly after, and the friendship between him and Hume was remarked on for its strength as well as for its peculiarity. Despite their shared reputation for daring views on religion, they made an odd pair. Hume was tall and big-boned with a dull expression and peculiar stare; Rousseau was short, delicate and timid with sharp black eyes (Mossner, 1980, p.516). Hume was affable and charming, an established historian and a diplomat; Rousseau was a Swiss refugee who walked around London in a fur cap and a long purple robe trimmed and lined with dark fur.

See Plate 5.1 in the Illustrations Book (portrait of Rousseau by Allan Ramsay), which relates to the comment below.

This is the finest surviving image of Rousseau, but neither the painter nor the sitter had much respect for one another. Hume arranged for Allan Ramsay, official court portraitist to George III, to paint the portraits of himself and Rousseau in 1766 (see Plate 4.1 for that of Hume). Rousseau felt he had been reduced to a caricature, and his suspicion is somewhat borne out by a letter Ramsay wrote to Denis Diderot, in which he mocks Rousseau's celebration of nature: 'Those who indulge in intellectual pursuits find little charm in the bare necessities of life. Reduced to bare necessity, one must bid farewell to poetry, painting, and all the agreeable branches of philosophy, and embrace instead Rousseau's Nature – Nature on all fours' (quoted in Warburton, 2002, p.40; in the final clause he is borrowing a quip about Rousseau from Voltaire). Ramsay only undertook to paint Rousseau at all as a favour to Hume, his friend and a fellow native of Edinburgh. Rousseau later (in Rousseau, juge de Jean Jacques [Rousseau, Judge of Jean Jacques]) describes Hume as having 'desired this portrait as ardently as a deeply smitten lover desires that of his mistress; through importunities he extorted his [i.e. Rousseau's] consent ... He [Rousseau] was made to wear a deep black cap and a deep brown garment, ... posed in a dark spot, and in order to paint him seated, he was forced to stand up, stooped over, supported by one hand on a low table, in an attitude where highly strained muscles altered the very contours of his face' (quoted in Mossner, 1980, p.538).

Rousseau also wore a caftan rather than breeches. In Rousseau's mind this was a reasonable response to a practical problem, a urinary complaint that had affected him since childhood. In the eyes of Londoners it was perceived as an affectation and a clear invitation to mockery. When this mockery began it was accompanied by bemusement at Hume's devotion to him. Hume guarded Rousseau's reputation on the many occasions it came under attack, and at the same time struggled to integrate him into London culture. He faced the difficulty that such integration was entirely contrary to Rousseau's own preference. In Rousseau's honour, Hume had arranged a special performance by the famous actor, Garrick, at the Drury Lane theatre with George III in attendance. He informed Rousseau at the last minute to catch him off guard; Rousseau resolved not to go because Sultan, his beloved dog, could not be locked up without howling. Hume won out that time, 'partly by ... [reasoning] and partly by force' (Hume, quoted in Mossner, 1980, p.518), but his efforts to keep Rousseau in London rather than a remote Welsh monastery had more mixed results. Rousseau resolved to move to Wootton in the Peak District, on the Derbyshire-Staffordshire border, 'situated amidst mountains and rocks and streams and forests' (Hume, quoted in Mossner, 1980, p.523).

In a lost cartoon Rousseau was represented as a Yahoo – that is, as a brute in human form as conceived in Jonathan Swift's 1726 novel, *Gulliver's Travels* – newly caught in the woods. Hume is a farmer, caressing him and offering him oats to eat, which he refuses in a rage (Hume to de Boufflers, quoted in Mure, 1854, p.104); the cartoon was in fact the work of the ubiquitous James Boswell. But it was a more sophisticated joke by Horace Walpole (1717–97) that led to the rapid and total breakdown in the friendship with Hume.

Walpole, a writer and man of letters, thought Rousseau a 'hypocrite' and a 'mountebank' (quoted in Mossner, 1980, p.513). As mentioned, Rousseau was known to have turned down a pension from the King of Prussia. Walpole wrote a letter purporting to be the one in which the offer was made. The document parodies the misplaced adulation Rousseau received from those like the king, as well as Rousseau's supposed preciousness. Had this really been the letter, its patronizing caveats would have enraged Rousseau's touchy personality.

> My Dear Jean-Jacques,
>
> You have renounced Geneva, your native soil. You have been driven from Switzerland, a country of which you have made such boast in your writings. In France you are outlawed. Come then to me. I admire your talents and amuse myself with your reveries; on which, however, by the way, you bestow too much time and attention. It is high time to grow prudent and happy; you have made yourself sufficiently talked of for singularities little becoming a truly great man. Show your enemies that you have sometimes common sense. This will vex them without hurting you. My dominions afford you a peaceful retreat. I am desirous to do you good, and will do it, if you can but think it such. But if you are determined to refuse my assistance, you may expect that I shall say not a word about it to anyone. If you persist in perplexing your brains to find out new misfortunes, choose such

as you like best. I am a king and can make you as miserable as you can wish. At the same time I will engage to do that which your enemies never will, I will cease to persecute you when you are no longer vain of persecution.

Your sincere friend,

Frederick

(Quoted in Mossner, 1980, pp.513–14)

EXERCISE   Reading between the lines of 'Frederick's' letter, what are some of Rousseau's purported character failings?

DISCUSSION   They include a vanity-driven persecution complex ('when you are no longer vain of persecution'); a desire to be unhappy ('I am a king and can make you as miserable as you can wish'); an overly serious and humourless character (Walpole is asking us to envisage Rousseau's enraged reaction to 'Frederick's' assertion that 'I admire your talents and amuse myself with your reveries; on which, however, by the way, you bestow too much time and attention'); cultivated eccentricity ('you have made yourself sufficiently talked of for singularities little becoming a truly great man'); a capacity for self-deception (e.g. about Switzerland, which rejected him); an over-stretched intellect ('if you persist in perplexing your brains'); an inability to know himself or his true interests ('it is high time to grow prudent and happy'; 'show your enemies that you have sometimes common sense'); a desire to annoy others just for the sake of it ('this will vex them without hurting you').

The letter quickly found its way into print in several places, usually with the true author's identity not revealed. The damage arose because Rousseau, when he saw it, suspected Hume of having had a hand in its composition.

Although it is true that Walpole had taken his joke on a dry run at a party in Paris at which Hume had been present, the evidence points very much against Rousseau's suspicion. Neither Rousseau's trying behaviour since they arrived in London, nor the fact that he had 'a hankering after religion and is little better than a Christian in a way of his own', had dampened Hume's enthusiasm for this 'wonderfully ingenious man' (Hume, quoted in Mossner, 1980, p.523). Hume's assessment of Walpole's game as found in a letter to Mme de Boufflers (February 1766) fits with this supposition. He is realistic and proportionate about the joke, but certainly does not condone it:

> It is a strange inclination we have to be wits, preferably to
> everything else. [Walpole] is a very worthy man ... Yet he could
> not forbear, for the sake of a very indifferent joke, the turning
> [Rousseau] into ridicule, and saying harsh things against him. I
> am a little angry with [Walpole], ... but the matter ought to be
> treated only as a piece of levity.

(Quoted in Mossner, 1980, p.514)

Ancien régime France was comparatively hierarchical and fixed; displays
of wit were cultivated in part because they provided a rare opportunity
for social advancement. Rousseau was either unable or unwilling to play
the game and acquired a reputation for being a killjoy. But Hume,
entertaining company by all accounts, is on Rousseau's side on this
occasion.

Rousseau's burgeoning paranoia about Hume was evident early on. In an
overnight stop en route to Calais, Rousseau had imagined hearing the
voice of Hume shouting over and over: *Je tiens Jean-Jacques! Je tiens
Jean-Jacques!* (the words one shouts on catching a thief, like 'I have
him!'), this at a time when Rousseau was fleeing the country. We have
also seen evidence of the mutual antipathy between Rousseau and the
philosophes, and of how Hume had been worthy of suspicion by
association in Rousseau's eyes. His conjecture that Hume had put
together the Walpole letter in collusion with Rousseau's enemies in
France so as to humiliate him thus formed part of a pattern.

Matters came to a head. Rousseau, pretending to be poorer than he in
fact was while at the same time refusing to accept the charity he did not
need, had declined to accept any mail (paid for by the receiver at that
time). Hume had been quietly holding Rousseau's mail so as to keep
Rousseau's secrets from the postal clerks who would no doubt have
opened this spurned post. Rousseau discovered this, without recognizing
it as a protective act. He suspected Hume himself of reading the post,
and this led him to the theory of Hume's involvement in the 'Frederick'
letter. Without saying exactly what he had in mind, he accused Hume of
treachery over dinner.

The historical record provides two different perspectives on what
happened next. According to Hume (in a letter to Joseph Blair), his
ineffective attempts to establish his innocence were followed by a long
and awkward silence that was resolved when Rousseau:

> sat down suddenly on my knee, threw his hands about my neck,
> kissed me with the greatest warmth, and bedewing all my face
> with tears, exclaimed: 'Is it possible you can ever forgive me, my
> dear friend? After all the testimonies of affection I have received
> from you, I reward you at last with this folly and ill behaviour.
> But I have, notwithstanding, a heart worthy of your friendship. I
> love you, I esteem you, and not an instance of your kindness is
> thrown away upon me.' [I was] melted on this occasion. I assure

you I kissed him and embraced him twenty times, with a
plentiful effusion of tears. I think no scene of my life was ever
more affecting.

(Quoted in Mossner, 1980, p.54)

Rousseau recalls the same events differently. His mistaken supposition
that Hume was engaging in mail tampering had led to an accusation of
treachery, meaning treachery over the Walpole letter. He did not say in
what respect Hume had been treacherous, and kept expecting to be
asked to elaborate. When Hume did not ask, Rousseau concluded that
Hume *already knew* what the accusation was, which would have meant
that the accusation was true. The emotional episode that Hume
interpreted as marking closure was, to Rousseau, a last desperate attempt
to get Hume to deny his guilt, or at least to ask for the specifics
concerning Rousseau's accusation. He reports himself as having cried out
in Hume's arms:

No, David Hume is not a traitor. That is impossible. If he is not
the best of men he must be the blackest.

(Quoted in Mossner, 1980, p.522)

Failing to get the reaction he sought (unsurprisingly given Hume's
perception of the episode), he went to bed 'sick at heart'. He left for
Derbyshire in the morning, and the two never saw one another again.

Hume had no idea that he had been written off by Rousseau, but a series
of increasingly acrimonious letters from Rousseau, and a fear of damage
to his reputation for probity as Rousseau's version of events crept into
the public domain, led him to send a complete account of his side of
events to a few key individuals. He came to regret doing so, since he
gradually settled on the view that Rousseau was mentally deranged.

Rousseau himself stayed at Wootton for a few months, then left as Hume
had already predicted he would. (Hume shared Ramsay's cynicism about
Rousseau's vision of nature, reported in the caption to Plate 5.1 above,
p.208.) He held to the theory that Hume was part of an international
conspiracy to discredit him. He persisted in interpreting events that had
taken place up to that final night as confirming this theory. He even
construed the portrait by Ramsay, the one for which Hume had insisted
he sit, as part of the grand scheme. After all, Hume had arranged for a
number of etchings of the painting to be made and sent out to
Rousseau's friends in Europe. Rousseau saw in the whole process an
attempt to make him seem ugly, especially when compared to Hume in
his bright red diplomat's tunic (see Plate 4.1 in the Illustrations Book).

Figure 5.1   Joseph Wright of Derby, Sir Brooke Boothby, *1781, oil on canvas, 148.6 x 207.6 cm, Tate Britain, London. Photo: © Tate, London, 2002.*

Rousseau's stay in Derbyshire was short-lived. While there, he continued to refuse to learn English, and only ever seems to have overcome his longstanding animosity to England for the few minutes of rapture upon landing at Dover. Local dignitaries came to him in Wootton to pay homage, but he would receive them in total silence until they left in embarrassment or annoyance. One exception seems to have been Sir Brooke Boothby (1743–1825), whom Rousseau trusted enough to make partial executor of his work. In return, Boothby became an early disciple and evangelist. In this portrait (by a fellow native of Derbyshire), Boothby is shown lying down in a country setting. He is primed for the contemplation of nature through having read from Rousseau, juge de Jean Jacques, *but is closing it so as to achieve a more direct experience, unmediated by books. The pose of chin in hand was a traditional representation of melancholy.*

Interpreting the events

It is important not to read too much into the events surrounding this shambolic friendship between Hume and Rousseau, particularly when it comes to evaluating their work. Reasoning does not stand or fall according to whether we approve of the behaviour of the reasoner. With that warning in place, what can we learn from the events just outlined?

One obvious lesson turns on the fact that Hume and Rousseau leave very different accounts of their falling out. If we had had to rely on Rousseau's account, we could have gone seriously awry. This demonstrates the importance of independent corroboration of descriptions of historical events, even when dealing with reports made at the time. (I have largely followed the version of events favoured by Mossner, 1980, chapters 35–6 and appendix F, who gives more details on sources than it would be appropriate for me to relay here.) This warning about the reliability of the historical record is taken up in the discussion of our knowledge of Napoleon's life in Block 2.

The friendship also illustrates the different attitudes Hume and Rousseau had towards evidence. Hume is generally more circumspect than Rousseau in reaching conclusions, both in his philosophy and in real life. Hume seeks sure evidence before he will dismiss a person, and expresses dismay at Rousseau's assumption that Hume is a rogue on the basis of such slim evidence:

> Was anything in the world so unaccountable? For the purpose of life and conduct, and society, a little good sense is surely better than all the genius, and a little good humour than this extreme sensibility.

(Letter to Mme de Boufflers, May 1766, quoted in Mossner, 1980, p.525)

Rousseau himself had stated that 'I know only what I feel' in a letter to Hume (quoted in Mossner, 1980, p.528). It is this appeal to feeling as a source of knowledge that Hume is criticizing in his reference to 'extreme sensibility'.

Trusting in what he felt was Rousseau's way of supplementing the traditional empiricist account of permissible evidence. In addition to the five 'outer' senses, in certain matters Rousseau was willing to trust the 'inner' voice of sentiment or feeling. Hume would have been as sceptical of Rousseau's reliance on an inner voice in the context of religious debate as in the context of his flight from Paris. Rousseau thought he heard Hume shouting 'Je tiens Jean-Jacques!', which seems to have been extremely unlikely, and we can readily guess at what Hume would have made of the fact that 'at times he [Rousseau] believes he has inspirations from an immediate communication with the Divinity' (Hume, letter to Blair, quoted in Mossner, 1980, p.512).

Rousseau's preparedness to allow sentiment to determine his opinions even in the face of a lack of evidence from the senses was allied to a preoccupation with himself that grew increasingly dominant with every book he wrote. Rousseau's early work, including the *Social Contract* of *c*.1755, is often fairly abstract. *Émile* (1762) is about the personal development of an individual child, though not necessarily Rousseau. Later still, his *Confessions* (written 1766–70, published posthumously) was an autobiography of a kind never seen before. Ceaselessly emphasizing the importance of personal integrity and honesty, it would have come across to many readers as self-indulgent. His *Rousseau, juge de Jean Jacques* (written 1772–6, also published posthumously) is put forward as a judgement on his own life by himself in the form of an intense dialogue. And his final work, *Reveries of the Solitary Walker* (written 1776–8 and published posthumously), would have struck many as a sequence of ravings.

Here he is in the *Reveries* recollecting his writing of the 'Profession of faith of a Savoyard vicar', which we are about to read:

> After what were perhaps the most ardent and sincere investigations ever conducted by any mortal, I made up my mind once and for all on the questions that concerned me, and if I was mistaken in my conclusion, I am sure at least that I cannot be blamed for my error since I did all I could to avoid it ... Sometimes [objections that I was unable to answer or had not foreseen] have worried me, but they have never shaken my faith. I have always said to myself: 'All these are hair-splitting metaphysical subtleties which count for nothing against the basic principles adopted by my reason, confirmed by my heart and bearing the seal of my conscience uninfluenced by passion. In matters so far above human understanding, shall I let an objection that I cannot answer overturn a whole body of doctrine which is so sound and coherent, the result of so much careful meditation, so well fitted to my reason, my heart and my whole being, and confirmed by that inner voice that I find absent from all the rest? No, empty logic-chopping will never destroy the close relation I perceive between my immortal nature and the constitution of the world, the physical order I see all around me.'

> (Rousseau, 1979, pp.55–6)

The passage shows how a total personal commitment was, for Rousseau, wrapped up with his adoption of a new account of how we should seek to ground our opinions, according to which not only reason and the outer senses but conscience, sentiment, feeling, conviction, an inner voice or sense – his 'whole being' – should serve as the sign of an opinion worth holding. Hume shared the view that philosophy could be an emotionally exhausting and transforming activity, but whereas Rousseau's response to this was to regard it the surest sign of truth, Hume's was to play cards with his friends for a few hours as a way of switching off.

2   Rousseau's profession of faith

Émile and the 'Profession'

The 'Profession of faith of a Savoyard vicar' is embedded in Book IV of Rousseau's hugely influential work, *Émile*. The book as a whole purports to describe the ideal education for a boy, Émile, through the first 20 or so years of his life. To the extent that any single lesson about education stands out from Rousseau's rich description of how to raise a person, it is a lesson that springs from an assumption about human nature.

The right conditions for Émile's growth are those that allow him to develop in accordance with his nature. Traditional educationalists sought to overcome the child's nature, mainly through discipline and control. Rousseau, instead of filling the child's head with facts and instilling in him desirable habits, seeks to cultivate his inner natural spontaneity. For this to be the right approach, Émile must be neither essentially corrupt, as the Christian doctrine of original sin implied, nor a *tabula rasa* (i.e. a blank slate) as empiricists following John Locke assumed the human mind to be prior to its receiving sensory input.

The role of the 'Profession' within *Émile* is nominally to deal with the nature of religious education, but it serves also as a self-contained expression and defence of a particular religious commitment. The segment falls into two halves. The first is a defence of Rousseau's own version of deism. The second is a critique of revealed religion, specifically of the Catholic Church, though it is a critique that is qualified by admiration for the non-revelatory elements of the New Testament. We will be looking mainly at the first half of the 'Profession'.

The publication of the book cost him dearly on several fronts, for reasons summed up by Hume:

> I am not in the least surprised that it gave offence. He has not the precaution to throw any veil over his sentiments; and as he scorns to dissemble his contempt of established opinions, he could not wonder that all the zealots were in arms against him.

(Letter to Mme de Boufflers; quoted in Mossner, 1980, p.508)

The reference to a lack of 'any veil over his sentiments' captures what offended Enlightenment thinking: the 'Profession' was grounded not in empirical reasoning but in the emotions, or the 'heart' as Rousseau often puts it. Relying on the sentiments to guide one towards the truth would have seemed utterly reckless. Prior to Rousseau, even deists sought evidence for their religious beliefs in the five 'outer' senses, not the 'inner' senses of personal conviction and feeling.

La nature étaloit à nos yeux toute sa magnificence.

Figure 5.2 Jean Michel Moreau, Nature Displayed all its Magnificence to our Eyes, *1778, Bibliothèque nationale de France, Paris.*

This is an illustration from an early edition of Émile *of the scene immediately before the Savoyard priest's profession. The narrator describes how he:*

> *indicated eagerness to hear [the priest's words on religious faith]. The appointment was put off till no later than the next morning. It was summer. We got up at daybreak. He took me outside of the city on a high hill, beneath which ran the Po, whose course was seen along the fertile banks it washes. In the distance the immense chain of the Alps crowned the landscape. The rays of the rising sun already grazed the plains and, projecting on the fields long shadows of the trees, the vineyards, and the houses, enriched with countless irregularities of light the most beautiful scene which can strike the human eye. One would have said that nature displayed all its magnificence to our eyes in order to present them with the text for our conversation. It was there that after having contemplated these objects in silence for some time, the man of peace spoke to me as follows: ...*

(Rousseau, 1991, p.266)

Rousseau viewed nature not merely as an object of investigation, but as a source of knowledge in its own right. Indeed, it could render as evident certain truths that we can only struggle to express through language.

The reference to his scorn 'to dissemble his contempt of established opinions' describes Rousseau's vulnerability to the assault of the Church once he had declared his identity as author. His sympathetic and personalized account of his relationship with God was perceived by the Roman Catholic Church as a threat to its role as mediator between heaven and the masses. Given the predictable failure of the *philosophes* to rally around, and his own paranoid refusal to look to them for support, his exile became almost inevitable.

Just before the 'Profession' begins, a narrator (the narrator for the rest of *Émile*) describes having met, in his own youth, an itinerant priest in the Italian Alps. This priest becomes the first-person narrator for the duration of the 'Profession'. The priest is based loosely on a real-life meeting Rousseau had with two priests in his youth. One further layer of complexity: Rousseau later acknowledged what many assumed at the time of publication, that the priest's profession is simply a statement of Rousseau's own views regarding religion.

The priest's journey

The priest's profession takes the form of an intellectual journey born of necessity. He describes becoming minister to a parish not out of a sense of calling but for the wage, then losing that ministry through a sexual scandal – independent evidence implies an act of indecency with a young boy – prompted by his respect for the marriage vows. The loss of his parish, his exile, and the perceived inconsistency and hypocrisy of the charge against him, shake his faith to such an extent that he ends up disbelieving everything he previously held true:

> I was born in a church which decides everything and permits no doubt; therefore, the rejection of a single point made me reject all the rest.

> (Anthology I, p.35)

He resolves to accept an opinion only if it is a reasonable one, and never merely because accepting it will lead him to a comfortable living.

Driven by a love for truth he will seek out how best to discover it. He looks first to the views of the *philosophes*, but is disappointed because their opinions are reached not out of a desire to discover the truth but – like his earlier self – out of a desire to live a comfortable life. In particular, they resort to rhetorical tricks or change their views from one day to the next according to their audience. Their sole aim is to appear clever, to win debating points, and so to promote their status in the *salons*.

Having resolved to accept only reasonable opinions – that is, opinions supported by evidence – and given the fact that neither the Church nor the *philosophes* can provide him with adequate sources of evidence, the priest decides to fall back on his own resources. He resolves 'to accept as evident all knowledge to which in the sincerity of my heart I cannot refuse my consent' (Anthology I, p.36), and to remain neutral on all the rest, neither accepting nor rejecting it.

EXERCISE   Read 'The priest's journey' from the 'Profession' in Anthology I (pp.33–6). (a) How, if at all, does Rousseau's style differ from Hume's? (b) How would Hume have reacted to the declaration of intent in the sentence 'I am resolved ... practice' (p.36)?

DISCUSSION   (a) Where Hume is ironic and occasionally offhand or bombastic, Rousseau is florid, earnest and sincere. Another difference is that Rousseau is for the most part easier to read, which is why you will find that the commentary below is less tied to the text than it was for Hume. Both, however, would wish their arguments to be the main engine of persuasion. (b) Hume would have been perfectly happy with most of the priest's account, but would not have been impressed with his plan to follow the 'sincerity of his heart'. Hume would have preferred a more focused endorsement of the outer senses as the sole source of evidence concerning 'matters of fact'. Rousseau is preparing to break away from the empiricist tradition.

The priest's search for knowledge in the remainder of the first half of his 'Profession' begins from this position of total scepticism about everything and progresses through four stages. At each stage he uncovers new opinions and principles that pass his test: in the sincerity of his heart he cannot withhold his consent. In turn he examines himself, God, his position in the universe and society, and how he ought to live. (These four stages are not labelled as such in the original text, which is a continuous treatise.)

Stage one: a sensing self

The main business of the 'Profession' opens with some influential but difficult discussions of the nature of perception and of the relation of perception to the self. This section has been quite heavily edited in the Anthology. You can, if you wish, skip immediately to stage two below, which begins with a short summary of what he achieves in stage one. But the ideas of this opening section have been enormously influential in discussions of empiricism, so you may wish to become acquainted with them.

Rousseau is starting from the position in which he has resolved to suspend every opinion he ever held true, save for those opinions he cannot in the sincerity of his heart abandon. He quickly finds that he cannot stop himself from supposing that he exists and that he has experiences ('sensations' or, as we might call them, 'perceptions').

These experiences are experiences *of* things; they feel directed towards objects outside him, objects that presumably cause him to have the experiences. When he has a certain kind of visual experience, for example, it feels to him as if there is a cloud up there in the sky that is causing him to have this visual experience. This, again, is something he cannot stop himself thinking. So he decides to accept the existence of a material universe, within which are objects that his experiences are caused by and representative of.

So far Rousseau has said nothing out of keeping with common sense. His next claim is more adventurous. He argues that there is an active component in our judgements about the external world. Many empiricists thought of judgement formation as an entirely passive process: the external world impinges on our sensory organs, causing sensations to take place within us, and thus causing us to make judgements about how the world is. They had two reasons for hoping this description of judgement formation was accurate.

First, many empiricists were also materialists: they believed that humans are not essentially different from the rest of the material world, making them susceptible to scientific investigation in the same way. Since the material world is essentially passive, humans would also need to be passive if they were made of matter. This was one reason for the orthodox view that human judgement formation is passive.

Second, empiricists thought that so long as our judgements are the slave of experience, they are unlikely to mislead us. Experiences are caused by the state of the real world and so are our surest route to correct opinion about the real world. If we start to form opinions that are not mandated by experience – that is, if we start making judgements that are not passively triggered by experience – then we are likely to end up with false views. (In truth, this is not really a reason for thinking that human judgement *is* passive; at best it is a reason for thinking that it *ought to be* passive.)

Rousseau agrees that sensations are caused in us without our playing any more than a passive role: '[sensations] affect me without my having anything to do with it' (p.36). This is why sensations are an accurate guide to the state of the external world. But he thinks that the objective judgements we make on the basis of these passively received sensations involve us in an active process. He offers two grounds for this claim, and you are asked to dig these out in the next exercise.

EXERCISE   Read 'A sensing self' from the 'Profession'. What are Rousseau's grounds for claiming that judgement is an active process? Look at the paragraphs beginning 'To see ...' and 'Add to ...' on p.37 for two distinct grounds.

DISCUSSION   The first ground involves giving examples of sensation unaccompanied by judgement. I can experience the presence of two sticks without yet having judged the one to be bigger than the other. I can witness a hand, but to judge how many fingers are held up requires me to count them actively in my mind. The second ground is more subtle. Our judgements about any given object can come through several senses at once: for example, when we judge there is a fire before us, this judgement is made on the basis of seeing a flickering light, feeling warmth and hearing crackling. The judgement that the sensations belonging to these different senses are caused by a single object (the fire) is something that we bring to the sensations, not something that we find in the sensations themselves.

This claim about the active elements in judgement has intrinsic interest, and its significance in the history of philosophy – particularly as developed by the German philosopher Immanuel Kant (1724–1804) – is hard to overestimate. The relevance it has for our discussion of religion is more confined.

Stage two: God and his properties

At the end of stage one, the priest has established that he exists, that he experiences the external world, and that he is an active, thinking being. He moves next to consider what religious opinions it would be reasonable for him to hold.

The route to his conclusion that God exists is initially quite conventional. He appeals first to the cosmological argument and then to the argument from design, leading to two 'articles of faith'. You may care to remind yourself of the content of the cosmological argument and the argument from design by consulting the glossary or by revisiting Unit 4, pp.175–6.

The priest's version of the cosmological argument is slightly more involved than the simple version outlined in Unit 4. He begins by offering a convoluted argument to the effect that the 'natural state of matter is to be at rest' (p.38). But matter, he observes, is in motion. So something must have caused matter to move out of its natural state and acquire this motion.

There are only two ways matter could have acquired motion: the motion could have been 'communicated' to it by something else, or it could have acquired the motion spontaneously ('voluntarily'). Communicated motion is the motion we see when one snooker ball hits another. Spontaneous motion is the motion we experience in our own actions, as when we move an arm intentionally, for example.

Motion cannot have arisen spontaneously in matter since the motion of matter 'is regular, uniform, and subjected to constant laws, it contains nothing of that liberty appearing in the spontaneous motions of man and the animals' (p.38). For this reason, something that *is* capable of spontaneous motion must ultimately have set the material world in motion.

Because he gets the idea of spontaneous motion from the example of his own wilful actions, he is led to his 'first article of faith': *that a will moves the universe and animates nature.* This is the conclusion of the cosmological argument.

EXERCISE   Read the extract entitled 'God and his properties' up to the paragraph ending '... absolutely nothing' (pp.37–9). The priest assumes that the natural state of matter is to be at rest, and that matter could not generate its own motion. Isolate how he defends these claims. Is this defence an empiricist one?

DISCUSSION   Yes. He is unwilling to give credence to the thought of spontaneous motion in matter because the motion of matter is dissimilar to the spontaneous motion that he has *observed*. In particular, it is 'regular, uniform, and subjected to constant laws'.

The priest sets out to show that this all-powerful 'first mover' has the other attributes of a traditional Christian deity: intelligence and benevolence. To arrive at the first of these attributes he turns to the argument from design.

Intelligence is manifest in the order and regularity of the material world. The priest does not attempt to piece together a rigorous defence of this 'second article of faith', the inference from order and harmony to the supreme intelligence of the creator. Instead he asks his audience to join him in:

> listen[ing] to our inner sentiment. What healthy mind can turn aside its testimony; to which unprejudiced eyes does the sensible [i.e. observable] order not proclaim a supreme intelligence; and how many sophisms must be piled up before it is impossible to recognize the harmony of the beings and the admirable concurrences of each piece in the preservation of the others?

(p.39)

This would have been frustrating to Rousseau's critics. Rather than offering a detailed argument for them to get their teeth into, he appeals to inner sentiment. Since inner sentiment is not recognized in the empiricist tradition as a reliable source of knowledge, Rousseau is radically at odds with that tradition. As the 'Profession' progresses, the extent of the departure increases.

We now have an argument for the existence of a God that is an intelligent will, responsible for having set in motion the inanimate matter of the universe. The third quality of God that Rousseau needs to establish is his goodness. He does not say much on this until the next extract. In the present extract he merely states without argument that God's essential goodness is a 'necessary consequence' of intelligence, power and will. These attributes he joins together to 'call *God*' (p.40).

EXERCISE Read the remainder of the extract entitled 'God and his properties'. Are there limits to our knowledge of God?

DISCUSSION There are. For example, the priest is resigned to his ignorance of whether there is just one God or many, or of whether the universe has always existed or was created (p.39). His ignorance of this latter fact explains his preference for the prime-mover version of the cosmological argument over the creator version (see the glossary definition of 'cosmological argument' if you need a reminder).

So far, Rousseau has done little more than endorse the traditional deist arguments and make some deviant assertions about listening to inner sentiment. From here on, this deviance becomes ever more pronounced.

Stage three: our position in the universe and in society

Rousseau now adopts a more open style than in stages one and two, and you should be able to read him without the need of detailed support. I will therefore limit myself to drawing attention to certain features of the text bearing on themes that have emerged already in the units.

For all his fame as a promoter of nature, Rousseau had very traditional assumptions about humanity's dominion over the rest of the universe (p.41):

> What is ... so ridiculous about thinking that everything is made for me ...?

What is most interesting about this claim in the present context is not its ego-centrism but the way in which Rousseau uses it to argue for a conclusion about God. Recognition of his own high status in the universe gives rise in him to gratitude to the creator of the universe, and confirms for him that God is a beneficent being (p.41):

> I adore the supreme power, and I am moved by its benefactions. I do not need to be taught this worship; it is dictated to me by nature itself.

This is quite explicitly an appeal to sentiment – and not the outer senses – to draw a conclusion about the deity. The priest is rejecting revealed religion as well as traditional empiricist thinking, and looking to different grounds for his opinions. In this case, the conviction of God's beneficence springs from his feelings of gratitude. A sense of gratitude can be called an 'inner' sense since it is distinct from the traditional five outer senses.

EXERCISE Read 'Our position in the universe and in society' up to the paragraph ending '... in him' (p.41). What are the 'two distinct principles' in the nature of man?

DISCUSSION The first is a commitment to sentiment, which reveals the eternal truths and consequently gives rise to a love of justice and moral beauty; the second is a restriction to the (outer) senses and the baser passions.

We saw in Unit 4, section 5 how Hume argued that divine providence must be present in every episode in the universe, including individual human actions. His grounds for this claim were that human affairs are, like the rest of the universe, marked by the harmony and order that are our best evidence for God's existence. This is precisely what Rousseau denies in a paragraph you have just read (p.41):

> [W]hen ... I seek to know my ... species, and I consider its various ranks and the men who fill them, ... What a spectacle! Where is the order I had observed? The picture of nature had presented me with only harmony and proportion; that of mankind presents me with only confusion and disorder! Concert reigns among the elements, and men are in chaos!

This forces him to reassess his judgement that God is a beneficent being. For why should he have allowed this to happen?

> O providence, is it thus that you rule the world? Beneficent Being, what has become of your power? I see evil on earth.

The answer he gives is that the source of evil is human freedom. Sentiment (once again) teaches him that humans are free, and this becomes a third article of faith: that 'man is ... free in his actions' (p.42) and not a mere material being.

But if God is supposedly beneficent, why would he create humans as free beings given that this will lead to evil in the world? The answer Rousseau provides is simple: a universe in which humans 'did not have the power to do evil' would be a less good universe than the one God has actually created, in which humans are 'made ... free in order that by choice ... [they] do not evil but good' (p.42). He ennobles us, and thereby himself, by creating us free; it is we who let him down, we who are the authors of evil, not God.

EXERCISE   Continue reading this extract up to the paragraph ending '... from yourself' (p.43). How does the priest seek to resolve the problem of evil?

DISCUSSION   The priest's solution to the problem is to identify human actions as the source of evil. The recipe for eliminating evil is to listen more to our sentiments and conscience, and less to our passions. Notice that if this solution to the problem of evil is accepted, the results of human actions should not be regarded as a part of divine providence. This is contrary to Hume's claim (see Unit 4, pp.197–200) that they should be so regarded.

The remainder of this extract concerns the topic of immortality. Once again Rousseau turns to his sentiments, his inner convictions, and finds that he cannot help believing that just actions on his part will be rewarded by God (p.43):

> The more I return within myself, and the more I consult myself, the more I see these words written in my soul: *Be just and you will be happy*.

The absence of reward in this life is therefore a clear signal that there is an afterlife in which justice is done.

The priest wonders about the nature of the afterlife, and concedes that there is little that can reasonably be said in detail. But on the ground that such a presumption 'consoles' him, he decides to yield to the thought that the soul will last forever, and not merely long enough for justice to be done. This, to an empiricist, is utterly facile, since finding a thought consoling is not a ground for adopting it as a truth.

You may be puzzled by the fact that Hume *was* prepared to appeal to sentiment in his discussion of immortality. He said that the traditional Christian conception of punishment was out of kilter with human sentiments on what is just, and that human sentiments should be given greater authority. Isn't this at odds with the assertion that Hume was an empiricist who gave credence only to the outer senses?

The resolution of this apparent contradiction is that Hume thought the outer senses were the only true guide to *matters of fact* (see the quotation from his *Enquiry*, p.172 above). Judgements about morality were not, in Hume's scheme, matters of fact at all. Hume was a subjectivist about moral judgement. He did not think moral judgements were, strictly speaking, judgements about an independent reality; they were just human responses springing from the sentiments. Many held the same view about artistic judgements (e.g. about what is beautiful) and made the same distinction between the realm of facts, which could be properly investigated only by using scientific methods, and the realm of those judgements that reflected no more than human sentiments. What is radical about Rousseau is the way he is prepared to let sentiment guide him in his judgements on matters of fact – e.g. the nature and existence of God – and not merely in his judgements on morality or art.

EXERCISE   Read the rest of this extract. Recall Hume's suggestion (Unit 4, section 4 and Figure 4.4) that an eternity of damnation is a disproportionate punishment for human sin. Does the priest's response in the final paragraph address this worry?

DISCUSSION   The priest admits he is unsure about what will happen to the wicked. But he is apparently oblivious to Hume's concern about the apparent lack of proportion of awarding them eternal damnation, saying he doesn't care what happens to the wicked. He also suggests that their punishment begins in this life through the effects of envy, avarice and ambition on their souls.

Stage four: how we should live

In this final stage the priest considers how to conduct himself in this life. It is here that Rousseau is most emphatic in his methodology of allowing his 'heart' to guide him rather than relying on traditional forms of reasoning alone.

Given his topic – proper moral conduct – this appeal to sentiment would not necessarily unsettle empiricists. As already noted, orthodox Enlightenment thinkers, and Hume in particular, did not want to trample on human sentiment as a guide. They merely wished to keep it in its place. So long as it is not taken as a guide to opinions on 'matters of fact', they would not object. Since moral judgements were deemed, by Hume at least, to be entirely subjective, he would be less troubled by these passages than by the appeal to sentiment as a guide to religious truth.

In the Anthology I have chosen extracts to reveal the extent to which the priest is prepared to appeal to sentiment, an inner voice, conscience, his soul, his heart and, most of all, what he calls 'nature' to guide him in his judgements about proper conduct. These appeals fill a role traditionally assigned to religious instruction.

EXERCISE   Read 'How we should live', which is self-explanatory. Attempt to find points at which the priest appeals to nature as a source of knowledge. Are you convinced by these appeals? Be as opinionated as you wish.

DISCUSSION   There is an appeal to nature in nearly every paragraph, though sometimes an appeal is made instead to nature's agents, the heart or an innate conscience: 'There is in the depths of souls, then, an innate principle of justice and virtue according to which, in spite of our own maxims, we judge our actions and those of others as good or bad. It is to this principle that I give the name *conscience*' (p.47).

I find such appeals to nature unsatisfying. Rousseau's priest provides no way of distinguishing between opinions that are the result of consulting his 'nature' and simple prejudice. Any connection with 'nature' or the 'heart' in a strict biological sense is entirely specious. But if 'nature' is not meant in a strict biological sense, the appeal to nature becomes hopelessly vague. For example, is using a light bulb 'natural'? If not, is doing so unnatural and therefore objectionable? Appealing to nature is often like saying: 'I can't come up with a good ground for thinking this, but I'm going to carry on believing it anyway.' Rousseau is right that the outer senses are a poor guide to correct moral judgement, but appealing to what it is 'natural' to believe adds nothing of value to the debate.

An exception is where the priest denies that naked self-interest is the sole end of human nature (p.47). This is a prescient antidote to those who think that Darwin, writing long after Rousseau, showed that altruistic behaviour is unnatural and selfishness natural. The fact that moral acts such as self-sacrifice can be found in all societies suggests this is a mistake.

It is sometimes said that Rousseau *opposes* reason, preferring instead to appeal to sentiment. I have offered a different interpretation, in which Rousseau is committed to believing only what it is reasonable to believe, i.e. to believing that for which there is evidence. It is just that he has a broader conception of what counts as evidence than was traditional at the time. Sentiment is not opposed to reason and evidence; rather, it is itself a source of evidence.

Against my interpretation, it could be pointed out that Rousseau occasionally explicitly contrasts reason with sentiment. Here is just such a passage (p.45):

> Too often reason deceives us. We have acquired only too much right to challenge it. But conscience never deceives; it is man's true guide.

However, I interpret him in these passages as using the word 'reason' as meaning reason *as it has been narrowly understood by empiricists*. For Rousseau, reason in this narrow sense was fine as far as it went; the mistake was to assume it went far enough, or that it was the only or the overriding source of acceptable evidence. Sentiment and conscience are needed to complete the picture of what should count as reasonable opinion, and in this broader sense are not opposed to reason.

Revealed religion and the model of Jesus

Rousseau's criticism of revealed religion is already implicit in the methodology of the first half of the 'Profession', in which he advocates relying on one's own resources rather than on external sources of knowledge – including not only the intellectually dishonest *philosophes* but also the disingenuous Catholic Church. In the second half he is more explicit in his rejection.

Throughout the second half, the priest qualifies his rejection of revealed religion. In the final section of the extract called 'Revealed religion and the model of Jesus', for example, he sees in Jesus a figure to follow, admire and learn from. The priest makes this judgement not because he trusts priests but because he consults his heart, which tells him to see Jesus and not Socrates as a model. For this reason, his endorsement of Jesus cannot really be classified as the adoption of a revelatory perspective.

In making this comparison between the two men, Rousseau is mocking those such as Diderot who attempted to adopt Socrates as a secular alternative to Jesus. Socrates was a slave not to some higher authority but to reason, making him a prime candidate for Enlightenment thinkers' admiration. The two also had similar deaths. Jesus was sentenced to death for what he preached; Socrates was sentenced to death for 'corrupting the youth' – that is, teaching them to value reason over mere opinion. Jesus had an opportunity to avoid death by not entering Jerusalem; Socrates could have fled Athens and lived in exile. Jesus accepted his death as a means of bringing salvation to those who carried out the killing, i.e. humanity, whose form he had taken on. Socrates chose to remain bound by the laws of the society that had made him, drinking the prescribed hemlock rather than fleeing in an act of disrespect.

EXERCISE   'Revealed religion and the model of Jesus' is more straightforward than the rest of the 'Profession', but reading it is *optional* save for pp.58–9, which you should now read. (The extract as a whole contains Rousseau's grounds for scepticism about Catholicism and about organized religion in general. Among them are his claims that there is no principle for choosing between the many organized religions on offer; that reports of miracles cannot be trusted; and that God would not resort to human mediators in communicating with us, his creation. Several of his criticisms of organized religion are taken up by Sade, as you will see.)

Read the assigned segment and study Plates 5.2 and 5.3 and their associated boxed captions here. In what ways is Jesus more worthy of our reverence than Socrates, according to Rousseau?

---

*See Plates 5.2 and 5.3 in the Illustrations Book (*The Death of Socrates *by Jacques-Louis David and* Christ on the Cross with the Magdalen, the Virgin Mary, and Saint John the Evangelist *by Eustache le Sueur), which relate to the comments below.*

These two paintings reflect contrasts in the standard characterizations of Socrates and Jesus respectively. In the crucifixion scene, the linearity of the work is vertical, upwards towards heaven. Socrates is also pointing upwards, also referring to an afterlife, but by contrast the main axis is horizontal and is formed by human bodies. This brings to mind the supposedly egalitarian aspect of human reason – reason was not held to be distributed according to social rank, and Socrates was reason's most famous advocate – to contrast with the essentially hierarchical and submissive requirements of faith.

There is also a difference in demeanour between the respective main characters. Socrates is a leader and chastizes the others for their failure to follow him in refusing to succumb to irrationality. (Socrates' wife Xanthippe, in particular, has been banished to another room for weeping at his determination to drink the hemlock poison. This aspect of the proceedings, reported in Plato's dialogue Phaedo*, would have chimed with eighteenth-century doubts about the rationality of women. Women were seen as primarily emotional beings, notoriously so in Book V of Rousseau's* Émile*.) But where Socrates is demanding respect, Christ's demeanour and posture invite pity.*

DISCUSSION   Jesus lacked Socrates' ostentation; he possessed majesty and gentleness where the philosopher was pompous and ambitious; Jesus suffered in ways that Socrates did not, the latter dying a 'sweet' and 'painless' death, and like Hume in exchanging quips with his friends (here Rousseau is repeating Plato's factual error in describing hemlock poisoning as painless); Jesus had a 'high' and 'simple' wisdom besides which Socrates' mere intelligence looks shallow; where Socrates succeeded in describing the good life, inspired by the example of others, Jesus lived it like no other around him; and because the facts of Jesus' death are supposedly better corroborated than are those of Socrates' death, he is more plausible as an object of reverence.

Ironically, Hume glowingly compares Rousseau to Socrates in a letter to Blair shortly after the two philosophers met (quoted in Mossner, 1980, p.512):

> I think Rousseau in many things very much resembles Socrates: the Philosopher of Geneva seems only to have more genius than he of Athens, who never wrote anything [i.e. since all we have are Plato's record of his conversations], and less sociableness and temper. Both of them were of very amorous complexions.

Rousseau's impassioned riposte to attempts to use Socrates to usurp Christ is targeted at the narrow and spiritless existence purportedly led by the majority of the *philosophes*, who are said to 'sow dispiriting doctrines in men's hearts under the pretext of explaining nature' (p.59).

Summary

Rousseau's purview was broad. He was, among other things, a novelist, a botanist, a composer, a political theorist, a philosopher, a theologian, an educationalist and a linguist. To focus on one section of one chapter of one book is to risk giving a distorted impression of his significance as a historical figure. One function of the video you viewed earlier was to lessen that risk. But my principal ambition in this unit has been not to give an overview of Rousseau's thinking, but to understand and assess the significance of the 'Profession' in its context. Rousseau gave voice to a form of deism that alienated him not only from the Church but also from many of his Enlightenment peers, including the atheists and agnostics as well as those deists who were uncomfortable with what he elected to regard as legitimate sources of evidence or inspiration. His declaration of faith was as revolutionary for its abandonment of the strictures of empiricism as for its break with traditional religion.

3   Sade's new religion

Our final text is an unusual one for its author. The Marquis de Sade (1740–1814) is better known for his attempts to eroticize violence and blasphemy than for his care and rigour as philosopher. The main use to which he put religion in his writing was as a sexual stimulant that could help his characters, usually violent thugs or cruel authority figures, achieve orgasm. The following passage from his novel *Juliette* is typical:

> Saint-Fond's discharge was brilliant, audacious, unrestrained; he pronounced the most energetic and impetuous blasphemies with a very loud voice; his emissions were considerable, his sperm was boiling, thick and savoury, his ecstasy strenuous, his convulsions violent, his delirium extreme.

> (Trans. and quoted in Plessix Gray, 1999, p.196)

Sade's insistence, in real life rather than just in his writing, on the erotic potential of blasphemy was what first brought him to the attention of the law.

But Sade did have a philosophical vision, and took it to vindicate these better-known aspects of his writing. The main message of his novels is that sensual pleasure is all that matters, and true sensual pleasure can take a violent form. This message is grounded in his claim that we are a part of nature, so it is nature that we ought to worship rather than any transcendent being.

Having a philosophical vision is not enough if it is an unreasonable vision, and Sade offered a defence of his. This required two things. First, he needed to undermine the traditional Christian conception of what matters, which is so opposed to sensual pleasure. This is his main agenda in the *Dialogue between a Priest and a Dying Man*, the final reading for these units. Second, he must defend his alternative religion. He undertakes some of this task in the *Dialogue*, but a broader discussion can be found in the audio recording that accompanies these units.

The *Dialogue* is considerably more sober than *Juliette*. Finished while Sade was incarcerated in the royal prison at Vincennes (Figure 5.3) just outside Paris, it describes an imagined exchange between a dying atheist and a priest who has come to administer the last rites. It ends with an orgy, but not one that is described in detail. Before this the dying man peddles a curious mixture of traditional anti-religious reasoning, venomous asides and an alternative sensualist credo, all designed to undermine the credibility of the priest's doctrines. Your main aim when working through the *Dialogue* should be to consolidate the appreciation you have built up of the nature of religious debate at the time.

Figure 5.3   Château de Vincennes, the royal prison, built fourteenth century. Photo: © Harald A. Jahn, Viennaslide Photoagency/CORBIS.

The Dialogue between a Priest and a Dying Man *was, like most of Sade's work, written in prison. Some have taken this to explain certain features of his writing style. A number fixation peculiar to some long-term prisoners shows up in the precision and frequent repetitiveness of his novels; this creates a sense of casualness and tedium that sits oddly with the extremity of what they depict. A discussion of the impact of prison and of the significance of repetition is found in Audio 2.*

EXERCISE   Now, or at some point before reaching the end of the units, read the AV Notes for, and then listen to, Audio 2, tracks 22–5: *The Marquis de Sade: Matter, Revolution and Vice.* As well as considering what I referred to as Sade's alternative religion, the recording compares Sade's libertinism with that of Don Giovanni and considers the relation between his violent and abusive vision and the French Revolution he experienced at first hand. It opens with a performance by actors of the opening of the *Dialogue between a Priest and a Dying Man* (Anthology I, p.61).

The *Dialogue*

The *Dialogue* begins with a dying man repenting for his human weakness and frailty after being requested to do so by a priest. After this promising beginning for the priest, things spiral quickly out of control.

The priest had meant weakness in succumbing to temptations of the flesh; the dying man clarifies that he regrets his weakness in not giving in far more thoroughly to these temptations. Elaborating, the dying man unveils his alternative credo (Anthology I, p.61):

> I repent only that I never sufficiently acknowledged the omnipotence of Nature and my remorse is direct solely against the modest use I made of those faculties, criminal in your eyes but perfectly straightforward in mine, which she gave me to use in her service. I did at times resist her, and am heartily sorry for it. I was blinded by the absurdity of your doctrine to which I resorted to fight the violence of desires planted in me by a power more divinely inspired by far, and I now repent of having done so. I picked only flowers when I could have gathered in a much greater harvest of ripe fruits.

Sade's other work is heavy with the 'ripe fruit' the dying man has in mind here: relatively speaking, the quotation above from *Juliette* is innocuous.

EXERCISE   Read the *Dialogue between a Priest and a Dying Man* up to the dying man's contribution ending '... no other to me' (p.61). How does Sade's style compare to that of the other readings for Units 4 and 5?

DISCUSSION   Sade's undertone of hostility to religious faith is unremitting. It is more pronounced, cruel and joyous even than anything found in Hume. The *Dialogue* lacks some of the sophistication of the pieces by Hume and Rousseau, but compensates in its directness.

Sade presents his case using the dialogue form rather than as a dissertation. Dialogues had become popular among Enlightenment writers (including Hume in his *Dialogues Concerning Natural Religion*) because they harked back to the classical age, and in particular to the Socratic dialogues of Plato. A dialogue supposedly showed how rational debate could drive a conversation to a reasonable conclusion. This wish to appear obedient only to reason is one factor in Sade's choice of the dialogue form. (Sade is not an irrationalist and is explicit on this: 'All other answers are the handiwork of pride, but mine is the product of reason', p.68.) But another is his fondness for theatricality. His less philosophical work is more often than not built into a dramatic framework, and he wrote and produced many of his own plays – most famously in the insane asylum at Charenton, with inmates playing the parts.

The priest, realizing that this is going to be an awkward ministration, endeavours to engage the man, now his opponent, in a theological debate. Perhaps he feels he will be on safe territory here, having the advantage of a seminary education. It is no surprise – given the identity of the author of the dialogue – that the dying man outmanoeuvres him at every turn. Much of the dialogue jumps quickly and freely between debates that you have come across already, such as the *argument from design*, the *cosmological argument* and the *problem of evil*. You may wish to quickly remind yourself of the content of these terms by looking at the glossary entries.

The priest's opening gambit is to diagnose Sade's mistake in worshipping nature instead of God. Sade, he says, sees properties in the created world (nature) that in truth belong to its creator (God). But in the course of laying out his objection, the priest invokes the Christian orthodoxy that nature is somehow 'fallen' or 'corrupt'. Sade jumps in with a query: if nature is so corrupt, how can it be God's creation? Sade is presenting the priest with a theological puzzle we have come across several times already: the problem of evil. If, as Christians maintain, God were all-powerful and benign, he would not have created a corrupt and evil world.

The priest's reply is the same as that deployed by Rousseau: evil exists, says the priest, because God saw fit to give humans free will. The evil that exists in the world is of humanity's making, not God's. The reason God saw fit to give humans free will is that in doing so he would give them the opportunity to do good.

The dying man is unconvinced by this reply. If humans are God's creation and they are disposed to bring evil into the world, then in effect it is God who is bringing evil into the world. Moreover, given God's supposed omniscience, he must have been fully able to predict that humans *would* bring evil rather than goodness into the world.

The priest falls back on mysticism (p.62): 'Who can comprehend the vast and infinite purpose which God has for man?' Aware that this may come across as something of a cop-out, he points out that our ignorance of God is unsurprising given how ignorant we are even of the natural ('visible') world.

The dying man reacts to this mysticism by asserting that we are *not* ignorant of the natural world. By divorcing investigations of the natural world from theological considerations – as the new sciences had begun to do – the natural world has finally become comprehensible. The only way to recognize this is to stop seeking a deeper underlying explanation of the behaviour of the natural world, an explanation that invokes something beyond nature (i.e. God). It is reasonable to reject this demand, Sade claims; and once we do so, God becomes unnecessary.

Sade's reasoning here echoes Hume's response to the cosmological argument in his *Dialogues Concerning Natural Religion*. Hume claims in that work that the laws of nature are explanation enough of the workings of the natural universe; we do not need to appeal to something beyond nature to explain the laws themselves. Once we recognize this, God becomes superfluous to explanatory requirements. As the dying man puts it later: 'Nature is ... sufficient unto herself' (p.63). And in any case, invoking God as the explanation of the laws of nature is no help since God himself is no less mysterious, no less in need of explanation, than these laws.

The priest calls the dying man a miserable sinner and prepares to bail from the conversation, which he regards as a lost cause. But the dying man is beginning to enjoy himself and so detains the priest. He explains that it is not that he is *refusing* to believe in God, but that he is *unable* to believe in God. To believe in something, one must be able to 'understand' it, and since he does not 'understand' religious doctrine, he is unable to believe in it.

This is an unusual claim and deserves scrutiny. Sade may be borrowing from John Locke's influential 'A letter concerning toleration' (1689). Locke argues that there is no point in torturing religious dissidents if the aim in doing so is to make these dissidents change their opinions. Opinions can be changed by reasoned persuasion and the presentation of good evidence, but physical force can only ever make people *pretend* to have changed their mind. No torturer could make us believe that, for example, we have two heads; we can't make ourselves believe such things even when we want to. Only reasonable evidence for an opinion can make us adopt it. The dying man is making a similar point: even if he wanted to change his beliefs into Christian ones, he would be unable to do so without suitable evidence. And not only does he lack decent evidence, the priest has just admitted that God is an infinite being beyond our capacity to comprehend. Christian doctrine is therefore both groundless *and* nonsensical.

Sade is making a pre-emptive strike against those who say we should give up on attempts to find evidence for religious doctrine and fall back on pure faith. Faith, conceived of as groundless belief, is not something humans are capable of. Or at least, it is not something he, as a reasonable person, is capable of.

EXERCISE   Read from 'To what a pass ...' on p.61 up to the end of the dying man's long contribution on p.64 ('... and her needs'). More is going on in this long contribution than the criticism of faith noted above. The dying man expresses a commitment to empiricism, and he repeats his commitment to nature as a replacement for God. Find a sentence expressing each of these commitments.

DISCUSSION   There are others you could have chosen, but the following would do:

Empiricism: 'I am convinced only by evidence, and evidence is provided by my senses alone' (p.63). *Nature worship:* '[S]ince Nature needs vice as much as she needs virtue, she directed me towards the first when she found it expedient, and when she had need of the second, she filled me with the appropriate desires to which I surrendered equally promptly' (p.64).

The priest seizes his moment when he hears the dying man talk of submitting to what is necessary. He treats this, tenuously, as an excuse to introduce the argument from design. In truth, of course, it is Sade putting words into his hapless character's mouth. And so predictably enough, the dying man makes the priest look dimwitted.

The priest says that only by relying on the assumption of a supremely wise being could we explain the order and 'necessity' – i.e. law-like behaviour – we see throughout nature. To this the dying man gives an example of a necessity – a law of nature – that has no intelligence lying behind it. Whenever a match touches gunpowder, an explosion ensues. There is no intelligence at work here, just chemicals. This shows that order and necessity can exist without hidden intelligence, and so it is contrary to an assumption at the heart of the argument from design.

The dying man does not rely on this example alone. Again echoing Hume, he says that appealing to intelligence to explain harmony is unnecessary and unhelpful. It is unnecessary because laws of nature do not need any further explanation: 'natural effects must have natural causes'. It is unhelpful because God 'would require a good deal of explaining' himself. In sum, God 'serves no useful purpose' (p.64). This dialogue was written some 70 years before Darwin's *Origin of Species*. We commonly assume that the only explanation of design in plants and animals available before this involved an appeal to the deity. So it is interesting to see how dissatisfied some were with religious explanations of natural order well before Darwin came up with his alternative.

The priest is, by now, desperate to escape, but the dying man, despite expressing a wish to be left in peace earlier on, is quite worked up and becomes steadily more obnoxious. So far he has been criticizing deist arguments. In a shift of emphasis he targets revealed religion, and specifically Christian religion.

European society during the eighteenth century had been attempting to come to terms with exposure to cultures other than its own. Reaction varied from distortion and rejection to sympathetic absorption. Nowhere was the significance of non-European cultures more transparent than in the field of religion. The Christian establishment suddenly needed an answer to the question: why is God, as conceived of by Christians, any more worthy of devotion than, say, an Islamic God? Embracing all religions was not an option, since they made mutually inconsistent claims. The dying man exploits the difficulty by listing several hugely different religions. Given their existence, along with that of different

Christian denominations, the choice of Roman Catholicism seems an arbitrary one.

The priest, condemned to lose every argument in the dialogue, thinks he can answer this conundrum with ease. He offers two reasons for regarding Christianity as unique and preferable. His first turns on an appeal to Christ's miracles.

The dying man dismisses these miracles as the work of 'the most transparent of swindlers and the most tiresome of humbugs' (p.65). After a sharp intake of breath from the priest, the dying man continues with a long discussion of the legitimacy that should be accorded to scriptural testimony of strange happenings. This section reiterates arguments found in Hume's chapter, 'On miracles', mentioned in Unit 4 above. But more generally it is an attack on the adequacy of divine revelation as a source of evidence. The existence of the supposed revelations – in particular, miracles and prophecies – is said to be as questionable as the thesis supposedly revealed through them. (Sade would perhaps have seen support for this contention in the reports by Rousseau and Hume of their final dinner together; the vast difference between these shows how unwise it can be to rely on isolated accounts of past events.) Even if one opts on balance to accept their legitimacy, the questionability of miracles reflects poorly on any God who has chosen to reveal himself in this manner. Their questionability is evident in, for example, religious differences across the globe.

A second attempt by the priest to say what is uniquely worthy about Christianity is met with what, to anyone sharing sympathies with the priest, is certainly the most offensive passage in the dialogues. Christ died for humanity, says the priest, and this fact sets the Christian deity apart from all others as worthy of our devotion. Sade replies that Jesus deserved to die, that the Romans were right to be firm with this 'seditious influence, an agitator, a bearer of false witness, a scoundrel, a lecher, a showman who performed crude tricks, a wicked and dangerous man' (p.67).

Sade seems to have several ambitions in this passage. For one, he intends without doubt to give offence for the sake of it. For another, he is being consistent with his view that the purported miracles were a sham. But a third function of the claim that the Romans were right to crucify Jesus is that he is implicitly declaring his loyalty to and love of terrestrial rulers – not the Romans in his case but Louis XVI. Sade was at the time locked in the Bastille under an order from the king (solicited by Sade's mother-in-law). Some grovelling in such circumstances is understandable. Moreover, though it was possible under Louis XVI to get away with anonymously publishing risqué anti-Christian sentiments, sedition against the Crown was ruthlessly put down. Sade's implicit endorsement of the monarchy may even have been heartfelt. In the run-up to the Revolution, many intellectuals looked to the Crown as a welcome source of political stability (Coward, 1992, p.273).

EXERCISE   Read from the priest's 'And so everything ...' on p.64 up to the end of the dying man's response ('... deserve to live', p.67). Unless you are interested in miracles, skip from the dying man's 'Quite so ...' (p.65) to the end of his long disputation ('... due process of law', p.67). What is the relevance of diverse forms of religion to this discussion between the priest and the dying man?

DISCUSSION   The dying man claims that the choice of the Roman Catholic form of Christianity, or of Christianity rather than some other world religion, is an arbitrary one.

The priest attempts to steer the conversation towards the afterlife, asking what expectations the dying man has if not an eternity of inconceivable pain and misery. Some of this territory was covered in Hume's essay, 'Of the immortality of the soul'.

In the commentary to Figure 4.5 (p.189) we saw how filial piety – survival in one's children – was advanced by some as an afterlife stripped of religious connotations. Here Sade offers a rather different form of surrogate post-death existence. In common with many thinkers at the time and since, Sade was a materialist: he denied that we have a soul that is distinct from the matter, the stuff, out of which our bodies are made. The dying man takes **materialism** for granted, and suggests that we have an eternal life because our material self survives in the worms that eat us after we die.

It seems unlikely that Sade was offering this as a serious position. Even materialists would have to accept that the state of repair of our bodies is essential to our continued existence. The persistence of our flesh in the flesh of a worm is not the kind of 'survival' many would regard as valuable. Sade is on safer ground in suggesting that all that awaits us is 'nothingness': that is, we do *not* survive.

The dying man also deploys a similar argument to that of Hume against the Christian account of an afterlife of punishment or reward (p.68; compare to section II of Hume's 'Of the immortality of the soul'):

> [W]hy do you believe that I should be rewarded for virtues I possess through no merit of my own, and punished for criminal acts over which I have no control?

I am subject to the laws of nature, the dying man is saying; so it is the laws of nature that should be punished, not me. Since the laws of nature are (allegedly) God's work, it is God and not us who should shoulder the blame for the sins 'we' commit.

The priest replies that we are not subject to the laws of nature since we have free will; he seems to have forgotten that the appeal to free will has already been rejected by the dying man. Without free will, he adds, we would not be responsible for anything; without free will, 'even the greatest crimes' would have to go unpunished. The dying man, says the priest, seems to be actively encouraging crime.

The dying man is anxious to avoid this consequence:

> God forbid that anyone should think that in saying this I seek to give encouragement to crime!
>
> (pp.68–9)

Religion, he implies, seeks to hijack morality, and we should not let it. Morality can be founded on principles that require 'no ... religion or God to appreciate and act upon' (p.69). The main principles he comes up with are (i) the so-called Golden Rule: *do unto others as you would have them do unto you* (or the dying man's variant, which is: *make others as happy as you yourself would be*); (ii) the willing submission to punishment *in this life* for immoral acts we have committed.

After reiterating the principles of his sensualist credo, the dying man invites the priest to indulge his own corrupted nature. The priest takes him up.

EXERCISE   Read the remainder of the essay, from the priest's 'But you do admit ...' on p.67. What is the dying man trying to show with his example of the scaffold on p.68? (Hint: the point of Sade's example is not as clear as one would like, but becomes clearer after rereading the dying man's comment immediately before the priest's claim that we are free to choose.)

DISCUSSION   Sade is using the scaffold example to support his claim that humans lack freedom. Instead, we are the slaves of our natural appetites or immediate desires. Away from the scaffold, criminals will obey their desires to benefit from crime; in the presence of the scaffold, they will never do so because they have an overriding desire not to be hanged. Sade wants to show that we lack freedom because he would thereby undermine the stock response to the problem of evil (see glossary; the problem is alluded to in the essay running up to the appearance of the scaffold example).

EXERCISE   Having read the essay in segments, go back and read it through from the beginning to consolidate your understanding. You should also use this as an opportunity to consolidate your understanding and estimation of the cosmological argument and the argument from design, as well as of the significance of the problem of evil. There are likely to be sections that remain unclear, but don't let this prevent you from getting into the critical habit of asking whether Sade's discussion is a valuable one in those parts that you do find clear.

Hume, Rousseau and Sade on nature

All three of our authors are positive about what they call 'nature', but what this positive attitude amounts to differs in each case. This is a term that will crop up over and over in the remainder of the course, which is one reason why it is worth appreciating these differences.

One obvious difference lies in the manner and enthusiasm apparent in their respective endorsements of nature. This difference can perhaps be put down to differences in temperament. Hume alludes all the time to nature but does so in a sober way, especially in comparison with Sade in the closing sections of the dialogue you have just read. Rousseau sits somewhere in between. These differences in expressiveness should not be trivialized, but they are less important than the distinctiveness of what it is that each is claiming in his use of the term 'nature'.

Hume, in common with other figures in the Enlightenment, uses 'nature' largely as a label to describe that which, so he believes, is susceptible to empirical investigation. This may sound slightly odd to us now, but it is a usage that would have been accepted by his contemporaries, and his claim that human beings cannot be understood save as natural entities was also widespread. This is implicit in the title of Hume's main philosophical work – *A Treatise of Human Nature* – as well as in his view that the methods of the natural sciences provided the only viable route to understanding anything at all.

Rousseau did not think humans were solely natural (i.e. material) beings. As we saw (in section 2), he thought of us as capable of active judgement in a way that matter is not, and from this was prepared to conclude that we have a soul which is able to rise above its material prison:

> The ... soul's liberty becomes both its merit and its recompense, and ... it prepares itself an incorruptible happiness in combating its terrestrial passions.

> (Rousseau, 1991, p.292)

Figure 5.4   Jacques de Vaucanson, mechanical duck (and detail), constructed c.1739. Photo: Alfred Chapuis and Edmond Droz, Automata: A Historical and Technological Study, *trans. Alec Reid, B.T. Batsford Ltd, London, 1958.*

In the eighteenth century there was a craze for automata: that is, mechanical models of humans or other living beings. The craze was driven by fascination with the thought that living humans are entirely mechanical or natural entities rather than souls temporarily inhabiting a body.

Although this fascination was shared by the philosophes, *they were supercilious about the automata themselves. Vaucanson, a renowned French engineer, took his duck on tour to demonstrate its capacity to eat, swallow, digest and excrete grain. Voltaire said that 'without the shitting duck, there would be nothing to remind us of the glory of France' (quoted in Wood, 2002, p.25). Vaucanson's duck was destroyed by fire in the nineteenth century, and the attribution of the photographic image is tentative.*

Another difference is that he saw nature as a source of knowledge and inspiration.

Both these features of Rousseau's conception of nature – its capacity to serve as a source of inspiration and knowledge, and the existence of a supernatural soul – are absent from Hume. They are combined by Rousseau in a supposition that natural scenes can trigger in us a sense of the sublime. The Latin word *sublimis* means uplifted or borne aloft through the sky. Confrontation with nature could cause the human soul to do just this, rising above the body. In an earlier draft of *Émile*, the penultimate sentence prior to the 'Profession' (see Figure 5.2 above) is:

> One would have said that nature displayed all its magnificence to our eyes in order to set aside low thoughts in our souls and lift us up to sublime contemplations.
>
> (Rousseau, 1991, p.490 n.41)

Sade took Rousseau's transfiguration of nature further in two respects. Nature for Sade was not merely a source of knowledge and inspiration; it was also something to be worshipped in its own right, a surrogate religion. Rousseau, it is true, often talks with reverence of nature *as if* he is worshipping it, in part because of the linguistic habit of personifying nature. But unlike Sade, Rousseau most definitely did not identify nature as the primary object of veneration, however admirable it is as God's creation.

Sade associates nature with cruelty, pain, suffering, degradation and decay, and not merely with 'virtue': 'Nature's mastery lies precisely in the perfect balance which she maintains between virtue and crime' (*Dialogue*, Anthology I, p.68). He values both associations equally. Rousseau also sees nature as having two aspects, but he venerates the one over the other:

> In meditating on the nature of man, I believed I discovered in it two distinct principles; one of which raised him to the study of eternal truths, to the love of justice and moral beauty, and to the regions of the intellectual world whose contemplation is the wise man's delight; while the other took him basely into himself, subjected him to the empire of the senses and to the passions which are their ministers, and by means of these hindered all that the sentiment of the former inspired in him.
>
> ('Profession', Anthology I, p.41; see also the exercise on p.224 above)

Rousseau sees 'subjection' to the passions as a 'hindrance'; Sade sees our submission to this side of our nature as a form of liberation:

> I was created by Nature with the keenest appetites and the strongest of passions and was put on this earth with the sole purpose of placating both by surrendering to them. They are components of my created self and are no more than mechanical parts necessary to the functioning of Nature's basic purposes.
>
> (*Dialogue*, Anthology I, p.61)

Sade's celebration of nature in all its aspects delivers a justification of sorts for the scenes of torment and lust that occupy the bulk of his writings.

See Plate 5.4 in the Illustrations Book (Saturn Devouring One of his Sons *by Francisco de Goya), which relates to the comment below.*

Goya's painting expresses nature's capacity for violence as well as any words of Sade. It was painted later than the period we are considering, and on some interpretations looks back to the French Revolution, with Saturn, a god associated with nature as well as with lack of restraint, representing the Revolution itself, and his son representing the Enlightenment. The Revolution championed the ideas of the Enlightenment as a father champions his son, but 'devoured' it in the sense that these ideas were often either distorted or applied with an extremity and force that was never originally intended. An example of distortion was the removal of Rousseau's remains to the Pantheon, a large classical building in Paris designed to pay homage to the forebears of the Revolution, disregarding Rousseau's own expressed wishes to remain on the Isle of Poplars (see Figure 5.5) forever. An example of force is the guillotining of the renowned scientist Lavoisier for serving as a part-time tax collector, notwithstanding his many important contributions to knowledge, such as discovering oxygen and laying the groundwork for modern chemistry.

Figure 5.5   Jean Michel Moreau, The Tomb of Jean-Jacques Rousseau, *1778, Bibliothèque Nationale de France, Paris.*

The Ermenonville gardens, just outside Paris, where Rousseau was entombed on the Isle of Poplars upon his death in 1778, became a site of pilgrimage for admirers of Rousseau and also helped to promote the cult of nature prefigured in his writings (see Video 1, band 3, on Rousseau).

4   Conclusion to the units

When evaluating religious debates of the kind we have been looking at, there is no getting around the need to go into details. Purported proofs of God's existence, solutions to the problem of evil, demonstrations of an afterlife and so forth all require careful examination before any general conclusions can reasonably be drawn. But stepping back from these details, it is possible to discern at least three broader developments at work in the writing we have been looking at.

The first is a shift in what is taken as good evidence for holding an opinion. Enlightenment thinkers such as Locke, Hume and most of the *philosophes* were empiricists. Impressed by advances in scientific understanding of the natural world occurring in their time, they came to think that *all* opinion should, like scientific opinion, be grounded in sensory experience. Rousseau (though not Sade) thought that it was sometimes reasonable to hold opinions that weren't grounded merely in sensory experience. Sense was joined by sensibility – variously called 'the faculty of sentiment', 'emotional judgement', 'inner sense' and so on – as a further source of evidence concerning matters of fact. Sensibility could reveal to us God's true nature. Strength of conviction, too, was regarded by him as an indicator of truth.

The second shift concerns changing conceptions of nature. These changes were detailed in the previous section. 'Nature' in the middle of the century was generally used as a label for that which is susceptible to investigation by the natural sciences. Judgements concerning the supernatural were automatically regarded as suspect by most empiricists because these would, by definition, be non-scientific. Stronger conceptions of nature involved its capacity to function as a source of inspiration and knowledge, and even as an object of reverence or worship. Though such conceptions were not unknown earlier on, they gained in currency as the century advanced.

A third trend has not played as central a role in our discussion as the first two, but is evident both in the writings we have studied and in the personalities of the authors: the move towards individualism. Hume, it is true, was a singular man, but Rousseau and Sade make him seem quite ordinary. The first half of the eighteenth century had already seen a growing and more open rejection of ecclesiastic and aristocratic authority. As the nineteenth century approached, society itself came to be seen by many as a fetter on individual expression, especially when contrasted with the inspirational power of nature. One manifestation of this growing celebration of individualism was the cult that grew up around Rousseau's memory, leading to his tomb at Ermenonville becoming a kind of shrine. A later one was the cult of Napoleon, which we will consider in the next block after having looked at the revolution that engulfed France in 1789.

References (Units 4 and 5)

Boswell, J. (1971) *Boswell in Extremes: The Private Papers of James Boswell, 1776–1778*, ed. C. McC. Weis and F.A. Pottle, London, Heinemann.

Boswell, J. (1986) *The Life of Samuel Johnson*, ed. C. Hibbert, Harmondsworth, Penguin (first published 1791).

Butlin, M. (1983) *William Blake*, London, Tate Gallery.

Clayton, G. (1812) *The Dreadful Sin of Suicide: A Sermon*, London, Black, Parry and Kingsbury.

Coward, D. (1992) 'Notes' to his edition of Sade's *The Misfortunes of Virtue and Other Early Tales*, Oxford, Oxford University Press.

Dufour, T. and Plan, P.-P. (eds) (1924–34) *Jean-Jacques Rousseau: Correspondance Générale*, 20 vols, Paris.

Fontaine, J. de la (1946) 'La mort et le bûcheron', in *Fables: Édition Complete*, London, Commodore Press.

Hampson, N. (1968) *The Enlightenment*, Harmondsworth, Penguin.

Horne, G. (1806) *Letters on Infidelity. The Second Edition. To which is prefixed a Letter to Dr Adam Smith*, Oxford, N. Bliss.

Hume, D. (1777) *The Life of David Hume, Esq., Written by Himself*, London, Strahan & Cadell.

Hume, D. (1947) *Dialogues Concerning Natural Religion*, ed. N.K. Smith, London, Collier Macmillan (written *c*.1750 and first published 1779).

Hume, D. (1962) 'My own life', in A. Flew (ed.) *David Hume on Human Nature and Understanding*, London, Collier Macmillan.

Hume, D. (1975) *Enquiries Concerning Human Understanding and Concerning the Principles of Morals*, ed. L.A. Selby-Bigge and P.H. Nidditch, 3rd edn, Oxford, Clarendon Press (first published 1748, 1751).

Hume, D. (1978) *A Treatise of Human Nature*, ed. L.A. Selby-Bigge and P.H. Nidditch, 2nd edn, Oxford, Clarendon Press (first published 1739).

Locke, J. (1975) *An Essay Concerning Human Understanding*, ed. P.H. Nidditch, Oxford, Clarendon Press.

Locke, J. (1991) 'A letter concerning toleration', in J. Horton and S. Mendus (eds) *John Locke: 'A Letter Conerning Toleration' in Focus*, London and New York, Routledge (first published 1689).

Moore, C. (1790) *A Full Inquiry into the Subject of Suicide*, London.

Mossner, E.C. (1980) *The Life of David Hume*, 2nd edn, Oxford, Oxford University Press.

Mossner, E.C. and Ross, I.S. (eds) (1987) *The Correspondence of Adam Smith*, Oxford, Oxford University Press.

Mure, W. (ed.) (1854) *Caldwell Papers*, Glasgow, Maitland Club.

Pinsky, R. (trans.) (1994) *The Inferno of Dante*, New York, Farrar, Straus and Giroux.

Plessix Gray, F. du (1999) *At Home with the Marquis de Sade*, London, Chatto & Windus.

Rousseau, J.-J. (1780) *Rousseau, juge de Jean Jacques: dialogues – premier dialogue*, Lichfield, J. Jackson.

Rousseau, J.-J. (1979) *Reveries of the Solitary Walker*, trans. P. France, Harmondsworth, Penguin (first published 1782).

Rousseau, J.-J. (1991) *Émile, or, On Education*, trans. and ed. Allan Bloom, Harmondsworth, Penguin, 1990 (first published 1762).

Scott, W.R. (1937) *Adam Smith as Student and Professor*, Glasgow, Jackson, Son & Co.

Smith, Adam (1982) *An Inquiry into the Nature and Causes of the Wealth of Nations*, Harmondsworth, Penguin (first published 1776).

Warburton, N. (2002) 'Art and illusion', *The Philosopher's Magazine*, 19, pp.40–2.

Wain, J. (ed.) (1990) *The Journals of James Boswell 1762–1795* (selections), London, Mandarin.

Wood, Gaby (2002) *Living Dolls: A Magical History of the Quest for Mechanical Life*, London, Faber.

Further reading (Units 4 and 5)

Hume, D. (1975) 'On miracles', in *Enquiries Concerning Human Understanding and Concerning the Principles of Morals*, ed. L.A. Selby-Bigge and P.H. Nidditch, 3rd edn, Oxford, Clarendon Press (first published 1748).

Rousseau, Jean-Jacques (1979) *Reveries of the Solitary Walker*, trans. P. France, Harmondsworth, Penguin (first published 1782).

Sade, Donatien Alphonse François, the Marquis de (1965) *Philosophy in the Bedroom*, trans. R. Seaver and A. Wainhouse, New York, Grove Press (first published 1795). (Warning: this could cause considerable offence or discomfort to some readers.)

Unit 6
The French Revolution

Prepared for the course team by Antony Lentin

Contents

Study components

Weeks of study	Supplementary material	Audio-visual	Anthologies and set books
1	AV Notes Illustrations Book	Audio 3	Anthology I

Objectives

By the end of your work on Unit 6 you should have:

- an understanding of the main events of the French Revolution 1789–99 and its significance in the shift in European culture from Enlightenment to Romanticism;

- an enhanced appreciation of the French Revolution and its significance through exposure to selected contemporary texts (documents and illustrations of the period).

1   Introduction

Unit 6 differs from the other units in this block and indeed in the course. While it makes reference to a variety of texts, it is not strictly speaking text-based in the sense that Units 2 and 3 are based on *Don Giovanni* and Units 4 and 5 on Hume, Rousseau and Sade.

The main aim of this unit is to provide basic historical background on the French Revolution, which marked a watershed in the history and culture of the period 1780–1830. An understanding of what happened in the ten years from 1789 to 1799 will enable you to appreciate some of the main themes of the course against the background of that watershed. The documents and illustrations associated with it are there to illustrate and bring out the points made. The first exercise is preceded by an extended preamble designed to facilitate your reading and understanding of the first document. This should in turn point a way towards engaging with other documents and illustrations associated with the unit. While you should attempt all the exercises, it is not essential to study all the documents and illustrations referred to. When TMAs and exam questions relate to a particular range of documents and/or illustrations, you will be clearly alerted to that range in advance.

The French Revolution, or at least its impact on France and Europe, lies at the heart of the cultural shift from Enlightenment to Romanticism. It not only marked a decisive break in the history of France and Europe, but also accelerated intellectual, cultural and psychological change. It opened up new horizons and possibilities. Indeed, while there remain much controversy and scepticism as to the real extent of underlying change in the social and economic structure of France, scholars generally agree that the Revolution brought a widening of expectations and imaginative awareness: a belief, inherited from the Enlightenment, in the possibility of progress, as well as a conviction that state and society could be reconstituted with a view to realizing social and individual aspirations and human happiness generally. As it degenerated into violence and bloodshed, however, the Revolution also provoked scepticism and pessimism about progress and human nature. The two basic types of modern political outlook, progressive and conservative, date from this experience. Which, if any, of these sets of beliefs was true is not at issue here. What matters is that the Revolution gave rise to them and gave them lasting life.

Enlightenment, liberty and revolution

It is not possible in one unit to do justice to the complexity of the French Revolution, whose significance preoccupied contemporaries and has continued to engage historians ever since. Suffice it to say that it was, and was considered by those who lived through it to be, the most momentous turning-point in modern history thus far, 'a traumatic convulsion' (Doyle, 2001, p.2) that made its impact on the way people lived and thought across Europe throughout most of the period covered by this course. Its impact and consequences are reflected in most, perhaps all, of the texts which you will go on to study in later units. The revolutionaries themselves recognized the break with the past by naming the social and political order before 1789 the 'Old Regime' (*ancien régime*).

The Revolution aroused the deepest passions, from ardent enthusiasm to inveterate hostility. Some of its enemies attributed it to a conspiracy hatched by freemasons or even by leading figures of the Enlightenment. Catherine the Great of Russia, once the darling of two of those leading figures, Voltaire and Diderot, was by 1794 voicing the suspicion 'that the aim of the *philosophes* was to overturn all thrones, and that the *Encyclopédie* was written with no other end in view than to destroy all kings and all religions' (Lentin, 1985, p.269). This was a wild exaggeration, but it illustrates the shock caused by the Revolution, and it raises the important question how far the Revolution was a result of the Enlightenment. Others stress the role of chance and personality in the Revolution (for example, the weakness or folly of the French king and queen, the fanaticism of the Jacobins) and the pressure of events and forces (mass violence, civil war, invasion) which took on a momentum of their own, often overwhelming and sometimes destroying the revolutionaries themselves. This unit condenses a sequence of tumultuous happenings in France and Europe in the decade 1789–99 (and a bewildering succession of political constitutions and legislative acts), in order to focus on the Revolution's more important stages or turning-points and their significance.

The main target of the Revolution was the political and social privilege entrenched under the Old Regime. Power in Europe rested, as it had for centuries, with a privileged nobility. Social status and political influence depended on birth, hereditary title to land or office (which could also be purchased), and unearned income derived from land and the right to peasants' contributions in cash, kind or labour. In France, in the generation before the Revolution, almost every one of the king's ministers, provincial governors and bishops was a nobleman.

You may remember from Mozart's *Don Giovanni* the rousing (and also ambiguous and potentially subversive) refrain, '*Viva la libertà!*' (long live liberty!)[35] The watchword 'liberty' sums up the main slogan and aspiration of the Revolution: liberation from political despotism, social exclusion and discrimination. The second watchword, closely related to 'liberty', was 'equality'. Both 'liberty' and 'equality' were supposed to be inspired by and suffused with a third – 'fraternity' or brotherly love. The

---

[35] You may also remember that in the version of *Don Giovanni* performed at Vienna, this was changed to the less controversial *Viva la società* (long live society).

historian François Furet insists that the appeal of liberty, equality and fraternity, which proved so infectious, stemmed from what he calls the Revolution's 'deepest motivating force: hatred of the aristocracy' (Furet, 1996, p.51). Be that as it may, on the eve of the Revolution, 'in all countries the distinction between the noble or gentleman and the rest of the population was the cardinal fact of social life' (Hampson, 1969, p.55).

2   Death of the Old Regime

The immediate cause of the Revolution was that the French monarchy faced imminent bankruptcy. (This was partly because of the enormous sums it had spent assisting the American Revolution between 1778 and 1781 in order to discomfort the traditional enemy, Britain.) Neither nobility nor clergy paid direct tax. Without the consent of the established orders of society to a reorganization of the tax burden so as to restore its finances, the government could no longer function. Successive ministers tried to win over influential sections of the nobility to various reform proposals, with inconclusive results. In 1788 the helpless King Louis XVI was advised to turn for help to the nation as a whole in the shape of its representatives duly elected and convened in ancient form: the **Estates-General**.

On 5 May 1789, this body was therefore assembled at Versailles for the first time since 1614. It consisted of elected representatives of the three orders or estates of the realm: clergy, nobility and the **Third Estate**, or commoners, the remaining 95 per cent of the population. The representatives of the Third Estate were mainly officials, lawyers, landowners and merchants. If the precedent of 1614 was followed, each of the orders would assemble separately, and if the clergy and nobility voted as estates, they could outvote the Third Estate by two to one. In 1789, however, 'nobody knew what the Estates-General would do ... There was a complete vacuum of power. The French Revolution was the process by which this vacuum was filled' (Doyle, 2001, p.36).

The Third Estate as the voice of the nation

Emmanuel-Joseph Sieyès (1748–1836) trained as a priest and became assistant to a bishop. He had no religious vocation, however, and his fame arose as the author of a highly influential pamphlet, *What is the Third Estate?* (Anthology I, pp.70–5), published in January 1789, on the strength of which Sieyès was elected a deputy to the Estates-General. Four editions or 30,000 copies of the book came out within months of its appearance, at a time of heightened consciousness that great changes were afoot. What is Sieyès's argument, how does he present it, and what is the significance of his book?

Sample analysis and discussion of 'What is the Third Estate?'

Let us take a closer look at part of this document before attempting the exercise below. This preamble should help you to relate to similar exercises in this unit and elsewhere (and to prepare for a TMA or exam question). The document is quite long, by far the longest one associated with this unit; but you should not find it difficult to read it through fairly quickly and to extract its main points, to grasp Sieyès's 'message', and to note how he conveyed it. *After you have read it through once, reread it from the beginning up to 'a nation within a nation' (p.71).*

The fact of its immediate success and large print run already suggests that *What is the Third Estate?* was crisply written, had a clear and timely message, and was readily and immediately understood and appreciated. Sieyès is methodical, concise and to the point. He tells us straightaway that 'we have three questions to ask ourselves' about the Third Estate. He sets out those three questions in numerical order. To each question he gives a one-word answer. He then states, 'We shall see if these are the right answers', and undertakes to provide 'the supporting evidence'.

This down-to-earth, systematic approach is very much in the style and spirit of the *Encyclopédie* in its clarity of presentation, its promise of logical argument based on supporting evidence, and its conclusions critical of existing institutions. Sieyès does not express his conclusions as views personal to himself but as demonstrable statements of objective *fact* (set out under points 4, 5 and 6).

In the next paragraph he asks, 'What is a nation?', and proceeds to give a definition. Again, his method and his objective are clear and logical. You will note, however, that this time he does not offer any supporting evidence for his statement. Why not? Presumably, he believed that his definition was self-evident and would be found so by his readers, as indeed it was.

Sieyès's basic idea of a nation was not new. It drew on Enlightenment concepts familiar to any educated reader. Diderot, in his article 'Political authority' published in the *Encyclopédie* in 1751, discussed terms and ideas which by 1789 had become the staple of political thought. He argued that sovereignty, or ultimate political power in a state, derives not from the monarch but from the 'people' or 'nation', that it must be exercised in their interest and for their benefit, that it should be controlled and circumscribed by laws, and that the ruler's tenure of office is in the nature of a trust exercised for the people's benefit and with their consent, underpinned by an implicit agreement or 'social contract' (Gendzier, 1967, pp.185–8).[36]

[handwritten margin note: Good starting point — See Diderot Political authority in the Encyclopédie]

[36] This reference to the *Encyclopédie* is included here in order to enhance your understanding of the background to Sieyès's book. When attempting an exercise or assignment, you are expected to draw on relevant texts and information provided in the course, and you will often be referred to them for guidance. You are not expected to draw on evidence not provided in the course.

Against this familiar background, Sieyès takes a further easy and logical step by postulating another characteristic of a nation: namely, that it has an elected, *representative* legislative (law-making) assembly. This too follows implicitly from ideas popularized in the *Encyclopédie*, but it received a tremendous additional boost, first from the success of the American Revolution and the summoning of a constitutional convention by the United States in 1787, and now in France by the summoning of the Estates-General. The French people, or nation, were at last to be 'represented' in an assembly or, as it was soon to be called, a **National Assembly**, through which it too would be enabled to express its political will, frame its own laws and shape its own national destiny.

After this definition of a nation, uncontroversial in its Enlightenment borrowings but now suddenly fresh and revolutionary in its immediate relevance in 1789, Sieyès makes a further claim, all the more unexpected because of the equable tone and calm logic employed by him thus far. He suddenly claims that the nobility, by reason of its 'privileges and exemptions', is not part of the nation at all, but 'a nation within a nation'. This, he states rhetorically, 'is only too clear, isn't it'. The reader will take the implicit point (soon to be made explicit) that not only is this indeed the case, but that such a situation is illogical, unjust and wrong, no longer tenable or tolerable. Sieyès's purpose is to isolate and marginalize the nobility in his readers' eyes, and to expose it to their critical censure. In the circumstances of 1789, his message took on startling implications about the respective roles of the nobility and the Third Estate in the Estates-General.

Now go to p.72 of the document (from 'To sum up ...' to '... becoming *something?*', p.73). We see here a reference to another Enlightenment touchstone – 'the rights of man' – and also to the 'petitions' (***cahiers de doléances***) which the representatives at the Estates-General brought with them from their constituents. In invoking 'the rights of man', Sieyès again draws on a common background and strikes a common chord with his readers in his references to the political terminology of the Enlightenment. Again, too, in mentioning the petitions, there is the striking topicality of his comments as the Estates-General assembled to air the nation's grievances.

But Sieyès refers only fleetingly to the rights of man. His main point in this passage relates to something else, though closely related to it: 'equality'. Equality was another emotive catchword derived from the Enlightenment. In his article on 'Natural equality' in the *Encyclopédie* (1755), de Jaucourt states that 'natural equality' is based on 'the constitution of human nature common to all men ... Each person must value and treat other people as so many individuals who are naturally equal to himself' (Gendzier, 1967, p.169).[37] True, de Jaucourt then goes on to say that 'I know too well the necessity of different ranks, grades,

---

[37] See footnote 36.

honours, distinctions, prerogatives, subordinations that must prevail in all governments' (Gendzier, 1967, p.170). De Jaucourt may be being ironic here, or he may be perfectly serious.[38] Be that as it may, Sieyès is certainly serious in his complaint concerning the *inequality* of representation in the Estates-General of the Third Estate in relation to the other two estates (church and nobility). The Third Estate, he says, '*demands* that the number of its representatives be equal to that of the two other orders put together' (emphasis added) (Anthology I, p.73).

EXERCISE   Now read from 'With regard to its *political* rights ...' (p.71) to '... going back in time a bit' (p.71). Briefly (in about 100 words) (i) explain in your own words what Sieyès has to say about the Third Estate and the nobility, and (ii) describe his tone.

DISCUSSION   (i)   Sieyès makes the revolutionary claim that the Third Estate itself constitutes the nation and should be adequately represented; that the nobility is over-privileged, exclusive, unrepresentative of the nation and over-represented in the Estates-General; and that the Estates-General should sit as a single integrated body, not divided into social orders and meeting in separate venues. Sieyès thus raises to the fore 'the quintessential revolutionary idea ... equality' (Furet, 1996, p.45).

(ii)   Sieyès's tone is confident, belligerent, uncompromising and inflammatory. His radical demands on behalf of the Third Estate largely take the form of blunt and open attacks on the nobility as a separate (and self-regarding) estate of the realm.

The significance of Sieyès's pamphlet lay in its 'consciousness-raising'. His defiant radicalism captured the mood of the 648 representatives of the Third Estate and inspired them to thumb their noses at the nobility or 'aristocrats', as he also calls them. (By 1789 and thanks partly to Sieyès, the word 'aristocrat' had become a term of abuse synonymous with undeserved privilege.)

On 17 June the deputies of the Third Estate unilaterally declared the assembly of their own members to be the true representative voice of the French nation: the 'National Assembly'. If the clergy and nobility wanted a voice in shaping the future of France, they must sit in the National Assembly as equals with the Third Estate. The pamphlet was both 'a treatise and a battle-cry' (Furet, 1996, p.48), a justification of and a summons to revolutionary action. On 20 June, finding itself locked out, the Third Estate, calling itself the National Assembly, withdrew to a

---

[38] The use of irony was a means of evading the royal censorship to which the *Encyclopédie* was subject.

nearby indoor tennis court and declared, in the so-called '**tennis-court oath**', that it would not disperse until it had provided France with a new, written constitution. It deliberately and expressly excluded the nobility and clergy as such from the body politic. The National Assembly had seized power in the name of the French nation. The Revolution had begun.

Fall of the Bastille, 14 July 1789

In a similar mood of aggrieved self-righteousness and revolutionary exultation came the fall of the Bastille, the medieval fortress and prison of Paris, on 14 July 1789. A catastrophic harvest in 1788 had provoked food riots in Paris and elsewhere. Louis XVI, alarmed both by this unrest and by the unexpected belligerence of the Third Estate, called troops into Paris to maintain order. It was feared that he also aimed to suppress the National Assembly, which rallied its supporters. The Parisian electors, those qualified to choose the city's representatives to the Estates-General, raised a militia of 48,000 men, the National Guard, to protect the Assembly. Its commander was the liberal-minded Marquis de Lafayette (1757–1834), who had fought as a volunteer with the American revolutionaries. The National Guard was short of arms. On 14 July, having ransacked the Invalides for muskets and cannons, it marched on the Bastille in search of gunpowder. When the governor, de Launay, appeared to offer resistance, it stormed the prison. De Launay and the chief city magistrate were lynched, their heads stuck on pikes and paraded about.

The event seemed to its supporters literally epoch-making. In fact, the Bastille in 1789 only contained eight prisoners (including lunatics and, until the week before its fall, the Marquis de Sade), but it had once briefly housed as state prisoners such leading figures of the Enlightenment as Voltaire and Diderot. Its fall was felt to symbolize the unstoppable might of the Revolution sweeping away the tyranny, oppression and injustice of the past. An English eyewitness reported that the news 'produced an impression on the crowd really indescribable ... such an instantaneous and unanimous emotion of extreme gladness as I should suppose was never before experienced by human beings' (quoted in Hampson, 1975, p.72). The British ambassador agreed: 'The greatest revolution that we know anything of has been effected with ... the loss of very few lives. From this moment we may consider France as a free country; the King a limited [that is, constitutional] monarch and the nobility as reduced to a level with the rest of the nation' (quoted in Townson, 1990, p.34). To Charles James Fox, leader of the English party in opposition, the fall of the Bastille was 'the most glorious event, and the happiest for mankind, that has ever taken place since human affairs have been recorded' (quoted in Rudé, 1966, p.181).

In France, the anniversary of the taking of the Bastille became an annual festival. Its significance as marking the passing of the Old Regime was commonly celebrated (as in the American War of Independence) by planting 'trees of liberty' as symbols of national regeneration. The king was constrained to accept the flag of the Revolution devised by Lafayette, the tricolour (red, white and blue), and to wear its colours on his cockade.

EXERCISE   Now read the second document (letter from Gustav III, absolute ruler of Sweden, August 1789, in Anthology I, p.76). Gustav had just learned of the event from his ambassador in Paris. Briefly state what the letter tells us (i) about the storming of the Bastille and (ii) about Gustav's reaction to it as compared with that of the British ambassador just quoted.

DISCUSSION   Factually, Gustav's letter provides an accurate account of the event. From his language, however, it is clear that, as he admits, he is a hostile commentator, deeply shocked at the breakdown of public order represented by the storming of the Bastille, the mob lynching of the governor, fraternization between the royal guards ('the French and Swiss guards') and 'the people', and the claims of the National Assembly ('the Estates'). He notes the role of popular violence and bloodshed, dismissed by the British ambassador as 'the loss of very few lives'.

Gustav is alarmed at the humiliation which all this represents for Louis XVI – a surrender of power by absolute monarchy. The French monarchy is on the way to becoming a constitutional monarchy, with ministers responsible to the Assembly. The British ambassador approves of the event as marking the advent of 'a free country'. Gustav abominates it, and laments Louis' appearance before the Assembly on 15 July not to give orders but 'to request assistance' and 'almost to apologise'. The letter confirms that the fall of the Bastille was seen by critics as well as enthusiasts as a significant (Gustav says 'terrible') blow to the Old Regime. Gustav fears for the king's throne.

Enlightened reformism – dismantling the Old Regime

The National Assembly, the self-proclaimed and now *de facto* supreme representative and legislative organ of state, set to work on the constitution which it had sworn to introduce. Calling itself the **Constituent Assembly** (to stress both its representative credentials and its constitutional mission), it consisted of 745 deputies elected for two years with virtually unlimited power to pass laws. The king, by interposing his veto, might delay but could not override laws passed by it.

Between 1789 and 1791 the Assembly implemented a transformation of French institutions, marking a clear break with the Old Regime by its sweeping application of the principle of equality. In a series of revolutionary decrees between 4 and 11 August 1789, it removed at one fell swoop the social and administrative foundations of the Old Regime. The Assembly decreed the abolition of 'the feudal system in its entirety' and with it the removal of privilege in France: the abolition of church tithes[39] and all rents, taxes and services due from peasants to noble landowners (notably rents paid in kind and the *corvée,* or forced labour on road repairs); abolition of seigneurial law courts; abolition of the sale of offices and an end to the exemption from direct taxation enjoyed by church and nobility. It proclaimed the comprehensive principle of equality: social equality, equality before the law, equal liability to taxation, and equality of opportunity. 'All citizens,' it decreed, 'without distinction of birth, are eligible for all offices, whether ecclesiastical, civil or military' (Hardman, 1999, p.113). The nobility thus lost its automatic monopoly of the higher offices of state.

Declaration of the Rights of Man

On 26 August 1789, the Assembly passed the Declaration of the Rights of Man and Citizen as the preamble to a constitution drawn up in 1791. (The Declaration also prefaced the later constitutions of 1793 and 1795.)

EXERCISE   Now read this document (Anthology I, p.77–9). How far do you see in it the influence of the Enlightenment? What was revolutionary about it?

DISCUSSION   The principles contained in the Declaration and described there as 'simple and incontrovertible' were familiar to the deputies from the *Encyclopédie* (and also from the American Revolution). They derived from the Enlightenment and were invoked in the petitions (*cahiers de doléances),* the lists of grievances which the delegates had drawn up for the meeting of the Estates-General. What made them revolutionary was that for the first time in European history they were formally incorporated and proclaimed in a document of state, which declared that the 'purpose of all political institutions' was to guarantee the citizens' 'natural rights' (civil rights or human rights, as we call them now). These rights were declared to be inalienable: that is, citizens could not divest themselves of them (for example, by selling them) or be deprived of them by subsequent legislation. They were to be entrenched in the constitution.

---

[39] In addition to drawing revenues from its ownership of a tenth of the land, the Church drew a tithe equivalent to one-tenth of the yield of the remaining land.

Article 1 reaffirmed the principle of equality: 'Men are born and remain free and equal in ... rights; social distinctions can only be based on public utility' (as opposed to noble birth or status). The rights of man included freedom from arbitrary arrest and imprisonment, freedom of opinion and speech, the right to a voice in the levying of taxes, the right to own property, equality before the law, and (as we have seen) equality of opportunity in access to government posts.

There was one crucial limitation: the rights of man did not apply to women. The (male) revolutionaries were largely hostile to the cause of women's suffrage, though women took part in some of the events of the Revolution and their cause was championed by such distinguished writers as Condorcet (1743–94), one of the younger *philosophes* of the Enlightenment. In 1793 women were to be expressly excluded from the rights of citizens. The feminist Olympe de Gouges, author of *The Declaration of the Rights of Woman and Citizen* (1791), was to fall victim to the Terror in 1793.

Also revolutionary in the European context was the assertion in the Declaration that sovereignty resided with the nation, not with the king (a claim made in the *Encyclopédie,* as we have seen, and vindicated in the American Revolution). In October 1789, absolute monarchy was formally abolished and replaced by constitutional monarchy. The Assembly decreed that Louis XVI was 'by the grace of God *and the constitutional law of the State*, King of the French' (emphasis added).

EXERCISE   Now read the decree on the abolition of nobility, June 1790 (Anthology I, p.79). Do you notice any similarity with *What is the Third Estate?* by Sieyès?

DISCUSSION The decree implements precisely what Sieyès and his fellow deputies of the Third Estate demanded: the outright abolition of the nobility as a separate social order. Henceforth everyone is simply a 'French citizen' without distinction of titles or armorial insignia. In tone the decree echoes Sieyès's uncompromising egalitarian hostility towards noble privilege.

The decree on the abolition of nobility drew the line at damage to property, ownership of property having been proclaimed a natural right in the Declaration of the Rights of Man. (The decree is evidence that, as is known from other sources, the crowd was taking the law into its own hands by ransacking châteaux, destroying records of seigneurial dues, etc.)

Revolutionary imagery

Figure 6.1   French School, Declaration of the Rights of Man and Citizen, *1789, oil on canvas, Musée Carnavalet, Paris. Photo: Giraudon/ Bridgeman Art Library.*

EXERCISE   Looking at Figure 6.1, what does the imagery of the Declaration of the Rights of Man appear to draw upon?

DISCUSSION   The basic form is biblical in inspiration: the well-known image of the two tablets of the law (the Ten Commandments) brought down by Moses from Mount Sinai. The implication is that the 17 rights of man parallel (or perhaps even supersede) the Judaeo-Christian decalogue. (In the preamble to the Declaration God is referred to as 'the Supreme Being', the divine creator of the universe postulated by Enlightenment deists.)

Other imagery is classical, drawn from motifs common in ancient republican Rome:

- the central pike (the weapon of the free citizen), surmounted by the Phrygian cap, or legendary red cap of liberty, associated with the freed slave;

- enveloping the pike, the *fasces* (upright sticks, bound together in a bundle, carried before the 'lictors' or senior magistrates and symbolizing solidarity and civic virtue);

- garlands of oak leaves, symbolizing victory.

Other symbols include a chain with a broken fetter, symbolizing emancipation from bondage; an equilateral triangle, symbolizing equality; and the all-seeing eye of Providence (a masonic symbol).

The revolutionaries thus drew on appropriate aspects of classical and religious imagery, familiar under the Old Regime, and adapted them to a new ideology after 1789.

Enlightenment, revolution and reform – the departments

Old Regime France was a confused welter of overlapping administrative, judicial and fiscal divisions and authorities (see Figure 6.2).

EXERCISE   Look at Figure 6.3, a map showing the departments (*départements*). These were the 83 new administrative units created in January 1790 by decree of the Assembly, most of which exist to this day. They were subdivided into districts, and these in turn into cantons and communes (or municipalities). Compare Figure 6.3 with Figure 6.2 (a map showing the 35 provinces of pre-revolutionary France). State what significant differences you notice. Give examples.

DISCUSSION   There are two main differences. First, the departments are of roughly equal size, in contrast to the haphazard former provinces, such as the Bourbonnais and Auvergne. Second, a department is usually named after a geographical feature, normally a river or mountain. For example, departments named after rivers include Gironde, Somme, Seine et Marne,

Figure 6.2 The French provinces, 1789. Photo: John Paxton, Companion to the French Revolution, *Facts on File, New York and Oxford, 1988. Reproduced by permission of John Paxton.*

Figure 6.3 The departments of revolutionary France, 1790. Photo: Franklin L. Ford, Europe 1780–1830, *2nd edn, Longman, Harlow, 1989. Reprinted by permission of Pearson Education Limited.*

Moselle, Upper and Lower Rhine (Haut-Rhin, Bas-Rhin). Departments
named after mountains include the High, Low and Eastern Pyrenees
(Hautes-Pyrénées, Basses-Pyrénées and Pyrénées Orientales), Vosges,
Jura, Higher and Lower Alps (Hautes-Alpes, Basses-Alpes). The
departments were established on the rational and scientific basis of equal
size,[40] and were named not after historical or traditional associations but
in accordance with natural features.

Power was decentralized and allocated to elected constituencies.
Administration was entrusted to officials elected by local taxpayers, to a
general council in the department and to a mayor in each commune.

3   From 1789 to the flight to Varennes

The moderate reformers

1789–92 was a period of relatively moderate reform in the spirit of the
Enlightenment – moderate, that is, compared with what followed. It was
certainly revolutionary in relation to what went before. The Constituent
Assembly (August 1789–September 1791) and its successor, the
Legislative Assembly (October 1791–August 1792), comprising educated
members of the Third Estate joined by liberal-minded nobles and clergy,
were satisfied with the transformation of absolute monarchy into a
parliamentary system, a constitutional monarchy under a constitution
introduced in 1791. Political power lay with the Assembly, which was
run by wealthy property-holders. Their object 'was not to effect a social
revolution but to create a more open society in which opportunities
previously restricted to birth, should now be open to talent' (Hampson,
1975, p.95).

Popular violence and the Revolution

The deputies were concerned to protect property and maintain order (as
the 1790 decree on the abolition of nobility suggests) in the face of a
growing breakdown of public order; and their attitude to the masses – to
what the demagogic journalist Jean-Paul Marat (1744–93) called *le petit
peuple* (the little people), the millions of propertyless, distressed, violent
and unpredictable 'fellow citizens' – was one of growing apprehension.
The people traditionally rioted when bread was short, and increasingly

---

[40] It was originally proposed to divide France into a grid of oblong departments,
nearly equal in shape as well as size.

they came out on the streets to take 'direct action' – that is, to take the law into their own hands – their expectations aroused by the sweeping changes taking place.

The masses were an ever-present threat to orderly reform. The leaders of the Paris crowd were political activists who called themselves **sans-culottes** (literally 'without breeches', because they wore trousers rather than the knee-breeches or *culottes* associated with the upper classes – see Plate 6.1 in the Illustrations Book). The *sans-culottes* were from what may be called the lower middle class – to be distinguished from the idle and the unemployed. The 'cream' of the *sans-culottes* included artisans and tradesmen, master craftsmen and small shopkeepers, but their followers were hired labourers, porters, waiters, janitors and barbers. Through demonstrations and street violence the *sans-culottes* forced events faster and further than the current leaders of opinion desired.

A nationwide panic or 'Great Fear' accompanied the Assembly's decrees of August 1789 abolishing feudalism and privilege in France. The king, unhappy at his new, diminished role and at being required to assent to so many revolutionary measures, and encouraged by his family and royalist supporters to resist, at first refused to promulgate the decrees of 4 August and the Declaration of the Rights of Man. 'I will never allow *my* clergy and *my* nobility to be stripped of their assets', he declared (quoted in Vovelle, 1984, p.114).

In October, when the king's personal guards at Versailles were seen to trample on the tricolour, the National Guard reacted, caught up in a revived fear that Louis might attempt to close the Assembly by force. A crowd of Parisian women, marching to the Assembly at Versailles to protest against rising bread prices, advanced on the royal palace. With the acquiescence and even co-operation of the National Guard, including Lafayette, they forced the royal family to return with them to Paris, where the king, virtually a prisoner in the Tuileries palace, now ignominiously assented to the decrees.

Edmund Burke's *Reflections on the Revolution in France* (extract in Anthology I, pp.80–1) became the bible across Europe of what was to become known as conservatism. From the first, Burke opposed the Revolution on principle. He deplored the sudden break with custom and tradition, and the implementation of change based on abstract principles (such as the rights of man) drawn from the Enlightenment. He abhorred the egalitarianism and lack of deference to nobility and monarchy, and the running amok of what he called 'the swinish multitude'. He foresaw bloodshed.

The majority of the deputies, under Lafayette, were determined to preserve order and to keep power in the hands of the representatives of the responsible and the propertied. Branches of the National Guard were established across France. In December 1789 the Assembly drew a distinction between 'active' (that is, monied) and 'passive' (propertyless) citizens. Only the former were eligible to participate in the election of deputies. An electorate of four and a half million male taxpayers chose some 50,000 'electors', who paid even higher tax and who in turn elected the deputies to the Assembly (and the candidates for public office). The deputies and office-holders themselves were qualified to stand by virtue of the still higher taxes which they paid. Even so, the electorate was far broader than any in the rest of Europe, where even these provisions seemed 'madly democratic' (Palmer, 1971, p.70). The French radicals, however, pointed to the 'aristocracy of the rich' (a phrase coined by Marat), which was replacing the old feudal 'aristocracy of birth'.

The divide over the Church, 1790

The revolutionaries of 1789 also aspired to reform the Catholic Church in France, though not to disestablish it, still less to de-Christianize the country. Many of the clergy themselves favoured reform. In August 1789 the Assembly deprived the Church of its income by abolishing the tithe. In November it decreed the sequestration (nationalization) of church lands, roughly 10 per cent of all land in France, for public sale. The Assembly was prompted by the same need to raise revenue to pay off the national debt which had led to the summoning of the Estates-General.

But the programme of church reform was also ideological, inspired by the rationalism and humanitarianism of the Enlightenment. In February 1790 the Assembly abolished the monastic orders and also proclaimed civic equality for Protestants. In July 1790 it introduced the **Civil Constitution of the Clergy**, which cut the number of Catholic bishoprics from 135 to 83, allocating one diocese for each department, and made provision for a salaried clergy appointed by popular election. These startling changes were introduced by the Assembly without consulting the Catholic Church.

A deep and lasting break between Catholic opinion and the Revolution came in November 1790, when the Assembly forced the issue by requiring the clergy to swear allegiance to the constitution (including the Civil Constitution of the Clergy). Almost half the ordinary clergy refused to take the oath, and only seven bishops assented, while the Pope denounced the Civil Constitution (and by implication the Revolution) in April 1791. The clergy who refused to take the oath (known as **non-jurors**) were imprisoned or went into exile – 30,000 priests had left France by 1799 – swelling the ranks of the émigrés and turning tensions between church and state into an ideological divide between supporters and enemies of the Revolution.

A published protest by a former deputy of the nobility to the Estates-General (Anthology I, p.82) shows how divisive the issue of the oath could be. The extract from Marat's *L'Ami du peuple* in December 1790

(Anthology I, p.83) provides evidence of the mounting extremism threatening the moderates.

Monarchy and the Revolution – the flight to Varennes, 1791

The task of the moderates was further complicated by the ambiguous attitude of the royal family. From the first there were royalists who refused to compromise with the Revolution, including Louis XVI's younger brothers, the comte de Provence (later Louis XVIII) and the comte d'Artois (later Charles X), who left France as émigrés and fomented counter-revolution from abroad. By 1791 half the noble officers in the French army had resigned their commissions. Weak, shifty and out of his depth, Louis XVI remained suspicious of the Revolution and hostile to the constitution. As a practising Catholic, he was profoundly disturbed by the Civil Constitution of the Clergy. Still more antagonistic was the queen, Marie-Antoinette, whose brother was the Habsburg emperor. Marie-Antoinette opposed any compromise with the Revolution. 'Only armed force', she wrote, 'can put things right' (Hampson, 1975, p.98). In June 1791 the royal family attempted to flee to a place of safety on the eastern frontier of France, from where Louis, with the implicit threat of armed foreign assistance, proposed to renegotiate terms with the Assembly. They were caught at Varennes (the episode is known as the flight to Varennes) and were returned to Paris under guard. Once more they were virtually prisoners.

'The flight to Varennes opened up the second great schism of the Revolution' (Doyle, 2001, p.47). The king's loyalty to the Revolution and his credibility as a constitutional monarch were fatally compromised. So was the cause of moderate, liberal constitutionalism in France. (See the article from *Le Père Duchesne*, 1791, a vicious personal attack on the king and queen after the flight to Varennes: Anthology I, pp.85–6.) In July 1791 an anti-royalist demonstration took place in the Champ-de-Mars in Paris. It was put down by the National Guard under Lafayette, and some 50 demonstrators were killed. What later became known as the massacre of the Champ-de-Mars further polarized opinion.

For the moderates of 1789, the Revolution had gone far enough. Confidence in constitutional monarchy would be restored, they hoped, by the king's formal assent to the new constitution in September 1791. From the spring of 1792 onwards, however, the cause of moderation was under continual challenge: on the one hand, from the king's unreliability and the threat of foreign intervention and counter-revolution, and, on the other, from the *sans-culottes*, militant agitators and radical intellectuals in and outside the Assembly.

4   Europe and the French Revolution

There was much sympathy among intellectuals abroad for the
Revolution, which seemed to be putting so many Enlightenment ideals
into practice. The German philosopher Immanuel Kant was among the
first to hail the Revolution as a unique historical phenomenon, and these
early reactions were shared by Fichte, Herder, Schiller and Goethe.
Enthusiasts in Britain included the radical Thomas Paine, author of *The
Rights of Man* (1791), Mary Wollstonecraft, author of *A Vindication of the
Rights of Men* (1790) and *A Vindication of the Rights of Women* (1792),
poets such as Burns, Blake, Coleridge and Wordsworth, and, initially, the
campaigner against slavery William Wilberforce, a man of deep religious
conviction. In later years Wordsworth recalled his emotions of 1789 in a
celebrated couplet:

> Bliss was it in that dawn to be alive,
> But to be young was very Heaven!

(*The Prelude*, XI.108–9)

What was the attitude of the French revolutionaries to Europe? In May
1790 the Assembly resolved that 'the French nation renounces
involvement in any war undertaken with the aim of making conquests'
and that 'it will never use force against the liberty of any people'
(Vovelle, 1984, p.123). This was not, however, regarded as incompatible
with wars of 'liberation' to spread the Revolution abroad. In the boast of
the radical deputy Pierre Chaumette: 'The land which separates Paris
from St Petersburg will soon be gallicized, municipalized, jacobinized'
(quoted in Furet, 1996, p.104).

How did the European monarchs react? A letter from Leopold II, Austrian
emperor, to Catherine II, empress of Russia, in July 1791 (Anthology I,
pp.83–4) and the Declaration of Pillnitz of August 1791 (Anthology I,
pp.84–5), written immediately after the flight to Varennes, indicate the
attitude to the Revolution of the monarchies of Austria and Prussia. Both
were 'open' documents, intended to influence public opinion across
France and Europe and to be understood as expressions of solidarity
between the rulers of Austria and Prussia, speaking on behalf of
European monarchs generally. In the letter to Catherine, Leopold
expresses indignation at the treatment of Louis XVI and Marie-Antoinette
and his fears for their safety. He sees in the 'dangerous excesses of the
French Revolution' a threat to monarchs and political stability generally.
The Revolution had thus become an international issue. The Declaration
of Pillnitz is an appeal for support by the Austrian and Prussian
monarchs to the other European monarchs and a warning of possible
military intervention in France.

The rulers of Britain and continental Europe in 1792 were alarmed by the
Revolution, but not so much that they took serious steps to suppress it.

Kaunitz, the Austrian chancellor, indeed protested against intervening in France's internal affairs as unnecessary. Austria, Prussia and Russia acted in traditional fashion by taking advantage of the weakness to which they supposed the Revolution had brought France, in order to complete the partition of France's former protégé, Poland, swallowed up by Russia and Prussia in the partitions of 1793 and 1795.

It was the French who declared war. They were not to know how far Austria and Prussia were serious in their threats. What they did know was that in 1787 the Prussians had intervened militarily in Holland, while the Austrians in 1788 had sent their troops into the Austrian Netherlands (Belgium), in each case to suppress a revolutionary uprising. In April 1792 France declared war on the Habsburg ruler of Austria, Emperor Francis (Leopold's successor), and invaded the Austrian Netherlands (present-day Belgium). (Anthology I, pp.89–90, shows a revolutionary proclamation to the people of Belgium inciting them against the Austrians.) In November the Assembly decreed that France offered 'fraternal assistance to all peoples wishing to recover their liberty'. Once hostilities began, the Declaration of Brunswick (August 1792) issued by the Duke of Brunswick, commanding the Prussian and Austrian armies, threatened to put Paris to sword and fire should any harm befall the French royal family. War between France and European monarchs spread the Revolution beyond France's frontiers, and inspired an ulterior goal of securing for France the 'natural frontier' of the Rhine.

Political polarization and the fall of the monarchy

By 1792 the liberal constitutionalists of 1789, men like Lafayette, found themselves increasingly on the defensive. There was growing hostility to the National Assembly, with its limited franchise and 'aristocracy of the rich'. A fringe of radical deputies seated on the left of the Assembly (the political terms 'left' and 'right' date from this period) were supported in Paris and across France by numerous radical political organizations or 'clubs', notably a club calling itself the Society of the Friends of the Constitution (and later Society of the Friends of Liberty and Equality) – better known as the **Jacobin** club. Foremost among the Jacobin deputies in the Assembly was Maximilien de Robespierre (1758–94), a fervent disciple of Rousseau, who seemed to believe himself the embodiment of the 'general will' and republican virtue.

In September 1791 the National Assembly, after the two years which it had allotted itself to enact a constitution, duly dissolved itself, transferring its powers to a Legislative Assembly, from election to which, at Robespierre's suggestion, it quixotically barred its own members. There were thus no experienced deputies, and there was an influx of younger radical revolutionaries. Half the deputies were under 30.

Outside the Assembly, the pressure of the 'clubs' and the growing politicization of the *sans-culottes* were accompanied by a torrent of publications released under the right to freedom of the press laid down in the Declaration of the Rights of Man. By 1791 there were 150 newspapers, including much inflammatory journalism, in which issues were personalized and political opponents were blackguarded. Notorious among these 'tabloids' of the day were Jacques Hébert's *Le Père Duchesne* (*Old Man Duchesne*), with a circulation running to 200,000, larded with foul invective, and Jean-Paul Marat's daily *L'Ami du peuple* (*The People's Friend),* both of which continually incited the *sans-culottes* to violence. As early as 1789 Marat had declared: 'The political machine can only be wound up by violence, just as the air can only be cleared by words' (Vovelle, 1984, p.209). Objects of attack included the usual targets – aristocrats and priests and increasingly the royal family (for example, see Anthology I, pp.83, 85–6) – and also extended to the 'active citizens' who supported and administered the new France – the authorities and members of the National Assembly (Anthology I, pp.83, 85–6).

In-fighting increased in the Assembly and radicalized it. By May 1792 the Assembly was falling under the influence of the Jacobins and other extreme factions such as the **Girondins**, who decreed the deportation of non-juring priests and the death sentence for counter-revolutionary émigrés. In June the Assembly called for a levy of 20,000 volunteers to defend Paris from its enemies at home and abroad. When the king vetoed the measure, the Girondins called for mass demonstrations outside the Tuileries. An armed crowd of *sans-culottes* broke into the palace and forced Louis to wear the red cap of liberty. On 10 August a body of *sans-culottes,* national guards and others sacked the Tuileries. The king's 600 Swiss guards, whom Louis ordered not to fire on the crowd, were massacred. The royal family took refuge in the Assembly, from where they were transferred, as prisoners, to a secure fortress in Paris. The cause of constitutional monarchy was drowned in violence and bloodshed.

Birth of the republic: war, civil war and terror

After the church and monarchy, 'war was the third great polarizing issue of the Revolution' (Doyle, 2001, p.50). With a declaration by the Assembly in July 1792 of *la patrie en danger* (the fatherland in danger), Prussian troops on French soil in August, and the fall of the border fortress of Verdun in September, there was mass panic in Paris, with accusations of treachery against the king and queen, Lafayette (who fled abroad), 'aristocrats' and priests. In the 'September massacre', some 1,400 priests and suspected counter-revolutionaries were dragged from prison by rampaging *sans-culottes,* and together with common criminals and prostitutes were wantonly butchered. *Le Père Duchesne* (Anthology I, pp.86–7) egged on the perpetrators, while the minister of justice, Georges Danton (1759–94), did nothing. 'The French Revolution, anti-noble almost from the start, had also turned anti-clerical, anti-monarchical and (with the September massacres) terroristic' (Doyle, 1999, p.xv).

On 20 September 1792, under pressure from Robespierre and the Jacobins, the Legislative Assembly was replaced by a **National Convention**. (The term was taken from the Constitutional Convention which drew up the US Constitution in 1787.) The significance of this appeared two days later, when the Convention duly decreed the abolition of the monarchy and the creation of the French Republic with a new constitution. Theoretically, the legislature was now – for the first time in modern history – elected by universal male suffrage. In practice, only one-tenth of the electorate – the *sans-culottes* – ventured to vote.

In January 1793 Louis XVI was tried by the Convention for so-called crimes against the nation. Addressed by his surname ('citizen Capet') just like any other citizen, he was, by a narrow majority vote, sentenced to death. He was guillotined in what became the place de la Révolution (formerly place Louis XV, now place de la Concorde). Marie-Antoinette, long defamed as 'the Austrian bitch' on suspicion of scheming for Austria's interests, was guillotined in October. Again, the Revolution made a violent break with the French past and in doing so issued a defiant challenge to the rest of Europe. In Danton's words, 'France threw down its gauntlet to Europe, and that gauntlet was the head of a king' (quoted in Doyle, 1989, p.4; see also Figure 6.4).

Attitudes became still more polarized. The Convention organized a determined resistance to foreign invasion, combined with action against those in France still loyal to the cause of monarchy. By 1793 France was not only at war with most of the European states, a war which continued until 1799, but also in a state of virtual civil war – and with intensified civil war came mounting violence and extremism. Figure 6.5 shows the invasion points of the **First Coalition** against France (Austria, Prussia, Holland, Britain, Spain and the kingdom of Sardinia) and the locations of internal resistance to the Revolution in 1792–3. There were two key centres of long-term resistance: the royalist insurgents, known as the 'Chouans', of Normandy and Brittany, and a massive uprising in the Vendée south of the Loire in 1793.

> From this time, until the enemies of France have been expelled from the territory of the Republic, all Frenchmen are in a state of permanent requisition for the army.

(Anthology I, p.90)

So began the decree on the *Levée en masse* issued by the Convention in August 1793, a compulsory call-up of 750,000 men (all single men aged 18–25) and the harnessing of all human and material resources. It was in effect a 'declaration of total war' (Blanning, 2000, p.253), which unleashed enthusiastic support from the forces of popular radicalism in Paris and elsewhere – notably the *sans-culottes* – and provoked armed resistance from the forces of counter-revolution in the Vendée and around Bordeaux, Lyons and Marseilles. The Mediterranean port of Toulon, occupied by the British fleet, defected to the British. By August

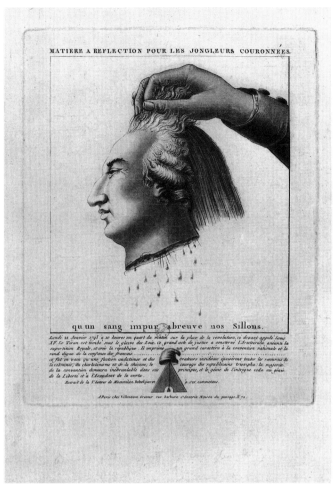

Figure 6.4   Villeneuve, Matière à réflection pour les jongleurs couronnées (Matter for thought for crowned twisters), *1793, engraving, Bibliothèque nationale de France, Paris.*

Beneath the severed head of Louis XVI are the words from the Marseillaise: *'Let impure blood water our furrows.' The caption reads: 'Monday 21 January 1793 at 10.15 a.m. on the place de la Révolution formerly called place Louis XV. The tyrant fell beneath the sword of the laws. This great act of justice appalled the aristocracy, destroyed the superstition of royalty, and created the republic. It stamps a great character on the National Convention and renders it worthy of the confidence of the French ... In vain did an audacious faction and some insidious orators exhaust all the resources of calumny, charlatanism and chicane; the courage of the republicans triumphed: the majority of the Convention remained unshakeable in its principles, and the genius of intrigue yielded to the genius of Liberty and the ascendancy of virtue. Extract from the 3rd letter of Maximilien Robespierre to his constituents' (trans. Lentin).*

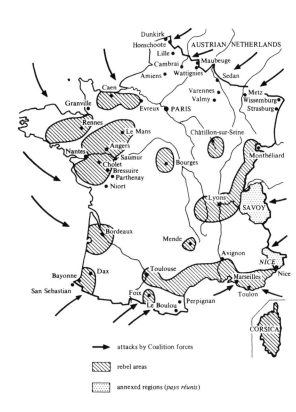

Figure 6.5   The republic under internal and external attack, 1793. Photo: Marc Bouloiseau, The Jacobin Republic 1792–1794, *Cambridge University Press, 1983.*

1793, 60 departments, or three-quarters of the total, were declared to be in a state of rebellion.

The Girondins, who dominated the Convention from September 1792, were ousted in May 1793 by the Jacobins under Robespierre with the help of 80,000 armed *sans-culottes*. A further constitution was introduced in June 1793, more democratic than that of 1791, but it was suspended for the duration of the war. The twelve months from July 1793 to July 1794 were known as the period of war government, revolutionary government, or simply **the Terror**. Real power was vested in a so-called **Committee of Public Safety**, in effect a war cabinet of 12 members of the Convention. The Committee took direct charge of mobilizing France's material and human resources, fixing wages and prices, calling up and provisioning the army – and eradicating internal opposition. (See Anthology I, pp.91–2, memorandum of Robespierre.)

The guillotine

The new system of departments introduced in 1790 removed the many differing and often overlapping jurisdictions of Old Regime France and replaced them with a uniform system of justice. Each department had its own criminal court, each district a civil court. All criminal cases were to be tried by jury, another revolutionary innovation. Enlightenment thinkers including Montesquieu and Voltaire had criticized the arbitrariness and brutality of penal practice in Old Regime France. Judicial torture as a means of exacting evidence in criminal proceedings and torture in general – notably the horrific penalty of breaking on the wheel (suffered in 1762 by the innocent Jean Calas, whose cause had been taken up by Voltaire) – were abolished in October 1789. There remained the question of capital punishment itself. The Legislative Assembly resolved by a narrow majority to retain the death penalty and adopted the guillotine as the instrument of execution, following a report from Dr Louis, secretary of the Academy of Surgeons and author of the article 'Death' in the *Encyclopédie.*

EXERCISE   Now read the decree concerning the death penalty, March 1792 (Anthology I, p.87–9). Why did the Assembly approve the guillotine?

DISCUSSION   The guillotine was adopted on expert advice and after experimentation on scientific and humanitarian grounds: as the quickest and least painful form of execution for victim, spectators and executioner alike ('humanity requires that the death penalty be as painless as possible'). It applied the fundamental principle of mechanics: Newton's law of gravitation. Newton's law was infallible, and so was the guillotine: 'the falling bevelled blade never failed to decapitate and there would be no more botched executions.'

The adoption of the guillotine was another example of legal and social equality in action. Nobleman and common murderer suffered the same penalty, and both were executed publicly. The king and queen were guillotined in the year after this decree. The guillotine was named after Dr Guillotin, a member of the Constituent Assembly, who enthused over the instrument as a symbol of the penal, technological and humanitarian progress inspired by the Enlightenment.

The *sans-culotte* as revolutionary hero

Revolutionary symbolism (which we noted earlier with reference to the Declaration of the Rights of Man) extended to clothing: the wearing of the tricolour cockade was made compulsory for men by a decree of July 1792. The red 'cap of liberty' became the normal headgear of the *sans-culottes,* now officially idealized as heroes of the people.

Plate 6.1 in the Illustrations Book shows an actor dressed as a *sans-culotte,* carrying the tricolour banner (on which is emblazoned the slogan 'liberty or death') at the 'festival of liberty' in Savoy in October 1792. (Savoy had just been annexed to France.) The pole supporting the banner may be intended to suggest a pike, a weapon associated with the *sans-culottes*. Robespierre called it a 'sacred weapon' (Vovelle, 1984, p.218).

EXERCISE   What other signs can you detect in Boilly's portrait of the *sans-culotte* (Plate 6.1) that differentiate him from an aristocratic hero?

DISCUSSION
- Trousers instead of knee-breeches (*culottes* – the term *sans-culottes* was originally used contemptuously by the nobility).

- Sabots, or wooden clogs, rather than buckled leather shoes.

- Natural hair instead of powdered wig.

- Tricolour cockade on the red 'cap of liberty'.

- Pipe stuck in mouth rather than, say, aristocratic snuff box.

- Short jacket (*la carmagnole,* also the title of a revolutionary song), rolled up sleeves, bare hands and forearms, open shirt and loose scarf: this is the hardy mountaineer (see the Savoy background) as opposed to the aristocratic fop with gloves and cravat.

The article 'What is a *sans-culotte*?' (Anthology I, pp.92–3), published in 1793, was a kind of Jacobin counterpart to Sieyès's *What is the Third Estate?*

Embodiment of the common man, the *sans-culotte* was held out in Jacobin ideology as the hero of the Revolution, the personification of 'liberty, equality and fraternity', the 'general will' and republican virtue. As an egalitarian, the *sans-culotte* made a point of addressing everyone, including deputies and officials, as *citoyen* (citizen – anyone saying *monsieur* or *madame* was liable to fall foul of the Law of Suspects, 1793: see Anthology I, p.93), and of using the familiar second-person singular – *tu* – not the polite form – *vous*.

The *sans-culotte* was an avowed political activist and militant. His duty, as defender of the Revolution, was to maintain an atmosphere of constant vigilance and suspicion, and if necessary to resort to violence and terror. The *sans-culottes* were championed by Marat in *L'Ami du peuple* and by Hébert, who urged in *Le Père Duchesne*: 'To your pikes, good *sans-culottes*! Sharpen them up to exterminate the aristocrats' (Vovelle, 1984, p.219). It was the *sans-culottes* who attended the revolutionary watch committees (they made up some three-quarters of the personnel, Rudé, 1966, p.150). Though often barely literate (Williams, 1989, p.30), they issued (or refused) certificates of good citizenship (*certificats de civisme*) to distinguish good citizens (revolutionaries) from 'enemies of the people'.

The *sans-culottes* were associated by their enemies with the street-mob excesses of the Revolution: the heads on pikes, the stringings-up on lamp-posts, the September massacres, the castration by frenzied women rioters of the corpses of the Swiss guards, the *tricoteuses* (women knitting around the guillotine as the heads rolled). It was poetic justice that, of those who had egged on the *sans-culottes*, Marat was assassinated by Charlotte Corday in 1793 (his death became the subject of a hagiographic picture by Jacques-Louis David – see Plate 9.7 in the Illustrations Book), while Hébert fell foul of Robespierre and was guillotined in 1794.

The Terror in action

The year of authorized state terror from July 1793 to July 1794 was 'the climactic year of the Revolution' (Palmer, 1971, p.113). Under the Committee of Public Safety, now including Robespierre, 'revolutionary tribunals', backed in every commune by a 'revolutionary committee' or 'watch committee' (*comité de surveillance*), were set up throughout France, staffed by members of the local Jacobin clubs and the *sans-culottes* to root out counter-revolutionaries, real and supposed. Deputies of the Convention were sent into the provinces as 'representatives on mission' to enforce the orders and reassert the control by the central government which had been devolved when the departments were created in 1790. The 'rights of man' were suspended. Anyone seeking public employment had to apply to the watch committee for a *certificat de civisme* as proof of ideological soundness. Possession of a certificate became virtually mandatory under the Law of Suspects of September 1793 (Anthology I, p.93), which authorized indefinite imprisonment without trial. It is reckoned that half a million men and women were detained under it (Jones, 1988, p.115).

A decree of June 1794 introduced by Robespierre declared that 'the tribunal is instituted to punish the enemies of the people' (Furet, 1996, p.146). The Law of Suspects defined 'enemies of the people' under a catch-all description as those who showed themselves to be 'partisans of tyranny ... and enemies of liberty'. Suspects were accused, tried and executed in batches. There was no appeal against sentence. The accused were deprived of the right to be defended by counsel and to call witnesses. To be accused was as good as to be condemned; conviction rates rose from 30 per cent to 70 per cent, and the Revolution began to devour its own – men who had played a leading part in events since 1789, particularly the Girondins. Jacobins such as Danton and Camille Desmoulins (1760–94), who tried to stem the tide of terror, were themselves denounced by Robespierre and condemned to death.

Between September 1793 and July 1794 perhaps 17,000 people were sentenced to death by revolutionary tribunals and executed, three-quarters for alleged counter-revolution. 85 per cent of those guillotined were commoners rather than nobles – note Robespierre's denunciation of 'the bourgeoisie' in Anthology I, p.91 – but in proportion to their number, nobles and clergy suffered most. Some 1,200 nobles were executed. Among the last victims of the Terror were the celebrated chemist Antoine Lavoisier (1743–94) and the poet André Chénier (1762–94). The Enlightenment philosopher Condorcet (1743–94), who laid the foundations of a system of universal education decreed in 1793, and who proclaimed his faith in humanity's future in an eloquent *Sketch on ... the Progress of the Human Mind* (1793), committed suicide while awaiting execution. Including 10–12,000 summary executions without trial, especially in western France, and another 10–12,000 deaths in prison among those detained for revolutionary offences, a total of around 35–40,000 seems a likely toll of those who perished under the Terror (Bouloiseau, 1983, pp.210–11; Jones, 1988, p.115). The farewell letters of Olympe de Gouges and Amable Clément (Anthology I, pp.94–6) attest to the indiscriminate savagery of the Terror. (There is a presumption in favour of the truth of 'deathbed' statements.) The victims protest their innocence, patriotism and loyalty to the principles of 1789.

Robespierre was foremost in whipping up passions for a campaign of extermination against counter-revolution. In Paris 1,376 people were guillotined in seven weeks in June and July 1794 – the so-called 'Great Terror' – more than in the preceding 15 months. In Lyons there were mass executions by firing-squad because the guillotine was considered too slow (taking around two minutes per victim). In the Vendée region the 'representative on mission' authorized mass drownings in the River Loire,[41] and a decree was implemented ordering nothing less than 'the destruction of the Vendée' (Furet, 1996, p.139). Rebellious Marseilles and Lyons were renamed respectively 'City-without-name' and 'Liberated City' (*ville-affranchie*).

François Furet sees the Terror as more than the suppression of political opposition by the Jacobin elite in power: the final 'Great Terror' was unleashed when it was already clear that the Revolution was emerging victorious against its internal and foreign enemies. The Terror, Furet argues, was part of a revolutionary philosophy, ultimately inspired by the Enlightenment. Its followers not only believed in the perfectibility of man and the regeneration of society on new lines, but in that cause and in the name of 'the people' also believed themselves justified in 'extirpating' through 'terror' all who stood in the way of that vision. (The documents in Anthology I, pp.96–9, exemplify Robespierre's faith in the ideals of 'revolutionary government' and his fervent justification of 'terror'.) Mme Roland, wife of the Girondin leader, and, like him, a victim of the Terror, exclaimed from the scaffold: 'O Liberty, what crimes are committed in your name!' (*Grand Dictionnaire Encyclopédique Larousse*, 1985, p.284).

---

[41] Nantes, at the mouth of the Loire, was an Atlantic slave port. Under the Terror, the hulks used to transport slaves were loaded with political prisoners, sunk in the Loire and refloated.

5   Enlightenment, universalism and revolution

Revolutionary calendar and metric system

We considered earlier the universalist principles of 1789 deriving from the Enlightenment that inspired the Declaration of the Rights of Man and the redivision of France into departments. As the dominant group in the Convention by 1793, the Jacobins regarded themselves as mandated to enact the 'general will' of the people in a sense inspired by Rousseau: not as the aggregate weight of the individual aspirations of 28 million Frenchmen, but as the expression of that which, as virtuous men and citizens, Frenchmen *ought* to want. Always confident of their own understanding of the 'general will', the Jacobins aimed to shape public consciousness and to propel it in given directions through art and the media. At the lowest level came the distribution to the army of *Le Père Duchesne* to stimulate the fighting men's revolutionary ardour.

The Jacobins revolutionized time itself. In October 1793 the Convention decreed the introduction of the revolutionary calendar based on a 10-day week (and originally even a 10-hour day) and a year of 12 months of equal length (30 days each, to which extra days were added at the end of the year).

EXERCISE   Examine Plate 6.2 in the Illustrations Book, headed *Calendrier pour l'an III de la République Française* (Calendar for year III of the French Republic). Why do you suppose 1795 became 'year III'?

DISCUSSION   The Convention sought to mark a clean break with the past by establishing a new revolutionary, *republican* era to replace the traditional Christian era. The use of Roman numerals also suggested a classical, pre-Christian epoch.

The new calendar was introduced in 1793 after the replacement of the monarchy by the republic. The year 1792 was retrospectively renamed 'year I' to mark a new era in the evolution of mankind dating from the establishment of the republic, and the year began on 22 September, the date of the founding of the republic.[42] Dates before 1792 – including

[42] The fact that 22 September also marks the autumn equinox was not lost on the revolutionaries, who compared 'equality of days and nights' with the 'civil and moral equality' proclaimed by the Revolution.

1789 itself – were expressed as, for example, 'the year 1789 of the Old Regime (*ancien régime*)'. To a deputy who argued that year I should be 1789 rather than 1792, another deputy replied, to applause: 'We have been free only since we have no longer had a king' (Furet, 1996, p.117). The cult of the republic, as Hampson puts it, was becoming 'something of a religion in its own right' (1981, p.20).

Names for the new months were invented to correspond with natural phenomena, climatic and agricultural. Autumn consisted of the months *Vendémiaire, Brumaire* and *Frimaire*, to signify respectively harvest, mist and cold. The winter months were named *Nivôse, Pluviôse* and *Ventôse*, months of snow, rain and wind. The three spring months signified seed time, flowering time and meadow – *Germinal, Floréal* and *Prairial* – followed by the summer months of *Messidor, Thermidor* and *Fructidor*, or summer harvest, heat and summer fruit.[43]

The new calendar lasted until 1806. The 10-hour day was particularly short-lived. The 10-day week, with a rest day occurring only on the tenth day (*Décadi*) instead of on the seventh, was not popular! Nor was the renaming of the weekdays popular (*Primidi, Duodi, Tridi*, i.e. first day, second day, third day), or the replacement of saints' days by days named after agricultural and botanical terms (25 November, St Catherine's day, became the day of the pig).

What characterizes these defiantly utopian reforms is the radical break with the past, the application of natural, mathematical and universal principles that would (in the words of the poet Fabre d'Eglantine, who devised the names of the months) 'enlighten the entire human race' (Kennedy, 1989, p.348). Similar thinking lay behind the metric system of weights and measures, introduced by decree in 1795, with its divisions and subdivisions into units of ten. It was intended to replace the multiplicity of weights and measures current in Old Regime France, about which complaints were common in the *cahiers de doléances* of 1789, and to be based on concepts of universal, albeit Franco-centric, validity. The arc of the meridian from the North Pole to the equator, measured at the Paris Observatory, became the basis of the metre. Area and volume were fixed by squaring and cubing the metre, and weight was calculated in units of a cubic decimetre of water.

Like the new calendar, the metric system was hailed by one member of the Convention as a 'benefit to humanity ... worthy of the Great Nation (*Grande Nation*) to whom it belongs and of other civilised people, who are also probably destined to adopt it sooner or later' (Kennedy, 1989,

---

[43] Britons scorned the revolutionary calendar. A satirical contemporary translation ran: Slippy, Nippy, Drippy; Freezy, Wheezy, Sneezy; Showery, Flowery, Bowery; Heaty, Wheaty, Sweety (Doyle, 2001, pp.116–17). The calendar was intended to be universal, but the names of the new months were inappropriate for the southern hemisphere, which is cold during the 'hot' month of *Thermidor*.

p.79). The metric system was indeed spread by the revolutionary armies across most of continental Europe, where it has become standard.

The cult of the Revolution

With the suppression of aristocrats, royalists and counter-revolutionary priests came a cultural revolution against symbols and monuments of the Old Regime, the monarchy and the Catholic Church (see Figure 6.6). Freedom of religion was decreed in 1793. The Abbey of St Denis outside Paris, burial place of the French kings since the sixth century, was despoiled of its corpses. The bodies of Henri IV, Louis XIV, Louis XV and others were tossed into a common grave. Royal statues and emblems were demolished or 'vandalized' (the word was invented in 1794). Such deliberate destruction and desecration suggest, again, a desire literally to root out the past and begin again.

Most churches were closed down, the *sans-culottes* making sure of that. Place names were changed. The town of St-Pierre-le-Moutier (St Peter's Monastery) became Brutus-le-Magnanime (Brutus the Magnanimous). Montmartre became Mont Marat. Around 1,400 Paris streets were

Figure 6.6   Joseph Chinard, La Raison sous les traits d'Apollon foulant aux pieds la Superstition *(Reason, in the person of Apollo, treading Superstition underfoot), 1791, terracotta model, 51.5 x 13.3 x 12 cm, Louvre, Paris. Photo: © RMN/C. Jean.*

Apollo, the sun god, the rays of the sun streaming from his head, strides across a cloud bearing a torch. Superstition, in a nun's habit and veiled, is unable to see the true light. Superstition holds two sacred emblems of Christianity, the cross and the chalice. Chinard, who was then at the French Academy (of art) in Rome, was for a time imprisoned by the papal authorities, almost certainly because of his blasphemous treatment of Christian emblems. (I am grateful for this information to Dr Linda Walsh.)

renamed: the rue des vièrges (virgins' street) becoming the rue Voltaire and the île Saint-Louis changed to the île de la Fraternité. There was a rue de la Liberté and a rue de l'Égalité. Even Christian names, strictly so-called, were discouraged in favour of the names of heroes of republican Rome or precursors of the Revolution: Jean-Jacques (after Rousseau) rather than Joseph. Men christened Louis tended to change their name.

Alternatives to Roman Catholicism were encouraged by the institution of revolutionary public 'festivals' with their own symbolism replacing Christian festivals and saints' days. The revolutionaries, like the thinkers of the Enlightenment, even if they believed in God, were mostly doubtful about the reality of an afterlife, and they felt the need for a secular alternative that would glorify the names of those who had contributed to the progress of humanity by immortalizing them in the nation's collective memory. Diderot had written that posterity was for the *philosophe* what heaven was for the believer. This was applied literally in 1791 when the church of Sainte-Geneviève in Paris became the Pantheon (temple of all the gods), rededicated as a final resting place for the 'great men' of the nation. The inscription on the portico reads: *Aux grands hommes la patrie reconnaissante* (to its great men – the grateful fatherland). Here the remains of Voltaire – whose name personified the Enlightenment as none other – were ceremonially reburied in July 1791 in a festival decorated with floats designed by the artist Jacques-Louis David and accompanied by brass and massed choirs singing the anthem *Peuple, éveille-toi!* (*People, awake!*) under the direction of its composer, François-Joseph Gossec. In October 1794 the remains of Rousseau were likewise transferred to the Pantheon with similar pomp. Thus while Louis XVI was decapitated and the bodies of his Bourbon ancestors were wantonly desecrated, those of the two best-known figures of the Enlightenment were reconsecrated as hallowed relics of the prophets of the Revolution. In November 1793 the metropolitan cathedral of Notre Dame was rededicated as the Temple of Reason.

In May 1794 the Convention passed a decree introducing the cult of the Supreme Being. This represented the triumph of the deist trend of the Enlightenment. Men might be sceptical of a particularist, sectarian concept of a Christian god, but that did not necessarily lessen faith in the Supreme Being of a natural religion. The climax came in June 1794 with the Festival of the Supreme Being, publicly celebrated by Robespierre.

The example of Paris was swiftly followed throughout France. On 19 December 1793, within six weeks of the rededication of Notre Dame in Paris, the commune of Aubenas in the department of the Ardèche held its own festival to celebrate 'the precious benefits of the Revolution and the abolition of the abuses of a hateful regime, remembered only with horror' (Charay, 1990, p.195; trans. Lentin). It was also agreed that 'in order to immortalize the memory of Marat, the friend of the people, there will be an apotheosis[44] on the day of the Festival of Reason, in honour of the martyr of liberty' (Charay, 1990, p.195). Marat too was buried in the Pantheon.

In 1795 the Catholic Church in France as reorganized under the Civil Constitution was formally separated from the state by decree of the Convention. The episode of de-Christianization was not long-lived, but it was significant of the utopianism which inspired many revolutionaries and which derived ultimately from the Enlightenment. In particular, this utopianism came from Rousseau: a belief in 'regenerated man', 'the people' and 'humanity', a return to the supposed virtues of Sparta or republican Rome (see Figure 6.7). It was accompanied by the ritual demonization of royalists, nobles and priests as 'enemies of the people'.

Figure 6.7 Jacques-Louis Pérée, Regenerated Man Gives Thanks to the Supreme Being, *1794–5, 41.5 x 29 cm, Bibliothèque nationale de France, Paris.*

With one hand he holds up the Rights of Man; in the other he wields a mattock. Beneath his feet lies the axed tree of the Old Regime, the debris of aristocratic privilege and luxury. A shaft of lightning sears a crown.

[44] Literally the granting of divine or elevated status. The apotheosis of Marat was the secular equivalent of canonizing a saint. Contrast the treatment by the artist David of the precious blood of the revolutionary martyr-hero Marat (Plate 9.7) with the treatment of the 'impure' blood of the executed and execrated Louis XVI in Figure 6.4. Under the Old Regime the French monarch enjoyed the traditional title of 'the most Christian king'.

Ideas of regeneration and reconstruction received further impetus during the Revolutionary Wars, in which, for example, the city of Lille near the Belgian frontier was damaged. Plans for rebuilding drew on the cult of the Revolution, on Rousseau, and on republican ideals with their strong classical associations. These ideals were eloquently expressed by Robespierre in his speech to the Convention of 5 February 1794 (Anthology I, pp.98–9):

> Now what is the fundamental principle of democratic or popular government, that is to say, the essential force that maintains and inspires it? It is virtue: I am speaking of public virtue, which brought about so many wonders in Greece and Rome, and which must produce even more astounding ones in republican France.

For an example of the reinterpretation of republican ideals in architecture, see Plate 6.3 in the Illustrations Book (Verly's design for a public bath and theatre in Lille). This design recalls the public buildings and monuments of ancient Rome (baths and theatre, obelisks, equestrian statues). The Roman republic was central to the concept of a modern republic of free and equal citizens inspired by 'public virtue'. The design is severely classical: symmetrical with arches and columns. (For other classically inspired republican symbols see Plates 6.4 and 6.5 in the Illustrations Book.)

The *Marseillaise*

During the Revolutionary Wars, as Robespierre insisted, 'republican enthusiasm must be exalted by all means possible' (Anthology I, p.92). The Jacobins encouraged a revolutionary solidarity and patriotism, expressed in the slogan 'Liberty, Equality, Fraternity'. The *Marseillaise* began as the 'battle-hymn of the army of the Rhine', composed by Rouget de Lisle in April 1792 immediately after France declared war on Francis of Austria. It acquired its name when a battalion of volunteers from Marseilles reached Paris in July 1792. It became the anthem of the Revolution, and the national anthem by a decree of the Convention in 1795. A choral version with orchestral accompaniment by Gossec was performed at the Paris Opera 130 times between 1792 and 1799 (Hemmings, 1987, p.51). You will almost certainly be familiar with its tune. (You can hear a few bars from it at the beginning of Audio 3, tracks 1–7: *Britain and the French Revolution*.) It is lively and rousing, magnificently evocative, as Simon Schama says, of 'the comradeship of citizens in arms' (Schama, 1989, p.598). What about the words?

EXERCISE   Read the words of the *Marseillaise* (Anthology I, p.100). How would you characterize them?

DISCUSSION   The words are an aggressive and sanguinary demonization of the enemy (in 1792 the Austrians) as tyrannous and cruel.

In the dynastic wars of the Old Regime, bloody as they were, monarchs did not normally encourage personal hatred of the enemy. The Revolutionary Wars were embittered by ideological zeal. By 'traitors' and 'conspiring kings', the author had in mind Louis XVI and his émigré supporters as well as counter-revolutionary monarchs abroad. At the same time, the words were general enough to serve for France's various enemies throughout the Revolutionary Wars, and the 'impure blood' of the invaders was identified (in Figure 6.4) with the blood of the executed Louis XVI.

The proclamation of 1792 to people of Belgium (Anthology I, pp.89–90) contains the same language of incitement. The Belgians are invited to defect to France in the cause of liberation from tyranny (the Habsburg emperor).

6   The Thermidorian Settlement and the end of the Revolution

In *Thermidor* (July) 1794 there was a further political coup, this time engineered by deputies in the Convention who felt that Jacobin fanaticism, mob violence and bloodshed had got wildly out of hand and feared for their own lives. They succeeded in outmanoeuvring Robespierre, who was arrested and (after a botched suicide attempt) guillotined together with over 100 other Jacobins. The Thermidorians then put a stop to show trials and bloodletting. They also called in the army to put down the *sans-culottes*: 'for the first time since 1789 the authorities felt they could rely on soldiers to restore domestic order' (Doyle, 2001, p.59). When the Paris *sans-culottes* twice took to the streets in 1795, they were ruthlessly suppressed. The slaughter continued in a so-called White Terror (so-called from the white flag of the Bourbons) by counter-revolutionaries in Lyons, Nîmes and Marseilles avenging themselves on their former persecutors.

Yet another constitution was introduced in 1795 which dismantled the dictatorship of the Terror and established a ruling executive committee, or **Directory**, of five and a bicameral legislature consisting of a **Council of 500** and an upper house, or **Council of Elders** or **'Ancients'**. Eligibility for public office was restricted to some 30,000 men of property. François Boissy d'Anglas (1756–1826), who drew up the constitution, equated 'a country ruled by property-owners' with rule by 'the best ... those with most education', concerned with law and order

(Hampson, 1969, p.118). The franchise of four and a half million male taxpayers was nonetheless still the widest in Europe.

In the words of Richard Cobb, 1795 was 'the decisive year of the whole revolutionary period, for it was basically the Thermidorian Settlement that survived into the *Restauration*' [Bourbon restoration of 1815] (Cobb, 1970, p.197). The main beneficiaries of the Revolution were in a broad sense bourgeois, but they were a landowning bourgeoisie, who had bought up land made available by the sequestration of church property, not an entrepreneurial bourgeoisie. The Revolution was disastrous to trade and industry, and a mercantile and industrial bourgeoisie did not come into its own in France before the 1830s. Men of means who qualified for the franchise – that is 'property-owners' and 'those with most education' – included members of the nobility, who re-emerged after Thermidor. The men of 1789 included nobles who had joined with the Third Estate and willingly jettisoned their privileges, and while events after 1789 had driven many nobles abroad, the émigrés constituted no more than 7 to 8 per cent of the French nobility. Most nobles remained, survived the Terror, participated in and even benefited from the Revolution – for example, as generals during the Revolutionary Wars. By the turn of the century, 'most of the wealthiest landowners in France were still the nobles of the Old Regime' (Blanning, 1987, p.55).

The energies of the French people as a whole were directed into spreading the Revolution abroad. As Gwynne Lewis puts it, 'after 1795, the French Revolution continued, but wearing a military uniform and without the active support of the masses' (Lewis, 1993, p.52). In so far as 'the masses' were identified with the excesses of the *sans-culottes,* the ruling classes were glad to see them put in their place.

In 1799 a fresh constitution entrusted supreme power to one of the successful generals who had been spreading the Revolution by military conquest in the neighbouring states: Napoleon Bonaparte. The author of this latest constitution was the abbé Sieyès, whom we met ten years earlier at the summoning of the Estates-General as the champion of the Third Estate. All that seemed a world away now, so much had happened in the meantime. Sieyès was asked, what did you do during the Revolution? 'I survived,' he replied (Caratini, 1988, p.507). What the propertied governing class in France desired now was to enjoy the gains which the Revolution had brought them and to keep them safe from the mob at home, from counter-revolution abroad, and from the possibility of a restoration of the Old Regime. Bonaparte would guarantee the new order in France and spread the Revolution abroad, incidentally securing France's 'natural frontier' on the Rhine. With Bonaparte's help – a 'whiff of grape-shot' – the lower chamber, which had royalist leanings, was dispersed in October 1795. In a *coup d'état* on 18 Brumaire (9 November) 1799, the upper chamber surrendered power to three 'consuls', the first of whom was Bonaparte. On 15 December Bonaparte issued a proclamation claiming that 'the Revolution is established on the principles with which it began. It is over'[1](Tulard, 1987, p.498).

7   Conclusion: the Enlightenment, the French Revolution, Britain and Europe

Je suis tombé par terre,
C'est la faute à Voltaire;
Le nez dans le ruisseau,
C'est la faute à Rousseau

[I've tumbled to the ground
thanks to Voltaire;
With my nose in the brook,
thanks to Rousseau]

(Quoted in Hugo, n.d., pp.204–5; trans. Lentin)

So ran a ditty popular after the Revolution, which blamed it on Voltaire and Rousseau. The idea was common among those hostile to the Revolution, including Catherine the Great, as we saw on p.250. But the idea was also long shared by historians that the Revolution took place *as a result of* the writings of the *philosophes*, who, it is said, undermined confidence in the institutions of the Old Regime and paved the way for its overthrow.

EXERCISE   The nature of the relationship between the Enlightenment and the Revolution remains a complex and controversial question. Without going into it in depth here, you might usefully address a related but slightly different question: how far did the *philosophes* intend to bring about a revolution?

Before attempting this exercise, reread the section of Unit 1 headed 'Enlightenment, humanity and revolution' and/or look again at Video 1, band 1, *Aspects of Enlightenment*, and the associated AV Notes. Make brief notes on points there which you think relevant to the present question. Then give your own answer to it in a few sentences.

DISCUSSION   Your notes probably included some of the following points:

• The *philosophes*, if not reformers themselves, pointed the way towards reform. They 'were convinced that their mission was for the benefit of their fellow human beings' (Unit 1, p.46).

• The *Encyclopédie* was intended to encourage a more informed, questioning and critical attitude towards existing institutions.

- Such articles as 'Inoculation', 'Fanaticism' or 'The slave trade' in the *Encyclopédie*, and Voltaire's role in the campaign to rehabilitate Calas, exemplify the *philosophes'* desire to lessen suffering, cruelty, injustice and unreason.

- In such articles as 'Natural equality' and 'Political authority' the *philosophes* promoted notions of human rights and natural equality.

But ideas of equality as conceived by most *philosophes* were moral rather than political in inspiration. What was meant was that human beings, whether religious minorities or black slaves, should be treated with 'humanity' (for instance, by according freedom of worship to the former and emancipation to the latter), not that social or economic distinctions should be abolished. Few *philosophes* were social or political radicals, and they were mostly open-minded or eclectic about forms of government. Few were out-and-out republicans (though Rousseau expressed more radical ideas on the good society, characterized by republican virtue).

In your brief answer, then, you may have said something on the following lines:

Certainly the revolutionaries hailed the Enlightenment as the precursor of revolution. This was symbolized by the ceremonial transfer of the remains of Voltaire and Rousseau to the Pantheon. Whether Voltaire or Rousseau would have recognized the revolution that erupted 11 years after their death as their legitimate progeny is doubtful. Neither had called for the overthrow of the Old Regime, still less for terror or bloodshed.

EXERCISE   According to R.R. Palmer, the French Revolution 'represented the Enlightenment in militant form' (1964, p.355). State briefly how far you agree with this proposition.

DISCUSSION   There are a number of possible ways of approaching this question. If you agree with Palmer's statement, you may have included something on the following lines:

The impact of the Enlightenment on the revolutionaries' way of thinking seems undeniable, notably their confidence in the efficacy of legislation to bring about conditions in which human rights and human happiness might be realized. This is evident, for example, in Sieyès's *What is the Third Estate?*, with its grounding in Enlightenment assumptions, or in the rational principles underlying the replacement of the provinces by the departments, or in the introduction of the metric system.

Broadly, Voltaire may be said to have influenced the first, reformist, liberal phase of the Revolution epitomized in the Declaration of the Rights of Man, while Rousseau's faith in mankind's innate goodness and his ideas of the regeneration of society both enhanced this general optimism at the outset of the Revolution and also affected leaders like Robespierre, attuned as he believed himself to be to the 'general will', during its more radical course after 1792.

What were the main consequences of the Revolution? Any answer demands so many qualifications that the question may be best answered in broad terms. 'The Revolution', says Norman Hampson, 'put an end to a way of life' (1975, p.174). Suddenly, the traditional assumptions of the Old Regime, the old certainties, were gone, transformed. New perspectives and new expectations took their place. 'In the long run,' Norman Davies argues, 'the Revolution probably had its greatest impact in the realm of pure ideas' (1997, p.713), and to William Doyle, 'the real message' of the Revolution was that 'the world could be *changed;* fresh starts *could* be made' (1989, p.8). Thomas Paine had said in *Common Sense* as early as 1776 under the stimulus of the American Revolution: 'We have it in our power to begin the world over again.' He expressed the same radical conviction with equal confidence in 1791 in *The Rights of Man,* his robust reply to Burke's *Reflections on the Revolution in France.* In *The Prelude* Wordsworth recalled

> ... a time when Europe was rejoiced,
> France standing on the top of golden hours,
> And human nature seeming born again.

(*The Prelude*, VI.352–4)

How people responded to the Revolution determined the shape of future political discourse in Europe. Broadly speaking, there were progressives – liberals and radicals on the left, who applauded its aims and achievements (or some of them) – and conservatives on the right, who did not. What was there in the Revolution to applaud or deplore? What precedents and challenges did it set to Europe as a whole?

- *Rule by divine right and absolute monarchy* were challenged by the principle of national sovereignty proclaimed by the Revolution. The nation, not the king, was recognized as the ultimate legitimate and legitimizing source of authority in the French state. This became explicit with the establishment of the republic in 1792. Written constitutions introduced a representative assembly, a legislature elected by popular suffrage.

- *A hierarchical society* juridically divided into social orders (estates), headed by a privileged nobility set apart by birth and caste, was challenged by the inclusive concept of citizenship and equality before the law. Offices of state were thrown open, theoretically at least, to individual merit, and the turmoil of events propelled new men into positions of authority in France.

- *The Catholic Church as an estate of the realm in a confessional state* was displaced by the concept of the French nation or people as a focus of common allegiance in a secular state. Church and state, identified for centuries, were separated. Freedom of religion was established and non-Catholics achieved civic equality. Civil marriage was introduced in 1792, together with divorce and *some* measure of greater equality between the sexes.

- *The rights of man,* drawn from Enlightenment ideals, were formally proclaimed. The French Revolution, as Robespierre declared, was, so far as Europe was concerned, 'the first revolution to be founded on the theory of the rights of humanity' (Furet and Ozouf, 1988, p.685).

- *Liberty, equality, fraternity:* these were among the potent revolutionary symbols and ideas for which people were willing to die – and to kill.

- *The people, the nation, the fatherland, the republic, citizens, the nation in arms:* these slogans had a revolutionary dynamic of their own. Under the Old Regime, government, especially foreign policy, was the private business of the king and his ministers. After the Revolution, domestic and foreign policy was something in which citizens were encouraged to feel they had a personal stake and a common interest as 'children of the fatherland' (in the words of the *Marseillaise*) and members of a national army of citizen conscripts marching to the strains of a *national* anthem.

Revolutionary changes were introduced by the French armies into the territories annexed by France. By 1799 the republic had incorporated the papal enclaves of Avignon and Comtat-Venaissin (1791), Savoy (1792), Nice (1793),[45] Belgium (formerly the Austrian Netherlands) (1795), the left bank of the Rhine and Geneva (1798). The same thing happened in the six satellite states or 'sister republics': Holland ('the Batavian Republic'), Switzerland ('the Helvetic Republic') and the four Italian republics (see Figures 6.8 and 6.9). Each republic had its constitution, based on the French model. The constitution proclaimed the sovereignty of the people, as laid down in article 3 of the Declaration of the Rights of Man, and 'the nation's rightful power to determine its own destiny' (quoted in Bouloiseau, 1983, p.10); that is, it invoked the principle of self-determination, denying the right of kings to dispose of peoples without their consent.

The expanded France, which styled itself the Great Nation, provoked a second European coalition against it, but by 1799 it had established itself as a force to be reckoned with: a military force in the first instance but also and not least a potent ideological force. Its influence and attraction spread far beyond its frontiers to other peoples under foreign rule, to

---

[45] The annexation of Avignon and Comtat-Venaissin, Savoy and Nice was accompanied by local plebiscites expressing the will of the people in favour of incorporation in the French Republic.

Figure 6.8 The departments of revolutionary France, 1793–9. Photo: William Doyle, The Oxford History of the French Revolution, *Oxford University Press, 1989. By permission of Oxford University Press.*

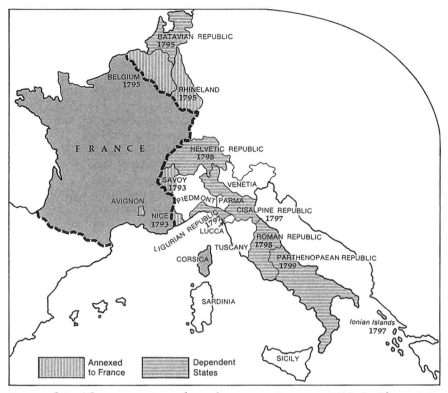

*Figure 6.9   The expansion of revolutionary France, 1793–9. Photo: E.J.
Knapton,* Revolutionary and Imperial France 1750–1815, *Scribner, New
York, 1972.*

Poland under the dominion of Prussia, Russia and Austria, to Greece
under the Turks, and to Ireland under the British. A Dublin ballad ran:

> Oh! May the wind of Freedom
> Soon send young Boney o'er,
> And we'll plant the Tree of Liberty
> Upon our Irish Shore!

(Palmer, 1964, p.336)

EXERCISE   For a detailed discussion of the impact of the Revolution in Britain, now
listen to Audio 3, tracks 1–7: *Britain and the French Revolution,* and
consult the related AV Notes. (Among other things, these refer you to the
illustrations discussed in the recording.) The following two paragraphs
are a summary of reaction in Britain to the Revolution.

In Britain the government was alarmed both by a revolutionary ideology which challenged its traditional political and social structure and by the re-emergence in a new form of the French threat to the European balance of power, signalled by French expansion into the Low Countries. Both factors explain Britain's participation in the wars against revolutionary (and then Napoleonic) France from 1793 onwards. A French attempt in 1796 to land troops at Bantry Bay was followed by rebellion in Ireland in 1798, leading to the Act of Union (1800) between Ireland and Great Britain. Naval mutinies at Spithead and the Nore in 1797 seemed to the authorities to reflect the influence of the Revolution.

Against this background arose a ferment of radical ideas, initially directed towards removing the civil disabilities suffered by Dissenters (Protestants outside the established Church of England) but rapidly spreading to encompass a reform of Parliament and a widening of the franchise. Inspired by the Revolution, radical political associations were established (notably the London Corresponding Society) and radical publications were circulated widely across the country. The government of Prime Minister William Pitt, in effect a coalition government after 1794, sensing a threat to law and order, imposed a variety of repressive measures: amendments to the law of treason, the partial suspension of the Habeas Corpus Act (prohibiting detention without trial), increased control of public meetings and publications. The London Corresponding Society was proscribed in 1799.

France had dictated the culture of civilized Europe since the seventeenth century. The eighteenth-century Parisian *salons* were at the heart of the Enlightenment. The French revolutionaries assumed that enlightened people everywhere would continue to look to Paris as the centre of progressive thought, would wish to be part of or at least associated with *la Grande Nation*. In August 1792 the National Assembly conferred honorary French citizenship on 17 assorted foreigners, as 'men who in various countries have brought reason to its present maturity' (Palmer, 1964, p.54). These included leaders of the American Revolution George Washington, Alexander Hamilton and James Madison; Swiss educational pioneer Pestalozzi; English utilitarian philosopher and legal reformer Jeremy Bentham; the radicals Thomas Paine and Joseph Priestley; leaders of the anti-slavery campaign Thomas Clarkson and William Wilberforce;[46] and German poet and playwright Friedrich von Schiller. In his *Sketch of a Historical Outline of the Progress of the Human Mind* (1793), Condorcet looked forward, in the cosmopolitan spirit of the Enlightenment, to a world in which national differences would be erased. In the same spirit of international fraternity, German admirers of the Revolution took up Schiller's *Ode to Joy,* best known in its later setting

[46] This was somewhat to Wilberforce's embarrassment, since he now had grave reservations about the Revolution. In 1794 the Convention decreed the abolition of slavery in the French colonies.

by Beethoven but in the 1790s sometimes sung to the tune of the *Marseillaise*:

> Seid unschlungen, Millionen
> Diesen Kuss der ganzen Welt!
>
> [Embrace each other, ye millions,
> Here's a kiss for all the world!]

(Palmer, 1964, p.445)

The Revolution, both in its original underlying principles and in its later excesses, was deeply divisive in France and Europe generally. It engendered conservatism and counter-revolution just as it did liberalism. Burke had from the first denounced the attempt to remodel society on abstract principles and preached the virtues of a settled, aristocratic society, of respect for precedent, tradition and time-honoured institutions. He deplored the example of 'those who have projected the subversion of that order of things under which our part of the world has so long flourished' (that is, the death of the Old Regime), and predicted that the Revolution would lead to bloodshed and tyranny (quoted in Welsh, 1995, p.114). Britain was to prove the most persistent enemy of the Revolution.

But even men passionately attracted to the Revolution became aware of the perils of violent change. 'I dreamed of a republic', Desmoulins wrote on the eve of his execution in 1794, 'that would have been the envy of the world. I could not believe that men could be so cruel and unjust' (quoted in Schama, 1989, p.xi). Even in 1794, however, when the Terror had alienated many, Wordsworth still declared himself to be 'of that odious class of men called democrats', the enemy of 'monarchical and aristocratical governments' and 'hereditary distinctions and privileged orders of every species' and therefore 'not amongst the admirers of the British Constitution' (Palmer, 1964, pp.22, 458). Wordsworth himself was soon to change his mind and to evolve a far more critical, reflective and conservative attitude to the Revolution, as you will discover in Block 4. Like it or not, however, everyone accepted that the French Revolution marked an epoch in world history and that things could never be the same again.

References

Blanning, T.C.W. (1987) *The French Revolution: Aristocrats versus Bourgeois?*, Basingstoke, Macmillan Education.

Blanning, T.C.W. (ed.) (2000) *The Eighteenth Century: Europe 1688–1815,* Oxford, Oxford University Press.

Bouloiseau, M. (1983) *The Jacobin Republic 1792–1794,* trans. Jonathan Mandelbaum, Cambridge, Cambridge University Press.

Caratini, R. (1988) *Dictionnaire des personnages de la Révolution*, Paris, Le Préaux Clercs.

Charay, J. (1990), 'Les cultes révolutionnaires à Aubenas', in *Salut Universel: Les Prêtres ardéchois dans la Révolution*, Aubenas en Vivarais, Imprimerie Lienhart.

Cobb, R.C. (1970) *The Police and the People: French Popular Protest 1789–1820*, Oxford, Clarendon Press.

Davies, N. (1997) *Europe: A History*, London, Pimlico.

Doyle, W. (1989) 'The principles of the French Revolution', in H.T. Mason and W. Doyle (eds) *The Impact of the French Revolution on European Consciousness*, Gloucester, Alan Sutton.

Doyle, W. (1999) 'Introduction', in Kirsty Carpenter and P. Mansel (eds) *The French Émigrés in Europe and the Struggle against the Revolution, 1789–1814*, Basingstoke, Macmillan.

Doyle, W. (2001) *The French Revolution: A Very Short Introduction*, Oxford, Oxford University Press.

Ellis, G. (1997) *Napoleon*, Harlow, Longman.

Furet, F. (1996) *The French Revolution 1770–1814*, Oxford, Blackwell.

Furet, F. and Ozouf M. (1988) *Dictionnaire Critique de la Révolution Française*, Paris, Flammarion.

Gendzier, S.J. (ed. and trans.) (1967) *Denis Diderot's 'The Encyclopedia': Selections*, New York, Harper Torchbooks.

Grand Dictionnaire Encyclopédique Larousse (1985) vol.9, Paris, Librairie Larousse.

Hampson, N. (1969) *The First European Revolution 1776–1815*, London, Thames and Hudson.

Hampson, N. (1975) *The French Revolution: A Concise History*, London, Thames and Hudson.

Hampson, N. (1981) *The Terror in the French Revolution*, London, The Historical Association.

Hardman, J. (ed.) (1999) *The French Revolution Sourcebook*, London, Edward Arnold.

Hemmings, F. (1987) *Culture and Society in France 1789–1848*, Leicester, Leicester University Press.

Hugo, V. (n.d.) *Les Misérables*, vol.3, Paris, Éditions Minerve.

Jones, C. (1988) *The Longman Companion to the French Revolution*, Harlow, Longman.

Kennedy, E. (1989) *A Cultural History of the French Revolution,* New Haven and London, Yale University Press.

Kennedy, M. (2000) *The Jacobin Clubs in the French Revolution 1793–1795,* Oxford, Berghahn Books.

Lentin, A. (1985) *Enlightened Absolutism (1760–1790): A Documentary Sourcebook,* Newcastle-upon-Tyne, Avero.

Lewis, G. (1993) *The French Revolution: Rethinking the Debate,* London and New York, Routledge.

Palmer, R. (1964) *The Age of the Democratic Revolution: A Political History of Europe and America, 1760–1800,* vol.II, Princeton, Princeton University Press.

Palmer, R. (1971) *The World of the French Revolution,* London, George Allen & Unwin.

Parker, H.T. (1937) *The Cult of Antiquity and the French Revolutionaries,* Chicago, University of Chicago Press.

Rudé, G. (1966) *Revolutionary Europe 1783–1815,* New York, Harper Torchbooks.

Schama, S. (1989) *Citizens: A Chronicle of the French Revolution,* New York, Alfred Knopf.

Townson, D. (1990) *France in Revolution,* London, Hodder & Stoughton.

Tulard, J. (ed.) (1987) *Dictionnaire Napoléon,* Paris, Fayard.

Vovelle, M. (1984) *The Fall of the French Monarchy 1787–1792,* Cambridge, Cambridge University Press.

Welsh, J.M. (1995) *Edmund Burke and International Relations,* London, Macmillan.

Williams, G. (1989) *Artisans and Sans-Culottes: Popular Movements in France and Britain during the French Revolution,* 2nd edn, London, Libris.

Further reading

Arasse, D. (1991) *The Guillotine and the Terror,* trans. Christopher Miller, Harmondsworth, Penguin.

Emsley, C. (2000) *Britain and the French Revolution,* Harlow, Longman.

Haydon, C and Doyle, W. (1999) *Robespierre,* Cambridge, Cambridge University Press.

McPhee, P. (2002) *The French Revolution 1789–1799,* Oxford, Oxford University Press.

Conclusion to Block 1

Prepared for the course team by Alex Barber and Antony Lentin

We suggested in the introduction to this block that a number of threads run through its three main components. Some of these were noted in the units; others you may have noted for yourself. One characteristic of the texts not so far mentioned seems to merit particular attention: their manifestation of a new emphasis on the relationship between liberty and happiness.

From the introductory video you may remember the Enlightenment cult of 'the noble savage', supposedly happy and free. Liberty, happiness and their interconnectedness were already common concerns during the Enlightenment. Liberty was a political ideal well before the end of the eighteenth century. The *philosophes* preached the possibility and desirability of a society of free and enlightened individuals. This was one of the ultimate aims of the *Encyclopédie*. The *philosophes* advocated happiness as a good in itself, indeed as the ultimate purpose and criterion of the good society. The *philosophes* Helvétius and Beccaria defined the object of government as 'the greatest happiness of the greatest number' (the belief known as utilitarianism). In the celebrated Declaration of Independence, drawn up in 1776 during the successful rebellion by the American colonies against what they saw as the despotism of Britain, the Founding Fathers of the United States pronounced the first aim of all government to be to promote the 'inalienable rights' of 'life, liberty and the pursuit of happiness'. America's example inspired the French revolutionaries and many others. The political philosopher and anarchist William Godwin, in his *An Enquiry Concerning Political Justice* (1793), also argued that individual liberty is a precondition of human happiness. The British utilitarian movement to which he belonged continued to regard liberty as important to the achievement of human fulfilment. As this movement gathered momentum, the social reformer Robert Owen designed a model society adapted to the new conditions of an industrializing Britain, and put it into action with high hopes at New Lanark (the focus of Units 18–19). Responsibility or self-determination was seen by him as an important ingredient of a happy existence.

The texts examined in this block point towards a new kind of link between liberty and happiness. The very process of achieving liberty, and not only liberty's exercise in a future idealized state, came to be associated with extreme pleasure, even delirium, as tyrannical barriers to freedom were knocked down and limitations transgressed. Most spectacularly of all, the fall of the ancient Parisian prison of the Bastille in 1789, the very symbol of despotism, was acclaimed with rapture by those present, hailed and toasted by thousands across Europe, and celebrated thenceforth as an annual festival in France, where 'liberty' was emblematically joined to 'equality' and 'fraternity' as fundamental human values. More chillingly, it is clear that a few years into the Revolution, the spectacle of aristocrats or their sympathizers being beheaded or lynched also gave rise to another kind of pleasure. A young officer stationed in Paris, Napoleon Bonaparte, reports witnessing with revulsion the sacking of the royal palace of the Tuileries by the mob in 1792 and the massacre of the king's Swiss guardsmen. The sinister imaginings of the Marquis de Sade are pertinent here, too. Transgression of virtue was for him a pleasurable undertaking in itself, to the point that the highest forms of pleasure actually *depended* on the existence of breakable constraints.

Another indication of this new association between liberty and the supposed pleasure of transgression is built into the very term 'libertine' (meaning both a freed, emancipated person and one not restrained by moral law). Don Giovanni is the obvious, indeed the proverbial, libertine. He embodies the abandonment of restraint in favour of sensual delight, delight that is enhanced in his case by the disruption its achievement gives rise to in others' lives. In a more measured way, Rousseau broke through the twin constraints of empiricism and the church to the pleasure of direct communion with God. Similar expressions of the joy associated with experiential religion are found in the Evangelical movement (examined in Unit 10).

This theme of transgression, liberty and euphoria continues through to the next block, which considers aspects of the life, image and mythology of Napoleon Bonaparte. He became an object of fervent, almost religious, veneration as he broke through France's borders to 'liberate' large swathes of continental Europe in a rush of military campaigns. Ludwig van Beethoven (1770–1827) dedicated his Third Symphony (1803–5, the 'Eroica', or heroic) to Bonaparte, and though he gouged out this dedication on learning that Napoleon had made himself emperor, he never entirely lost his enthusiasm for what Napoleon represented. In one of his most inspirational works, his ninth and final symphony (1823–4), Beethoven set to music the words of Friedrich von Schiller's 1785 poem, *Ode to Joy*. The words in this musical setting gave an eloquent voice to the new association we have suggested between happiness and the process of liberation:

> Freude, schöner Götterfunken,
> Tochter aus Elysium,
> Wir betreten feuertrunken,
> Himmlische, dein Heiligtum!
>
> Deine Zauber binden wieder
> Was die Mode streng geteilt;
> Alle Menschen werden Brüder
> Wo dein sanfter Flügel weilt.

[Joy, beautiful divine spark,
Daughter of Elysium,
Drunk with fire, Goddess,
We approach your holy shrine!

Your magic binds together once more
What convention has split apart;
All men become brothers
Where your gentle wings abide.]

(Schiller, *An die Freude*, quoted in Davies, N. (1997) *Europe: A History*, London, Pimlico, p.684; trans. Barber and Lentin)

Glossary

Units 2 and 3

Accompanied recitative (also *accompagnato* recitative): recitative, usually for one operatic character alone, accompanied by the orchestra. The accompaniment often involves sustained chords under the singer, or orchestral interjections punctuating the singer's phrases.

Aria: solo operatic song.

Baroque: period of European musical style between *c.*1600 and 1760, represented in the first half of the eighteenth century by the music of J.S. Bach and Handel.

Cadence: clear formula of chords marking the end of a phrase; the final cadence of a movement brings the music to rest in the 'home' key.

Classical: period of European musical style between *c.*1780 and 1820, represented in the last decades of the eighteenth century by the music of Haydn and Mozart.

Compound time: a metre in which each beat can be divided into three equal shorter notes (see Example 2.4, p.95) rather than two (the latter giving **simple time**).

Da capo: a form of aria in **Baroque *opera seria*** comprising three sections: a first section to one set of words, a second section to another text, and then a repeat of the first section in which the singer was expected to elaborate the melody with additional musical decoration that demonstrated their technique and good taste.

Libretto (plural: librettos or libretti): the literary text of an opera.

Metre: the underlying beat-structure of the music, involving regular but subtle emphasis on the first beat of each bar.

Opera buffa: 'comic' genres of eighteenth-century opera.

Opera seria: 'serious' genres of eighteenth-century opera.

Recitative: sections of music that do not form complete regular musical movements (e.g. **arias**), but are more freely delivered and often involve the musical setting of conversations between two or more characters. See also **simple recitative** and **accompanied recitative**.

Ritornello: orchestral section introducing and concluding a vocal movement (**aria**). Some arias also have orchestral ritornellos within the movement.

Simple recitative (also *semplice* recitative): conversational exchange which is accompanied by a keyboard instrument rather than the orchestra.

Simple time: any musical **metre** whose main beats are divisible by two (see Example 2.3, p.95).

Sonata form: musical structure that was typical for orchestral music of the **Classical** period; it is based on two themes (or groups of themes) with a clear return to the first theme and the tonic key later in the movement.

Units 4 and 5

Agnosticism: the claim that we do not know that God exists or that he does not exist. (**Atheists**, by contrast, deny that God exists.)

Arguments for the existence of God: see independent entries for **argument from design**, **cosmological argument** and **ontological argument**.

Argument from design ('teleological argument'): the universe can be seen to be ordered and harmonious; the only possible explanation of this order and harmony requires that we accept the existence of an intelligent, powerful, and benign creator, i.e. God.

Atheism: belief in the non-existence of God.

Cosmological argument: in its simplest form, the argument runs as follows. Something has to have created the universe (the 'cosmos'); that creator is God. A common variant of this is: something has to have first caused the inert universe to move; that 'first mover' is God.

Deism: a form of **natural religion**, especially as pursued in Europe in the eighteenth and nineteenth centuries.

Empiricism: the view that opinions are acceptable only if backed up with evidence that is grounded *either* in experience *or* in one of some small number of permitted principles of abstract reasoning (e.g. mathematical principles).

Materialism: the view that, if we have a soul at all, it is built up out of the matter of our bodies; more generally, the view that there is nothing beyond matter.

Natural religion: religion the evidence for which does not depend on the testimony of historical scripture. Evidence for natural religion will come, rather, from what is available to everyone, such as reason or immediate experience. (Contrast with **revealed religion**; see also **arguments for the existence of God**.)

Ontological argument: God, by definition, is perfect; failing to exist is an imperfection; so God exists.

Philosophe: one of a number of participants in the French Enlightenment. The term *philosophe* was used because a preparedness to engage with philosophical topics was a hallmark of the movement in

France. Prominent among the *philosophes* were Diderot, Voltaire, d'Holbach, la Mettrie, and d'Alembert.

Problem of evil: most Christians and deists claimed that God was both good and all powerful. The problem of evil is to reconcile this with the existence of evil in the world. If God were both good and all powerful, he wouldn't allow bad things to happen. A common response to the problem is to insist that it is humans rather than God who make bad things happen. God has given us freedom to do as we see fit, but is not responsible for our actions. (This response requires adoption of Rousseau's account of divine providence and not Hume's – see **providence**.)

Providence: the term 'divine providence' refers to the measures God supposedly puts in place to ensure that events in the universe turn out as he wishes. Different accounts are available as to the nature and extent of these measures. Some (e.g. Hume) argue that he has input into every single episode that takes place in the universe, including our own actions. Others (e.g. Rousseau) claim that human actions are our responsibility and ours alone. On this latter view, the results of human action do not belong to divine providence.

Reason: a reasonable (or 'rational') opinion is one that is based on good evidence. This leaves room for disagreement over what counts as good evidence. Hume and Rousseau both thought of themselves as holding reasonable opinions, but disagreed over whether the only acceptable sources of evidence were the outer senses. (See also **empiricism**; **sentiment**.)

Revealed religion: religion the evidence for which comes primarily from reports – especially reports in historical scripture – of God supposedly *revealing* himself to a particular individual or group of individuals. (Contrast with **natural religion**.)

Rule of analogy (often known today as the 'principle of induction'): the rule of reasoning according to which it is legitimate to expect, for example, that the next snow one encounters will be cold, given that all snow previously encountered has been cold. More generally, if all experiences of one type (e.g. seeing snow) have been followed by experiences of some other type (e.g. feeling it to be cold) *in the past*, then experiences of the first type will be followed by experiences of the second type *in the future* (so that, in the example, all snow, even that which we have yet to observe, will turn out to be cold).

Sentiment: an emotion; more broadly, an 'inner' feeling. Often contrasted with the traditional five 'outer' senses. Rousseau, unlike Hume, held that sentiment could provide good evidence of 'matters of fact', e.g. of God's existence. (See also **reason**.)

Unit 6

Cahiers de doléances: literally 'books of grievances', the 'petitions' which the representatives at the Estates-General of 1789 brought with them from their constituents.

Civil Constitution of the Clergy: in July 1790 the Assembly cut the number of Catholic bishoprics from 135 to 83, allocating one diocese for each department, and made provision for a salaried clergy appointed by popular election.

Committee of Public Safety: power was vested in a so-called Committee of Public Safety 1793–4, in effect a war cabinet of 12 members of the Convention.

Constituent Assembly: the National Assembly, the *de facto* supreme representative and legislative organ of state from June 1789, set to work on the constitution which it had sworn to introduce. Calling itself the Constituent Assembly (to stress both its representative credentials and its constitutional mission), it consisted of 745 deputies elected for two years from August 1789 to September 1791 with virtually unlimited power to pass laws.

Council of 500: the lower chamber of the bicameral legislature established in 1795 by the Thermidorian Settlement.

Council of Elders or **'Ancients'**: the upper house of the bicameral legislature established in 1795 by the Thermidorian Settlement.

Directory: the ruling executive committee of five established in 1795 by the Thermidorian Settlement.

Estates-General: pre-revolutionary elected representatives of the three orders or estates of the realm: clergy, nobility and the **Third Estate**, or commoners.

First Coalition: Austria, Prussia, Britain, Spain, Holland and the kingdom of Sardinia joined forces against France in 1793 (see Figure 6.5).

Girondins: one of the Revolution's extreme factions, whose leaders included Roland.

Jacobin: member of a radical political organization or 'club' under the leadership of Robespierre calling itself the Society of the Friends of the Constitution (and later Society of the Friends of Liberty and Equality).

Legislative Assembly: successor to the Constituent Assembly (October 1791–August 1792).

National Assembly: In June 1789 the assembly of the deputies of the **Third Estate** became the National Assembly, the *de facto* deliberative and legislative assembly of the French nation.

National Convention: On 20 September 1792, under pressure from Robespierre and the Jacobins, the Legislative Assembly was replaced by a National Convention (1792–5), which abolished the monarchy and proclaimed the republic.

Non-jurors: the clergy who refused to take the oath to the constitution and the **Civil Constitution of the Clergy**, 1790.

Sans-culottes: literally 'without breeches', because they wore trousers rather than the knee-breeches or *culottes* associated with the upper classes; the *sans-culottes* were radical revolutionaries who practised direct action and street violence. See Plate 6.1 in the Illustrations Book.

'Tennis-court oath': on 20 June 1789, finding itself locked out, the Third Estate, calling itself the National Assembly, withdrew to a nearby indoor tennis court and declared, in the so-called 'tennis-court oath', that it would not disperse until it had provided France with a new, written constitution.

The Terror: the twelve months from July 1793 to July 1794 known as the period of war government, revolutionary government, or simply the Terror.

Third Estate: in pre-revolutionary France, the commoners, the remaining 95 per cent of the population after the nobility and clergy.

Index

Page numbers in *italics* refer to illustrations.

Acknowledgements

Grateful acknowledgement is made to the following sources for permission to reproduce material within this book.

pp.118, 119 and 141: *Don Giovanni, Opera in Two Acts by Wolfgang Amadeus Mozart.* Words by Lorenzo da Ponte, English version by Edward J. Dent, vocal score by Ernest Roth. Reproduced by kind permission of Boosey & Hawkes Music Publishers Ltd.

p.131: Plath, W. and Rehm, W. (1968) *Wolfgang Amadeus Mozart*, Serie II, *Bühnenwerke*, Bärenreiter-Verlag Karl Votterle GmbH & Co. KG, Kassel.

pp.148–53: Arblaster, A. (1992) 'Mozart, class conflict and enlightenment', *Viva la Libertà! Politics in Opera*, Verso.

Every effort has been made to contact copyright holders. If any have been inadvertently overlooked the publishers will be pleased to make the necessary arrangements at the first opportunity.